ENLIGHTENED DEMOCRACY

ENLIGHTENED DEMOCRACY

THE CASE FOR THE ELECTORAL COLLEGE

TARA ROSS

Foreword by George Will

World Ahead Publishing, Inc.

For Adam
My partner in all
of life's endeavors

CONTENTS

FOREWORD

Mr. George Will

A MERICA'S constitutional system aims not merely for majority rule but for rule by certain kinds of majorities. It aims for majorities suited to moderate, consensual governance of a heterogeneous, continental nation with myriad regional and other diversities. All 537 persons elected to national offices—the president, vice president, 100 senators and 435 representatives—are chosen by majorities that reflect the nation's federal nature. They are elected by majorities within states or within states' congressional districts.

American majorities are not spontaneous; they are built. A two-party system builds moderate majorities by assembling them from coalitions of minorities. In multiparty systems, parties proliferate, each representing intense minorities. Then a group of parties strives to govern through (often unstable) coalitions improvised after the election.

A two-party system is buttressed by an electoral system that handicaps minor parties by electing a single person from each jurisdiction, chosen by majority or plurality. In presidential elections, states are the jurisdictions. Forty-eight of them have chosen a winner-take-all allocation of electoral votes: The presidential candidate winning the state is awarded its entire slate of electors. So in 1992 Ross Perot won 18.9 percent of the popular vote but carried no state and won no electoral votes.

Bill Clinton's 43 percent of the popular vote won him 68.8 percent of the electoral votes. In 1912 Woodrow Wilson's 41.8 percent of the popular votes produced a strong presidency based on 81.9 percent of the electoral votes.

Political scientist Judith Best notes that the electoral-vote system, combined with winner-take-all allocation, creates a "distribution condition." Candidates cannot just pile up popular votes in the most populous states. They must win many states, because legitimacy, and the capacity to govern this extensive republic, involves more than crude arithmetic. The federal principle, Best argues, prevents the most dangerous kinds of factions—racial, religious, economic—"from uniting their votes across state lines. It confines them within little republics and forces them to compromise early and often with their fellow state citizens."

The 2000 election, the sixth in which the popular-vote margin between the winner and runner-up was less than 1 percent, was a reminder that the electoral-vote system quarantines electoral disputes. Imagine a close election—2000, or the 1960 election, in which Kennedy's margin over Nixon was just 118,574—under direct popular election. With all votes poured into a single national bucket, there would be powerful incentives to challenge the results in many thousands of the nation's 170,000 precincts. The outcome could remain murky for months, leaving whoever wins crippled by attenuated legitimacy.

America *has* direct popular election of presidents, but has it *within* the states. As Best says, the states are not mere administrative agencies for a unitary government; they are components of a compound—a federal-republic. And today's electoral-vote system is not an 18th-century anachronism. It has evolved, shaping and being shaped by a large development the Constitution's Framers did not foresee—the two-party system.

Tara Ross' book, *Enlightened Democracy: The Case for the Electoral College*, celebrates this important bulwark of America's federalist republic. The Constitution provides for the election of Presidents by states' electoral votes, rather than individual popular votes, for an important reason: It enables citizens of a heterogeneous, free society to live peacefully alongside each other.

Proposals have recently been made that would undermine the protections provided by America's unique presidential election system. Some Coloradans, for instance, seek to do away with the winner-take-all allocation of their state's electoral votes, replacing it with a proportional division. Such proposals appeal to single-minded—hence simple-minded—majoritarians. The wiser path is to study the logic and rationale that prompted the Founders to avoid a national popular election, settling instead upon a federal process for presidential selection.

ACKNOWLEDGMENTS

F AMILIES should always be first on a list of acknowledgments, and I owe many thanks to mine. To my dear husband, Adam, who sacrificed the most for this book. We don't have to eat carry-out for several months now, I promise. To the Branum side of the family and the Ross side of the family: Thank you for understanding the lack of phone calls from this general direction this summer. I will make it up to you, too.

I owe many thanks to several lawyers and academics who helped in the completion of this project. First and foremost to Mr. George Will, who took the time to contribute a foreword for my book: I cannot tell you how much I appreciate your taking time out of your busy summer to help with this effort. To Attorney General Edwin Meese III, Judge Robert Bork, Judge Kenneth W. Starr, Professor Lino Graglia, Mr. Leonard Leo, and Mr. Todd Gaziano, who all helped in a variety of ways at various points during this endeavor: I am profoundly grateful for your faith in me. To Mr. John Fortier, Mr. Patrick O'Daniel, Mr. Doug Wilson, Ms. Elizabeth Kovacs, and Ms. Rachael Branum, who reviewed drafts of this work in its early stages: You have helped to make the book better than it otherwise would have been, and I am thankful for your hard work on my behalf.

Among the most important contributors to the project were those who supplied me with caffeine. I surely would not have survived the extremely tight deadlines without coffee and a comfortable locale at which to work! To my Starbucks baristas, who have become friends during the course of this endeavor: Ms. Beth Daugherty, Mr. Sanjay Dharmapal, Ms.

Samantha Garland, Ms. Kourtney Karvas, and Mr. Albert Po-
males: Don't worry. Book or no book, I still need coffee. You
can't get rid of me that easily.

To the many good and dear friends who have supported
me and endured my discussions of life in the year 1787 over
the course of the past several months: I know you have
wanted to see a completed book out of me for months now. I
hope you enjoy the end result.

INTRODUCTION

The mode of appointment of the Chief Magistrate of the United
States is almost the only part of the system . . . which has escaped
without severe censure . . . . I venture somewhat further,
and hesitate not to affirm that if the manner of it
be not perfect, it is at least excellent.

— Alexander Hamilton[1]

F OUR YEARS have passed since the eventful election of 2000.
The story of that election is well known by now. Returns
were close throughout election night. As in other years, media
coverage focused on predicting state-by-state results. American
presidential elections are, after all, a battle to win the most state
votes (called electoral votes), rather than the most popular votes
nationwide.

The networks called many of the so-called "swing states" for
Democratic candidate Al Gore early in the evening.[2] One of these
critical states, Florida, was first called for Gore at 7:49 p.m.
Eastern Time by NBC. Other networks quickly jumped on board
with the prediction, despite the fact that polls had not yet closed
in the state's Republican-leaning western panhandle, which is in
a different time zone. Within a matter of hours, the call for Gore
was deemed premature, and it was rescinded. Shortly after 2
a.m., the networks declared Republican candidate George W.
Bush the winner of Florida and, hence, the presidential election.

By 4 a.m., they had withdrawn their prediction—again. The country went to bed without knowing the name of its next President.

The final results of the election remained in doubt days later. Neither candidate had yet obtained a majority of at least 270 electoral votes, which would be needed to win. To that point, Bush had earned a total of 246 electoral votes, while Gore had earned 262 electoral votes. Two state elections remained undecided: Florida (25 electoral votes) and New Mexico (5 electoral votes).[3] The outcome of the national election would turn on the results in Florida, with its large bloc of unclaimed votes. Florida's election, however, was unusually close. Bush was ahead in the state tally, but his lead was razor-thin. Lawsuits were filed, and recounts were requested. Weeks of doubt followed as state officials and judges attempted to determine whether Bush or Gore had won the state's electoral votes.

The legal wrangling and recounts endured in Florida for more than a month. The U.S. Supreme Court was asked to intervene, not once, but twice.[4] The Court's final ruling essentially stopped the Florida Supreme Court from ordering hand recounts in addition to the mechanized recounts that had already been completed. In doing so, it brought a halt to the legal contest in Florida.

Throughout this entire process, Gore remained ahead in the national popular vote tally. His popular vote lead has no legal significance under the American state-by-state presidential election system; nevertheless, it gave Gore supporters ammunition in the forthcoming public relations battle against Bush. Many argued that the system is unfair; Gore should not have to fight to win a majority of the states' votes when he was virtually certain to win the popular vote tally among individual voters. America's system of electing Presidents (referred to colloquially as the Electoral College) took a pounding in the press.

In the end, Florida's 25 electoral votes were awarded to Bush. Certified results held that he had won the state by 537 votes.

Bush's win in Florida pushed him to a majority of 271 electoral votes and ultimately gave him the presidency, despite the fact that he finished more than 500,000 votes behind Gore in the nationwide popular vote tally.[5] Bush's Electoral College win made him the first President in more than 100 years to ascend to the presidency despite the fact that he had garnered fewer individual popular votes, overall, than his opponent.

The close and disputed nature of the Bush-Gore election arguably pushed the American presidential election system to its limits, but it was not the only one of its kind. Elections in 1876 and 1888 also resulted in Presidents who lost the recorded popular vote, but won the electoral vote. The 1876 election resulted in many weeks of post-election uncertainty, as did the 2000 election.

The last "popular vote loser" President was Benjamin Harrison. In 1888, Harrison defeated Grover Cleveland in the Electoral College vote, but he lost the popular vote by nearly 100,000 votes. Yet the outcome of this election between Harrison and Cleveland was not surrounded by the controversy of post-election disputes and recounts, as was the Bush-Gore election. The most recent election to face post-election disputes on the scale of those faced in Florida was the election of 1876, in which Rutherford B. Hayes defeated Samuel J. Tilden.

The 1876 and 2000 elections were comparable, but the Hayes-Tilden election was arguably even more controversial than the Bush-Gore election. In 1876, the country waited for weeks to see which candidate would be declared the victor; it did not get an answer until two days before President Ulysses S. Grant's term expired.[6] Imagine if Bush and Gore had continued fighting over the 2000 election outcome through Christmas and New Year's. What if Gore had conceded the election in the middle of January 2001, rather than the middle of December 2000? This is a taste of what the 1876 election was like, although 19th century Americans did not have CNN, Fox News, and MSNBC to add 24-hour drama to the process, as 21st century Americans do.

3

The 1876 election was similar to, although perhaps more suspenseful than, the 2000 election in another way. In 2000, the outcome in Florida was disputed. In 1876, not only Florida, but also two other states remained undecided after Election Day.[7] When the Electoral College met, multiple sets of election returns were generated by these three states. It was left to Congress to sort out which of the conflicting sets of returns to accept. Congress dealt with the problem by creating an Electoral Commission to determine which slates of electors should be certified from each of the three contested states. This controversial Commission was composed of 15 Senators, Congressmen, and Supreme Court Justices. Although it was meant to be composed of equal numbers of representatives from each party, plus one independent, it ended up with one extra Republican. This Republican reliably voted with the Republicans (not surprisingly), causing the Commission's votes to fall along party lines. Congress eventually accepted its determinations, but not before a filibuster nearly sidetracked even this final decision.

One last resemblance exists between the 2000 and 1876 elections. In 2000, Bush's popular vote loss was challenged by some who claimed that such a result might not have occurred were it not for the networks' early calls for Gore. These erroneous predictions, commentators argue, discouraged Republicans in western time zones from going to the polls. Former Speaker of the House, Newt Gingrich, observed in 2000: "I feel pretty strongly that had the networks not called Florida early that night, [Gore] wouldn't have won the popular vote. We wouldn't be in this mess. And I think Bush would be above 300 electoral votes."[8] Others hypothesize, specifically, that Bush lost anywhere from 8,000 to 37,000 votes in the Republican-leaning western panhandle of Florida due to the early call.[9] A similar situation existed in 1876, although voters then cared less about the outcome of the national popular vote.[10] Hayes won the electoral vote and lost the popular vote by more than 250,000 votes, but these totals don't tell the whole story. The country was still in the midst of Reconstruction, and disputes surrounded the voting in many southern states, making it impossible to know what the outcome of a truly free election would have been.

As with the 1876 election, Gore supporters have continued to protest the results of the 2000 election, even after the election results have been relegated to the history books. Many of these Americans have focused on the controversy surrounding the recount in Florida; however, a smaller number of dissenters take the argument a step further. Gore's popular vote win, they stress, should have guaranteed him the presidency, regardless of how the states' votes came out. The popular vote totals, these individuals believe, show that he was the true choice of the people. The 2000 election results have led many to denounce a unique American institution: the Electoral College.

Lack of Understanding Equals Lack of Support

Gore's campaign indicated its intent to abide by the results of the electoral vote throughout the recounts in Florida. Yet he and his campaign still took jabs at a system that would allow a popular vote winner to lose the presidential election. As the recounts began in Florida, Gore noted: *"Despite the fact that Joe Lieberman and I won the popular vote,* under our Constitution it is the winner of the Electoral College who will be the next president."[11] On November 12, his campaign chairman, William Daley, reminded Wolf Blitzer that "Al Gore got more votes in this election than anyone in the history of our country running for president except Ronald Reagan. He is ahead in the popular vote. . . . He, clearly, at this point, was favored by the majority of the people who went to the polls."[12] The constant reminders of Gore's popular vote lead served to mitigate any potential public irritation with his continuing legal challenges to the outcome of the vote in Florida.[13]

Outside the Gore campaign team, the rhetoric against the Electoral College was more direct. Many Democrats (and even a few Republicans) lost no time in demanding that the Electoral College be replaced with a direct voting system. Newly elected Senator Hillary Rodham Clinton derided the Electoral College as an institution that does not "respect the will of the people."[14] Senator Richard Durbin of Illinois introduced a constitutional amendment to abolish the Electoral College. His direct vote proposal, he explained, "reflects more what a democracy should represent, the voice of the people and the vote of the people, instead of an electoral college which has become a constitutional dinosaur."[15] House Minority Leader Richard Gephardt concurred, "[W]e ought to get rid of the Electoral College. . . . [W]hoever wins the vote should be the next President of the United States."[16]

Calls to abolish the Electoral College are not new. Over the years, the Electoral College has been consistently criticized by some academics and political commentators. It is an "anachronism" that "thwarts" democratic principles,[17] or a "sign[ ] of constitutional stupidity,"[18] or even a "dangerous game" with "many built-in pitfalls" that are "bound to destroy us."[19] The American Bar Association has called the Electoral College "archaic, undemocratic, complex, ambiguous, indirect, and dangerous."[20] Opponents argue that the Electoral College allows a President to be selected who is not the popular vote winner "and thus is not the first choice of the voters."[21] These critics seek to support their cause by building a picture of the Electoral College as a "hastily-drawn compromise[ ]" of the 1787 Constitutional Convention that should never have lasted so long.[22] Some critics go even further and claim that the Electoral College was included in the Constitution as an appeasement to southern slaveholding interests. This "structural 'badge[ ] and incident[ ]' of slavery" should be eliminated as quickly as humanly possible.[23]

Many Americans do not understand the origins or logic behind the Electoral College, nor are they taught about the history of this constitutional device in many schools. One law professor,

Professor Abner Mikva of the University of Chicago Law School, made a similar point prior to the 2000 election. In 1997, he complained that the Electoral College is "secret because a majority of the American people don't even know it exists, let alone how it works."[24]

The lack of understanding discussed by Professor Mikva has led to a general lack of support for the Electoral College among the public. Instead, polls consistently show support for a switch to direct popular election of the President. For instance, in 1988, an ABC and *Washington Post* poll showed that 77 percent of the public was in favor of direct election, rather than the Electoral College system.[25] Indeed, as early as 1944, 65 percent of the American public wanted to abolish the Electoral College.[26]

A close election in 1968 caused opposition to the Electoral College to hit one of its high points. At that time, 81 percent of the American public was in favor of abolishing the Electoral College, according to one estimate.[27] The furor over the Electoral College that year was caused by the campaign of third-party candidate Governor George Wallace.[28] He earned enough support to cause fears that the election would essentially be decided by the Governor himself. Many worried that Wallace would obtain enough electoral votes to prevent either the Republican or the Democratic candidates, Richard Nixon and Hubert Humphrey, from obtaining a majority in the Electoral College. In such circumstances, the presidential election would move to the Constitution's secondary election procedure in the House of Representatives. The situation could have put Wallace in a position to cut a deal because his endorsement could swing the votes of his electors and prevent the necessity of a contingent election. Such a situation never came about, however. On Election Day, Wallace won 46 electoral votes, but these votes were insufficient to prevent Nixon from winning the presidential election with a majority of 301 electoral votes.

Following Bush's defeat of Gore, a Gallup poll again showed that a majority of Americans, 59 percent, would support abolition of the Electoral College.[29] A *Time*/CNN poll showed a greater majority: 63 percent in support of abolition, compared to 29 percent in favor of retaining the Electoral College.[30] This number is lower than it has been in the past, despite the turmoil surrounding the 2000 election.

Today's negative views on the Electoral College are ironic, given the universal admiration in which the system was held at the time of the Constitutional Convention. One influential delegate to the Constitutional Convention, Alexander Hamilton, publicly deemed the Electoral College "excellent." The other Convention delegates agreed with him; they viewed the Electoral College as one of the great achievements of the Constitutional Convention.[31] Transcripts of the ratification debates do not record much opposition to the presidential election process, although other aspects of the proposed Constitution were debated intensely. Both at the Convention and during the ratification debates, the Electoral College was considered a clever solution to one problem facing the new nation: It would allow the will of the people to be expressed, but would still provide sufficient safeguards to protect minority interests. The unenthusiastic views of today's citizenry on this topic would almost certainly surprise the founding generation.

Judging Institutions, Not Individuals

Prior to the 2000 election, speculation was rampant that Bush would win the popular vote, yet lose the presidency to an Electoral College win by Gore. Several news outlets reported that each candidate was preparing for exactly this situation. The *New York Daily News* quoted a "Bush aide" as saying that the campaign would seek to discredit a Gore Electoral College win. "The one thing we don't do is roll over," the Bush aide allegedly stated, "We fight."[32] Several days later, the *Scripps Howard News Service* reported that the Gore campaign was also preparing for a popular vote loss prior to the election. According to this report,

Gore requested that a legal brief be prepared "detailing why the Constitution and the Electoral College must be the final arbiter of a presidential race."[33] Before the election, then, he was reportedly preparing to justify the legitimacy of his presidency, despite an anticipated popular vote loss. Following the election, of course, the positions of the candidates were reversed.

Neither of these stories gained steam in the media, although rumors regarding these preparations still survive on the Internet today. Whether they are truth, rumor, or a little of both,[34] these stories illustrate an important point: When evaluating constitutional provisions, it is foolhardy to base one's opinion on how one situation may or may not come out. After all, the situation can easily reverse itself the next time around.

The pre-election speculation in 2000 does make one wonder. How many Gore supporters would have called for changes to the presidential election process if their candidate had won during 2000? Conversely, would so many Bush supporters have become instant Electoral College supporters if Gore had won the electoral vote, but lost the popular vote?

Most Americans did not seem to have strong feelings about the Electoral College one way or another prior to 2000. Following the election, however, many voters quickly developed passionate opinions on the wisdom of awarding the presidency based upon the votes of the states, rather than the combined votes of individuals nationwide. One suspects that many Americans became instant Electoral College opponents or supporters, depending on which candidate they had backed in the voting booth on November 7.

Such a situation is unfortunate. The Electoral College is a brilliant constitutional device that deserves the support of the American people. It does not deserve such support, however, simply because one man in one year won one election—nor does it deserve to be opposed because one man lost one election. It should be evaluated and judged on its own merits, regardless of which candidate a person voted for in 2000.

It is dangerous to keep or change constitutional provisions just to accommodate one person. Good arguments can often be made for one trustworthy or sympathetic individual—but the status of one individual in one situation is never the primary concern. After all, others may later come along who are *un*trustworthy or *un*sympathetic. The most important goal of the Constitution is to protect the freedom of Americans from these latter individuals or situations, even if it sometimes means placing restrictions on people who have elicited our compassion or confidence.

Americans would not, for example, consider repealing their right to be free from "unreasonable searches and seizures,"[35] simply because the current Attorney General is an upright and moral man who has promised to use his newfound freedom solely to fight terrorists. Even if that Attorney General is truly honorable, what guarantee is there that his successor will not abuse the power? Nor would Americans give up their right to a trial by jury simply because the current batch of judges seems especially fair and impartial.[36] These and other provisions in our Constitution exist to protect Americans' freedom when undeserving people follow principled people into office. In many cases, the Constitution may even provide two or three layers of security against those individuals who would abuse the power of government once given the opportunity to do so.

The Electoral College serves as one of these many layers of protection. Americans should not decide to alter it based upon the outcome of one election that may or may not have gone their way—even if a popular vote winner faced with legal disputes in one state cuts an extraordinarily sympathetic figure. A more honest intellectual exercise is to consider carefully the benefits and protections offered by the presidential election process as a whole, over time, regardless of the caliber of candidates who seek the office of President.

INTRODUCTION

On a Personal Note

This book was not originally intended to be a book at all. Instead, it was meant for possible publication in a legal periodical. When I started the project, my views on the Electoral College were fairly ambivalent. In the interest of full disclosure, readers should know that I voted for Bush in the 2000 election, so I was rather pleased about that election outcome. At the time, however, I realized how very close the country came to the precise opposite result. I was, in fact, feeling a bit irritated about the Electoral College in late October 2000. I was worried that Gore would win the electoral vote, leaving Bush with a useless popular vote win.

By the time I plowed through my research, my views were no longer ambivalent. To the contrary, I had absolutely convinced myself of the immense value of the Electoral College to our republican democracy.

My research revealed one additional point. I came to realize that my legal research piece, if completed, would fill a need that had already been fulfilled. Most works available on the Electoral College are law review articles for lawyers or textbooks for political scientists. Few other options are available to those who would like to better understand this aspect of the American voting system. My law review article became a book, intended to fill that gap.

This book is not intended to be a treatise on the Electoral College. Many of those have already been written and are listed in the endnotes for those who are interested. Instead, this book is a primer, a summary of the history of and justifications for preserving our unique presidential election system. It is my hope that this book will help reveal the invalidity of the criticisms that are often thrown at the Electoral College. Americans can learn much from the historical results of their presidential election system, just as the founding generation learned much from the political systems that preceded their own.

The Founders deemed the Electoral College to be one of the best features of the Constitution that they created. I imagine they would consider it a great pity that most Americans now believe the Electoral College to be an anachronism, an institution that serves no real purpose in a global economy transformed by wireless Internet access, 24-hour information outlets, email, beepers, cell phones, and Blackberrys.

The world has changed since that summer in Philadelphia when the Founders drafted a new form of government. As a result, the Electoral College does not operate exactly as anticipated. It does, however, still serve the purposes that it was intended to serve. The world has changed, but the humans in it have not.

Ambition, power, and greed are still dangerous to self-government. Minorities still need to be protected. Rhode Island and Delaware are still smaller than their neighbors, and they still have unique interests that should be represented in the federal government. Moderation and compromise among federal officials and candidates are still beneficial. Americans still need a President who represents the variety of subcultures that span the nation. We need an *American* President, not a Californian or Texan President. The Electoral College ensures that Presidents develop a national base, rather than a regional one.

I was admittedly annoyed in 2000 at the thought of a President Gore, elected by the Electoral College. I will no doubt be unhappy if my candidate loses the electoral vote in future elections. Any such future frustration, however, will not be directed at the country's presidential election system. Instead, it will simply be the disappointment of a voter whose candidate lost the national election. Nothing more. The Electoral College is a clever device that works to protect the freedom of Americans. I believe it would receive a great deal more support if it were better understood.

As the 2004 election draws near, the Electoral College question is sure to be debated yet again. Is the Electoral College an institution that is out-of-date? Does it undermine democratic principles and subvert the will of the people, or is it in fact an ingenious method whereby the will of the people can be expressed while the freedom of Americans is protected?

The Electoral College is an institution worthy of respect, but it does need to be better understood by those that it serves. It is the hope of this author that this book will help Americans in 2004 to better understand the election system that was deemed "excellent" if not "perfect" in 1787.[37]

PART ONE

THE ORIGINS OF THE ELECTORAL COLLEGE

CHAPTER ONE

THE CONSTITUTION'S ELECTION PROCESS

M ODERN-DAY American presidential elections are governed by the 12th Amendment to the U.S. Constitution;[1] however, this provision was not adopted and ratified by the states until 1804. The framework for the nation's first four presidential elections was instead provided by Article II[2] of the Constitution, first created at the Constitutional Convention during the summer of 1787.

The 12th Amendment and Article II procedures are fairly similar, except the original Article II provision did not provide for separate voting for the President and Vice President. Instead, the candidate with the most votes became President and the runner-up became Vice President. During the country's fourth presidential election in 1800, this combined voting procedure created problems. As a result, the 12th Amendment was adopted and governed the next presidential election in 1804.

Despite claims to the contrary, the constitutional process of selecting a President, while not as straight-forward as a direct popular vote, is not terribly complicated either. It is perhaps easiest to think of the election in two phases: First, the Electoral College vote, and second, the contingent election procedure, which is used only if no candidate wins a majority of electoral votes.

Unintended Consequences in 1800

The country's first two elections were relatively uneventful. Nearly everyone expected that the revered General, George Washington, would be the nation's first President. The bigger question was who would serve as his Vice President. John Adams was elected to the post. By the time Washington retired in 1796, political parties were coalescing, and they were identifying specific nominees for President and Vice President. In 2004, voters expect each party to nominate one person for President and one for Vice President. In 1796, however, this practice was just taking shape. The emergence of separate nomination processes for President and Vice President caused an unanticipated conflict with the new Constitution's presidential election provision. At that time, electors were not allowed to differentiate between their votes for President and Vice President. Instead, each elector was to cast two ballots for President. When these electoral votes were tallied, the first place winner became President and the second place winner became Vice President.

Two major party candidates competed for the presidency during the country's third presidential election in 1796. The Federalist Party nominated then-Vice President Adams for President, and the Democratic-Republican Party nominated Thomas Jefferson. When the electors cast their votes, Adams placed first with 71 electoral votes, and he became the country's second President. The Federalist Party's vice presidential candidate, Thomas Pinckney, did not place second, however. Instead, that honor went to Jefferson, who won 68 electoral votes. His second place finish made him Vice President, even though he and Adams were from different political parties. Pinckney placed third with 59 electoral votes. The remainder of the electoral vote was divided among ten men.

The Federalist Party avoided a mistake that the Democratic-Republican Party would later make in the election of 1800. Yet its actions, ironically, contributed to Pinckney's loss of the vice presidency. Recognizing the possibility of an unintended tie if all Federalist electors voted both for Adams and Pinckney, the Federalist Party instructed some of its electors to vote for Adams with one ballot, but to cast a blank second ballot in place of their vote for Pinckney. Unfortunately for the Federalists, too many Pinckney votes were held back, and Jefferson squeaked in between the two men to place second in the balloting.[3]

The fourth presidential election was more eventful,[4] and it brought the flaw in the Article II process more sharply into view. In 1800, the Democratic-Republican Party nominated Jefferson for President and Aaron Burr for Vice President. The Democratic-Republican slate defeated the Federalist Party candidates, Adams and Charles Pinckney, by eight and nine electoral votes, respectively. The presidential election should have ended there—but it didn't. Unfortunately, the Democratic-Republican Party failed to ensure that one elector would abstain from casting his vote for Burr. The result was an electoral tie: Jefferson and Burr each received the same number of states' electoral votes. Although the electors had intended to elect Jefferson for President and Burr for Vice President, the constitutional provision did not allow them to distinguish between their votes for the two offices. The election was thrown into the Constitution's secondary election procedure, known as the House contingent election.

More trouble brewed in the House, which was still controlled by the outgoing Federalist Party. Many Federalists searched for a way to thwart Jefferson's election. Eventually, these Congressmen decided to throw their support behind Burr. Other Federalists, relegated to the minority for the first time, sought concessions from Jefferson in return for their vote.

A stalemate continued for the better part of a week.[5] Nine state votes were needed to win the election in the House, but neither candidate could obtain this majority. Over five days of voting, 34 ballots were taken, but the vote remained unchanged: Eight states for Jefferson, six for Burr, and two states divided. The sixth day of voting opened with yet another unchanged ballot, but after this 35th ballot, one Congressman yielded. James Bayard, the only Congressman from Delaware, indicated his decision to switch his vote to Jefferson. His action would place the critical ninth state in Jefferson's column. His decision broke the deadlock, which in turn made his vote for Jefferson unnecessary. In the end, he abstained from voting on the 36th ballot, as did Congressmen from Maryland, Vermont, and South Carolina. Jefferson ultimately won, ten states to Burr's four.

Results: Election of 1800

	Party	Nominee For	Electoral Votes	House Votes
Thomas Jefferson	Democratic-Republican	President	73	10
Aaron Burr	Democratic-Republican	Vice President	73	4
John Adams	Federalist	President	65	—
Charles C. Pinckney	Federalist	Vice President	64	—

Allegations later surfaced that the impasse had been broken because Jefferson cut a deal with Bayard via an intermediary, General Samuel Smith of Maryland. Jefferson, however, denied these claims. In a letter to Dr. Benjamin Rush, he later described his reaction to Adams at the time of the House deliberations, "I will not come into the government by capitulation. I will not enter on it, but in perfect freedom to follow the dictates of my own judgment."[6]

In all likelihood, Jefferson did not cut a deal, but Smith may have taken it upon himself to ascertain and pass on Jefferson's views regarding certain matters of concern to Bayard. Bayard, finding Jefferson's views satisfactory, eventually decided to change his vote.[7] Jefferson's election may also owe much to the intercession of Alexander Hamilton, who had no great fondness for Burr. Hamilton wrote many letters to Congressmen, urging them to obtain concessions from and vote for Jefferson instead. To Bayard he wrote a scathing letter alluding to Burr: "'[G]reat Ambition unchecked by principle, or the love of Glory, is an unruly Tyrant.'"[8] The new Vice President had no great fondness for Hamilton, either. He would later kill Hamilton in a duel during July 1804.

To an American voter in the year 2004, passing a constitutional amendment to separate the voting for President and Vice President might seem like an obvious solution to these electoral problems, but many congressional representatives in the early 1800s did not see the issue in such black and white terms. To the contrary, a fair amount of argument over the subject ensued in 1801 and following.[9] The minority party, the Federalists, did not want to approve the proposed amendment. They argued that the election process, as it then stood, made it possible for the minority party to have a representative in the executive branch of the government. In all likelihood, they feared that the Democratic-Republicans were taking advantage of the situation to deprive them of such an advantage in a future presidential administration. Some Democratic-Republicans, for their part, could see the possibility that they would be in the minority again some day. They hesitated to change the election procedure as well. After all, the Article II process had helped them to gain the vice presidency in 1796, when Jefferson defeated the Federalist vice presidential candidate, Thomas Pinckney.

An amendment to the election procedure failed to pass the Senate by a single vote when it was first proposed in 1801. In 1803, however, with the specter of a new presidential election on the horizon, the 12th Amendment gained enough support in the Congress to pass both the Senate and the House. North Carolina became the first state to ratify the amendment on December 21, 1803. The amendment became effective when New Hampshire ratified it on June 15, 1804. Tennessee ratified it later, on July 27, 1804. Three states rejected the amendment.[10]

The 12th Amendment still provides the framework for American presidential elections today.[11] Its procedures are virtually identical to those in the original Article II provision adopted at the 1787 Constitutional Convention, except the 12th Amendment procedures provide for separate voting for the President and Vice President in the Electoral College; they also made minor changes to the contingent election procedures, used when no candidate wins a majority of the electoral votes.[12]

The election process was tweaked and adjusted following the election of 1800, yet today it remains largely as the Founders created it. As a first step, the states cast electoral votes in the nationwide presidential election. If no candidate wins a majority of these state votes, then the House of Representatives must decide which of the top candidates will be the next President.

The Electoral College Vote

The Constitution does not provide for a national, direct popular vote to determine the winner of the presidency. Instead, it provides for an election in which each state is granted a certain number of representatives, called electors, to cast votes on its behalf.[13] This vote is national in nature, but it is a tally of states' votes, not individuals' votes. This national vote among the states is often referred to as the Electoral College vote.

States are allocated one elector for each of their representatives in Congress — both Senators and Congressmen.[14] Each state therefore automatically receives a minimum of three votes, as it is entitled to at least two Senators and one Congressman in the Congress, regardless of population.[15] Puerto Rico and the Island Areas are not given electors, as they are not states. The District of Columbia did not initially receive votes because it is not a state;

however, adoption of the 23rd Amendment in 1961 provided it with at least three electoral votes, as if it were a state.[16] At this time, there are 538 total electors. Following the 2000 Census, California has the most electors (55), while seven states plus the District of Columbia have the minimum number of electors (3).[17]

It is left to the state legislatures to decide how to appoint their electors for this national election,[18] and it is generally agreed that the legislatures may appoint their states' electors in any manner that they choose. The Supreme Court reaffirmed this principle in the litigation surrounding the 2000 election. In *Bush v. Gore*, the Court stated: "The individual citizen has no federal constitutional right to vote for electors for the President of the United States unless and until the state legislature chooses a statewide election as the means to implement its power to appoint members of the Electoral College."[19] Indeed, the Court noted, "[The state legislature] may, if it so chooses, select the electors itself."[20]

This is exactly what happened in the first presidential election when the legislatures of Connecticut, Delaware, Georgia, New Jersey, and South Carolina each appointed electors on behalf of their citizens.[21] On the other hand, Pennsylvania, Maryland, Virginia, and Massachusetts appointed their electors through popular vote; this vote took a different form in each of the four states.

In Pennsylvania, electors were elected on a general ticket by popular vote. Maryland provided for the election of electors on a general ticket, but directed that five were to be residents from the Western Shore and three were to be from the Eastern Shore. Virginia created 12 districts specifically for the election of electors. One elector was elected from each of these 12 districts. These elector districts were separate from the ten districts created for the election of Congressmen. In Massachusetts, the state was divided into congressional districts. On Election Day, voters cast two ballots for elector in addition to the votes cast for Congressmen. The names of the two electors receiving the most votes in each congressional district were submitted for a second election, this one before Massachusetts' general court. From this list of names, the general court determined which elector would represent each congressional district; they also selected two at-large electors to represent the state.

A fifth state attempted, but failed, to implement a popular vote in this first presidential election. New Hampshire passed a statute providing for an election by a majority popular vote, but it also made provision for legislative selection in the event that the election resulted in no choice. Ultimately, the legislature appointed the electors in the 1789 election. Of the other three states, New York lost its vote altogether due to disagreement in the legislature regarding how to proceed, and North Carolina and Rhode Island did not vote, as they had not yet ratified the Constitution.

The second presidential election saw a similar variety of elector selection methods. Of the 15 states that voted, nine states relied upon their legislatures to choose their electors. Maryland, New Hampshire, and Pennsylvania elected their electors by general ticket, while Virginia elected them by districts. Massachusetts held an election for the selection of electors, but divided its state into two five-elector districts and two three-elector districts for this purpose. North Carolina was divided into four districts. The members of the legislature in each district selected three electors to represent the district.

The states continued to rely upon a wide variety of methods for the appointment of their electors through the first several presidential elections; however, it did not take long for each state to move to statewide direct, popular elections instead. Most states had taken this step by the 1830s, although South Carolina did not utilize popular elections until after the Civil War.[22] Today, each state except Maine and Nebraska uses a "winner-take-all" system, whereby the presidential candidate winning the state's popular vote is awarded the state's slate of electors in its entirety. Maine and Nebraska give two electoral votes to the winner of the state's popular vote and select the remaining electors by congressional district.[23] Despite the technical possibility that their electoral votes could be divided among candidates, neither state has done so since they implemented their district systems in 1972 and 1992, respectively.[24]

While the state's authority to determine a method for appointing electors is not in doubt, one issue is unresolved. Some dispute remains regarding the extent of Congress' constitutional authority (or lack thereof) if there is controversy regarding which of two slates of electors rightfully represents a state.[25] The controversies surrounding the election of 1876, discussed in the introduction, were made worse in large part due to this unresolved issue. The Congress created an Electoral Commission to resolve the problems in 1876, but only after many other House and Senate proposals had been defeated. No one seemed to know how to handle the election dispute.[26] Following the chaotic election proceedings, Congress enacted the Electoral Count Act of 1887.[27] In this statute, Congress claimed authority to supervise the Electoral College process. The law it passed limits state discretion as to issues of timing and grants Congress final authority in counting electoral votes. This federal law, as updated and expanded through the years, currently provides a timeline for the various procedures described in the Constitution.

Election Day is the Tuesday following the first Monday in November in any given presidential election year.[28] In 2004, the election date is November 2, and in 2008, the election will be held on November 4. On Election Day, voters in the states are not voting for the presidential candidate himself. They are actually voting for a slate of electors (Republican, Democrat, or third party), even though the names of the electors themselves are not on the ballot in most states.[29] Once the votes have been tallied, each state (except Maine and Nebraska) will certify the entire slate of electors for the party that won a majority of that state's popular vote. A "Certificate of Ascertainment" with the names of these electors is forwarded to Washington, D.C.[30]

The electors affiliated with each party were appointed prior to the election, usually at the state party convention during the election year. In some states, these electors are committed to vote for their party candidates by state law, although it is unclear whether these pledges can constitutionally be enforced. At other times, the elector is bound by a pledge to his party, but in still other cases, the elector is bound by nothing more than his conscience.[31]

These electors assemble in their state on the first Monday after the second Wednesday in December.[32] In 2004, these meetings are on December 13, and in 2008, they will be held on December 15. On this day, the electors cast the votes that officially determine who will be the next President of the United States. These votes are recorded on "Certificates of Vote," one of which goes to the President of the Senate.[33] These votes must be received by the Senate by the fourth Wednesday in December,[34] and they are counted on the January 6 following any meetings of the electors. The Congress meets in joint session to count the votes.[35] The President of the Senate presides at this meeting. Ironically, on January 6, 2001, then-Vice President Al Gore presided over the joint session that declared his opponent, George W. Bush, the winner of the 2000 election.

To be elected President, a candidate needs a majority of the states' electoral votes, which are cast in December. He does not need a majority of the direct popular vote on Election Day.[36] At this time, 270 votes constitute a majority of the Electoral College and will win the presidency for a candidate.[37]

The Contingent Election

If no candidate wins a majority of the Electoral College vote, the Constitution provides a back-up method for presidential selection. This procedure is often referred to as the Constitution's contingent election procedure. In this secondary election, the election of the President is sent to the House and the election of the Vice President is sent to the Senate.[38]

In the House vote for President, each state delegation is granted one vote.[39] California, with its current delegation of 53 Congressmen, would cast one vote, as would South Dakota, with its single Congressman. In the event that a state's delegation is evenly divided, that state cannot vote until and unless the tie is broken. For instance, Maine's vote will result in a tie if one of Maine's two Congressmen votes Republican while the other votes Democrat. One of the Congressmen will have to agree to abstain or switch his vote before Maine's vote can be cast for a candidate. Otherwise, the State of Maine will abstain from the election.

A President is elected when one candidate wins a majority of the votes of state delegations (currently 26). State delegations may vote for any one of the top three presidential candidates in the Electoral College vote, and re-votes are taken until a majority is achieved. A similar procedure is employed for election of the Vice President, except that each Senator is granted one vote and only the top two vice presidential candidates from the Electoral College vote are candidates in the Senate vote.

The Constitution provides this outline for the contingency procedures that are to be employed in the House and Senate, but it does not delineate all the logistical aspects of this secondary election. If a contingent election were required in the House in 2004, there would be numerous questions regarding what specific procedures should be followed.[40]

First, are state votes determined by majority or plurality within each state delegation? A closely related question is whether a quorum is required within each state delegation before the delegation may take its vote. The Constitution does not provide an answer, so the House would likely turn to the rules that it passed during the contingent election of 1825 (discussed more in Chapters Four and Twelve). Under these rules, a state could not cast a vote except by "'majority of the votes given.'"[41]

For instance, in Massachusetts, which has ten Congressmen, six Congressmen constitute a majority and are therefore needed to cast the state's one vote (assuming that all Congressmen vote). If four Congressmen vote for Kerry, three for Bush, and three for Nader, the state's vote is deemed "'divided'" and is not counted because Kerry has only a plurality of the votes within the state delegation. The state may vote in the election if, for instance, two Congressmen switch to Kerry. Alternatively, if the three Nader Congressmen abstain from the state balloting, then Massachusetts' vote will go to Kerry because four votes constitute the "'majority of the votes given.'"

Second, are states' votes taken by secret ballot? Similarly, are the votes of individual Congressmen within each state delegation taken by secret ballot? In 1801 and 1825, many Congressmen felt that votes within state delegations should be cast by secret ballot, but the rules that they passed do not necessarily require the ballots to be secret. In fact, many newspapers in 1801 and 1825 reported the votes of Congressmen.[42]

Last, is the contingent election conducted in the new or old House of Representatives? The Constitution provides that the new House is sworn in on January 3,[43] and federal law provides that the electoral votes are counted on January 6.[44] Accordingly, many scholars believe that the new House is responsible for conducting the contingent election. A few others, however, observe that the counting of the votes on January 6 is a mere formality. The outcome of the Electoral College vote is generally known much sooner. It is possible that, under the right set of circumstances, some might urge that the contingent election be held earlier, in the lame-duck House.

When Ross Perot entered the 1992 presidential race, the House did some investigation into the logistical aspects of a contingent election. Unfortunately, it dropped the issue when Perot dropped out of the race (temporarily, as it turns out).[45] The issue was never raised in any serious manner again. The lack of consideration regarding this issue is unfortunate. Obviously, fair and impartial contingent election procedures can most easily be identified before the outcome of any one election hangs in the balance. Once the procedures are actually needed, partisan considerations are certain to taint any discussion of logistical procedures that remain unresolved. The House of Representatives should consider these logistical issues and adopt procedures for a contingent election, even though no immediate need for them appears on the horizon.

<><>

America's method of presidential election remains largely as it was first conceived by the Founders in the summer of 1787. The procedure seems unnecessarily complicated to many modern-day Americans, yet the Founding Fathers believed the Electoral College to be an ingenious solution to the problems facing the new country. Max Farrand, in his *The Framing of the Constitution of the United States*, reports: "[F]or of all things done in the convention the members seemed to have been prouder of that than of any other, and they seemed to regard it as having solved the problem for any country of how to choose a chief magistrate."[46]

The Founders spent months of extensive deliberation on the topic of presidential election. They found it to be one of the hardest topics facing the Convention, because of the necessity of incorporating so many conflicting values into the election system. When the Electoral College proposal was completed, they viewed it as a unique and commendable solution—a solution that came as close to perfection as possible in an imperfect world. More importantly, creation of the Electoral College allowed the Founders to reflect the many, apparently contradictory, goals of the new republic in their presidential election process.

CHAPTER TWO

AN AMERICAN BALANCING ACT

D EAN CLARENCE MANION of the Notre Dame University College of Law once observed:

> The honest and serious students of American history will recall that our Founding Fathers managed to write both the Declaration of Independence and the Constitution of the United States without using the term "democracy" even once. No part of any one of the existing forty-eight State constitutions contains any reference to the word.[1]

Half a century later, his statement remains true, with the exception of two recent additions to the California and Oregon Constitutions.[2]

This fact may come as a surprise to many Americans, who mistakenly believe that the United States was established as a democracy. The founding generation, however, intentionally omitted the word "democracy" from their governing documents. The Founders, by and large, were opposed to pure democracies, which allow bare majorities to tyrannize over minority groups. Instead, the founding generation intended to create a republic—or, arguably, a republican democracy—which would incorporate a spirit of compromise and deliberation into decision-making.

Such a form of government, the Founders believed, would allow them to achieve two potentially conflicting objectives: Avoiding the "tyranny of the majority" inherent in pure democratic systems, while allowing the "sense of the people" to be reflected in the new American government.

Before traveling any further into the tangled thicket of the "intent of the Founders," it is important to recognize that an element of difficulty always exists in attempting to summarize the collective thoughts and deliberations of a group of individuals. Certainly, opinions among the delegates to the Constitutional Convention, the state ratifying conventions, and the general public differed widely on many issues. Indeed, some early Americans were opposed to adoption of the Constitution altogether. These early Patriots had differences of opinion, but their differences were, in many respects, transcended by shared concerns. One concern that was shared by many in the founding generation was how to resolve the tension between allowing self-government and providing protection for the political liberties of minority groups.

Members of the founding generation thought of themselves as having more reason than any other to know what it was like to have no voice in their own government. They themselves had been abused by a tyrannical monarch who took no account of their needs and opinions. As a result, self-governance was an important principle to these Founders. Yet their experiences in England had taught them another important lesson: They knew what it was like to be an ill-treated minority. After all, even if England had been a pure democracy rather than a monarchy, the American colonies, relegated to minority status, would have been quickly trampled by the majority of citizens at home in England.[3]

What form of government allows the people to govern themselves, but also prevents democratic majorities from endangering the freedom of minorities? How can the evils of democracy be avoided, while the benefits are allowed to flourish? The conflict was very real to many of the Founders. At one point during the Constitutional Convention in Philadelphia (one can almost imagine his exasperation), Colonel George Mason, delegate from Virginia, was led to observe: "It is curious to remark the different language held at different times. At one moment we are told that the [democratically elected] Legislature is entitled to thorough confidence, and to indifinite power. At another, that it will be governed by intrigue & corruption, and cannot be trusted at all."[4]

The Founders were students of history. They knew that democracy, in its purest from, could allow even "inflamed" majorities and "unreflective mob[s]" to rule.[5] Any majority, even a bare majority, always wins—even when they do so at the expense of rather large minority groups. The authors of the Constitution realized that freedom and self-government can only co-exist if devices are created to temper the momentary passions of the public. Only "reasonable" majorities should be allowed to rule. The Founders had another important incentive for establishing such a system: It would enable the country's most permanent minority constituency, the small states, to exist peacefully alongside their larger neighbors.

The importance of protecting both the majority and the minority, of allowing self-government but protecting political liberties, was summarized by Thomas Jefferson in his first inaugural address: "All, too, will bear in mind this sacred principle, that though the will of the majority is in all cases to prevail, that will, to be rightful, must be reasonable; that the minority possess their equal rights, which equal laws must protect, and to violate which would be oppression."[6]

The Founders would find encapsulating these conflicting values in the presidential election process to be especially difficult. When they finished crafting the Electoral College, however, it was nearly universally agreed that they had successfully created an election process that reflected the competing values of democratic self-government and the preservation of political liberty for minorities. The Electoral College made it nearly impossible for a presidential candidate to rely upon unreasonable or regional majorities at the expense of minorities or the small states. Instead, a candidate would need to generate national support before he could be successfully elected.

The Evils of Democracy

The Constitution does not guarantee "every State in this Union" a democratic form of government, but rather "a Republican Form of Government."[7] The difference is more than merely semantic. Republicanism expects that a country will thrive when the people are governed by representatives who are elected based on their wisdom, integrity and civic virtue. These representatives are intended to deliberate and reach wise compromises with other representatives.

A democratic, or populist, theory of government, by contrast, would assume that the "main repository of wisdom and virtue" is in the people themselves.[8] Representatives in a democracy merely carry out the majority will and are not expected to independently deliberate. Thus, 51 percent of the people can rule the other 49 percent without any need for compromise, even when the majority will tramples the rights of the minority.

The authors of the Constitution were opposed to the concept of a pure democracy. They had studied the history of many failed democratic systems, and they strove to create a form of government that would be quite different. Indeed, James Madison, delegate from Virginia, argued that unfettered majorities such as those found in pure democracies tend toward tyranny. Madison stated it this way:

> [In a pure democracy], [a] common passion or interest will, in almost every case, be felt by a majority of the whole; a communication and concert results from the form of government itself; and there is nothing to check the inducements to sacrifice the weaker party or an obnoxious individual. Hence it is that such democracies have ever been spectacles of turbulence and contention; have ever been found incompatible with personal security

or the rights of property; and have in general been as short in their lives as they have been violent in their deaths.[9]

The rhetoric against democracies became quite strong during the Constitutional Convention. Early in the debates, Elbridge Gerry, delegate from Massachusetts, forcefully asserted that "[t]he evils we experience flow from the excess of democracy."[10] Edmund Randolph of Virginia concurred that "the general object was to provide a cure for the evils under which the [United States] laboured; that in tracing these evils to their origin every man had found it in the turbulence and follies of democracy."[11] Later in the Convention, Randolph reaffirmed his words, noting that the "democratic licentiousness of the State Legislatures proved the necessity of a firm Senate. . . . to controul the democratic branch of the [National] Legislature."[12]

Other delegates also sought to encourage creation of a system that would control the impulsiveness and emotion that they believed would sometimes characterize public opinion. Gouverneur Morris of Pennsylvania remarked that "Every man of observation had seen in the democratic branches of the State Legislatures, precipitation—in Congress changeableness, in every department excesses [against] personal liberty private property & personal safety."[13]

The arguments against pure democracy continued after the Constitutional Convention had concluded. Madison spoke to Jefferson of the dangers that could be created when the Government becomes "the mere instrument of the major number of the constituents."[14] Alexander Hamilton continued these arguments against democracies in a June 21, 1788 speech before the New York ratifying convention:

> It has been observed, by an honorable gentleman, that a pure democracy, if it were practicable, would be the most perfect government. Experience has proved that no position in politics is more false than this. The ancient democracies, in which the people themselves deliberated, never possessed one feature of good

government. Their very character was tyranny; their figure, deformity.[15]

Other early Americans concurred in the judgment of these Convention delegates. John Adams, who signed the Declaration of Independence and later became President, declared, "[D]emocracy never lasts long. It soon wastes, exhausts, and murders itself. There never was a democracy yet that did not commit suicide."[16] Another signatory to the Declaration of Independence, Benjamin Rush, stated, "A simple democracy . . . is one of the greatest of evils."[17] A third signer, John Witherspoon, agreed: "Pure democracy cannot subsist long, nor be carried far into the department of state—it is very subject to caprice and the madness of popular rage."[18] Fisher Ames, a member of the Massachusetts convention that ratified the Constitution, agreed: "A democracy is a volcano, which conceals the fiery materials of its own destruction. These will produce an eruption, and carry desolation in their way."[19]

The concerns of these pro-Constitution Americans were shared, at least to some degree, by those who opposed ratification of the Constitution. Historian Paul Johnson once described the American form of government as one of "republican structure" and "democratic content."[20] True, those who opposed the Constitution (then referred to as "anti-Federalists") were perhaps more likely to emphasize Johnson's "democratic content," as when Patrick Henry declared in a moving speech before the Virginia ratifying convention that the proposed government "is not a democracy, wherein the people retain all their rights securely."[21] Despite such statements in favor of the people's rights, however, these anti-Federalists did not dismiss the importance of "republican structure."

The opposition of anti-Federalists often centered on one of two perceived shortcomings in the federal Constitution. First, its (then-existing) lack of a Bill of Rights; or, second, the "consolidated" form of the new government. Anti-Federalists feared that the new government attempted to span too much territory; they argued that the new centralized government would have too much power over the state governments. The benefits of republicanism versus democracy were not dismissed; they were often assumed. Indeed, many anti-Federalists promoted a "confederation of republics" instead of the Constitution that had been proposed.[22] The day before Patrick Henry's statement in which he condemned the new Constitution as "not a democracy," he took to the convention floor to declare, "[Y]ou ought to be extremely cautious, watchful, jealous of your liberty; for, instead of securing your rights, you may lose them forever. If a wrong step be now made, *the republic may be lost forever.*"[23] His concern in both speeches was "[t]hat this is a consolidated government . . . ; and the danger of such a government is, to my mind, very striking."[24]

Another anti-Federalist, who wrote under the pen name "Brutus," was more explicit in acknowledging the dangers of democracies. In his argument to do away with the consolidated federal government, he stated, "In every free government, the people must give their assent to the laws by which they are governed."[25] Unfortunately, he concluded, "in a large extended country, it is impossible to have a representation, possessing the sentiments, and of integrity, to declare the minds of the people, without having it so numerous and unwieldy, as to be subject in great measure to the inconveniency of a democratic government."[26]

The pro-Constitution and anti-Constitution forces, then, generally agreed on the principles of republicanism versus democracy. Their disagreement lay in how to express the principles of "republican structure" and "democratic content" in the new government that was to be created. They also disagreed about the wisdom of attempting to create a republic that would cover such a large territory. In the end, obviously, the arguments of the pro-Constitution forces carried the day, and the Constitution was ratified.

The Founders determined that democracy, in its purest form, is dangerous. The Constitution they crafted, therefore, explicitly rejected simple democratic rule by the majority in favor of a system that would require deliberation and compromise. Walter Berns of the American Enterprise Institute has summarized these conclusions reached by the founding generation as they drafted, debated, and ratified the Constitution. He stated:

> The American idea of democracy cannot be expressed in the simple but insidious formula of the greatest good for the greatest number. What the greatest number regards as its greatest good might very well prove to be a curse to those who are not part of that number. . . . [G]overnment is instituted to secure the rights of all.[27]

Reflecting the Sense of the People

These men who spoke so forcefully against the vices of a pure democracy were, however, the same men who supported the signing of the Declaration of Independence, a document that proclaimed: "[Governments] deriv[e] their just powers from the consent of the governed."[28] The Founders' statements against democracy were not indicative of opposition to self-government. To the contrary, the Founders knew and often spoke of the need to allow the will of the people to operate in the new government that they were crafting.

At the Constitutional Convention in Philadelphia, Virginia delegate George Mason often emphasized the importance of retaining a democratic principle in the government. "Notwithstanding the oppressions & injustice experienced among us from democracy," he declared, "the genius of the people must be consulted."[29] One legislative branch, he argued, should be directly elected by the people. This branch would serve as the "grand depository of the democratic principle of the [Government]."[30] It would be able to "know & sympathise with every part of the community."[31] He admitted that the state governments "had been too democratic"[32] in the past, but cautioned the

Convention delegates not to use these past failures as an excuse to "incautiously run into the opposite extreme."[33]

He need not have worried. Other delegates also realized that the government would not be legitimate or sustainable if it failed to reflect the voice of the people. James Wilson, delegate from Pennsylvania, argued that the "most numerous branch of the Legislature [should come] immediately from the people," because "[n]o government could long subsist without the confidence of the people."[34] James Madison "considered the popular election of one branch of the National Legislature as essential to every plan of free Government."[35] He reiterated these thoughts later, as the states considered whether to ratify the Constitution. In *The Federalist No. 39*, he described the "honorable determination which animates every votary of freedom to rest all our political experiments on the capacity of mankind for self-government."[36]

The delegates, then, faced a dilemma. Their fierce opposition to simple democracy ran headlong into their determination to allow the people to govern themselves. Fearful of tyrannical majorities, they distrusted straight democracies. However, they strongly advocated for the right to self-government—and they were faced with the challenging task of reconciling these two positions. How could they let the people rule themselves, while protecting the country from momentary passions or irrational majorities? The Convention delegates addressed the conflict by creating a republican government in which minorities would be given many opportunities to make themselves heard.

James Madison later described the solution that had been sought: "But it is the reason, alone, of the public, that ought to control and regulate the government. The passions ought to be controlled and regulated by the government."[37] James Wilson concurred, as he defended the proposed Constitution before his state's ratification convention: "The advantages of *democracy*," he noted, "are, liberty, equality, cautious and salutary laws, public spirit, frugality, peace, opportunities of exciting and producing abilities of the best citizens."[38] However, he added, democracy has disadvantages, such as "dissensions, the delay and disclosure of public counsels, the imbecility of public measures, retarded by the necessity of a numerous consent."[39] The Constitution, Wilson concluded, proposes a government that "[i]n its principle, it is purely democratical. But that principle is applied in different forms, in order to obtain the advantages, and exclude the inconveniences, of the simple modes of government."[40]

A Republic, If You Can Keep It

When asked by a Philadelphia matron what the Constitutional Convention had produced, Benjamin Franklin famously responded, "'A Republic, if you can keep it.'"[41] The American republic that Franklin described is a blend of contrasts: It takes the will of the majority into account, but then ensures that the voice of the minority will also be heard and not stifled. The political well-being of the country would best be nurtured, the Founders believed, if they provided both the majority and the minority with a voice in their government.

More than one constitutional provision reflects the intent of the Founders to give minorities more influence than they would have in a simple democracy. For instance, the legislative power is divided between a House, in which representation is based on population, and a Senate, in which each state is equally represented.[42] The Constitution divides powers between the state and the federal governments, which allows states to govern themselves in some areas—most notably in the exercise of their police power—without seeking compromise or input from other states or the federal government. In addition, the Constitution sometimes requires a supermajority for action, rather than a simple majority, as when the legislature attempts to override a presidential veto or when states approve a constitutional amendment.

The Founders buttressed the new government with one last protective device: The Electoral College. The new presidential election system provided at least two reasonable concessions to the minority. First, a presidential candidate cannot be elected simply by gaining a majority in a handful of states. Instead, the presidential candidate must garner support across the nation to have a reasonable probability of being elected. Second, the minority is provided with several methods by which it may amplify its voice, allowing it to make a statement that would otherwise go unnoticed in a direct popular vote.

For instance, minority groups that congregate in one state or region of the country may increase their impact in the presidential election. The Hispanic vote has greater weight than it might otherwise have, as it can be influential in determining the outcome of Texas' and California's votes.[43] The Jewish vote in New York carries similar influence.[44] Farmers in the Midwest have the ability to make a statement as well because they can affect the votes of several states.

The election of 1948 demonstrated the great weight that a minority can carry if its population is concentrated in one region of the country. Strom Thurmond received 2.4 percent of the vote in the 1948 election,[45] a relatively small percentage that could have gone unnoticed in a direct popular election. However, the Electoral College system enabled him to capture the votes of four states,[46] victories that allowed him and those he represented to capture national attention. The election outcome is a remarkable demonstration of what a minority can achieve in our presidential election system, at least under certain circumstances. (At the same time, it demonstrates the manner in which the Electoral College controls extremist or unhealthy third parties. The benefits of moderation and compromise in politics, as encouraged by the Electoral College, are discussed more in Chapter Six.)

Some critics, however, continue to advance the notion that the Founders had dishonorable motives for creating the Electoral College. According to this view of the founding, the Founders were an "elitist" group of white men who deliberately sought to take the election of the President out of the hands of the people.

In pursuing their politically correct theory, these critics frequently cite George Mason, who (in addition to his statements that "the genius of the people must be consulted") stated, "it would be as unnatural to refer the choice of a proper character for chief Magistrate to the people, as it would, to refer a trial of colours to a blind man."[47]

This negative view of the Founders as an elitist group has been reinforced at a level as high as the Supreme Court. In 1963, the Court, then led by liberal Chief Justice Earl Warren, stated that the "electoral college was designed by men who did not want the election of the President to be left to the people."[48] The Electoral College, under this view of the Founding, is an institution that should be eliminated—a fate befitting its undemocratic and anti-proletarian roots.

These critics have misinterpreted the role of the safeguards inserted into the presidential election process by the Founders. The Founders, as students of history, felt that its verdict was clear: A presidential election process would fail if based on the untempered expression of the people's will; however, the Founders also strongly felt that the voice of the people could not be removed from presidential election altogether. The system that they devised sought to reconcile these potentially contradictory goals. The Convention delegates knew precautions were necessary, but these protective measures could not filter out the will of the public and replace it with the will of the few. Instead, they should merely filter out public passions of the moment, while enabling the less volatile aspects of public opinion to emerge as the expressed will of the people. The system should allow the majority to win, but it should not exclude the minority altogether.

Discussions regarding the mode of presidential election emphasized the importance of providing the people a voice in the process. The delegates' praise for the final product reflected the importance that they placed upon electing Presidents chosen by the people. James Madison declared, "[T]he President is now to be elected by the people."[49] Alexander Hamilton promoted the Electoral College as an institution that would allow the "sense of the people" to "operate in the choice of the [President]."[50] James Wilson of Pennsylvania supported the proposed election system during the ratification debates, noting that the President "may be justly styled *the man of the people*."[51]

In the American republic created by the Founders, majorities can—and should—rule, but only while they are reasonable. The minority views in a 1970 Senate report reflected this sentiment:

> Accordingly, the crucial question in considering electoral reform is whether one method of election is better than another at creating *reasonable* majorities. One method might be better at obtaining a strictly numerical majority, but only at the price of failing to protect minorities; another might protect minorities very well indeed, but only at the price of frustrating a truly *reasonable* majority.[52]

The Electoral College was considered by the Founders to have struck the perfect balance between minority protection and majority rule. It was a balance that they hit upon only after several months of deliberation and compromise in Philadelphia during the summer of 1787.

CHAPTER THREE

THE GREAT COMPROMISE

T HE CONSTITUTIONAL CONVENTION of 1787 got off to a slow start.[1] At the urging of James Madison and Alexander Hamilton, a convention had been called by the Confederation Congress, which governed (in name, if not in practice) the American colonies immediately following the Revolutionary War. The Confederation Congress, however, did not want the nation's then-existing charter, the Articles of Confederation, replaced. It had instead restricted the purpose of the Convention to "the sole and express purpose *of revising the articles of Confederation* and reporting to Congress and the several legislatures such *alterations and provisions therein* as shall ... render the federal Constitution *adequate to the exigencies of government and the preservation of the Union.*"[2]

It is doubtful that Madison and Hamilton ever intended to abide by these limited instructions. In their view, a stronger national government was needed to handle issues of interstate commerce and foreign relations, among other matters. The directive from the Confederation Congress, however, served as an excuse to convene delegates from all the states. Once they convened, it became clear to the delegates that the Articles of

Confederation could not be successfully amended; instead, a new government would need to be created and proposed. Of course, this dawning revelation—plus the exigencies of travel—all took time, which caused an initial languid pace to the Convention's proceedings.

The meeting was scheduled to begin in Philadelphia on May 14, 1787, but on that morning, only a handful of delegates had arrived. By May 25, a quorum of seven states was present. The 29 delegates determined to proceed with the Convention, despite the fact that six states had no delegates in attendance. Eventually, 55 delegates attended at least some portion of the Convention. Nineteen delegates never made an appearance, and Rhode Island refused to send delegates at all. The average age of these delegates never exceeded 43. Benjamin Franklin, at 81, was the oldest, while Jonathan Dayton from New Jersey was the youngest at 26. Despite their young average age, the delegates were unusually accomplished. Most of these delegates had served in Congress or the colonial or state legislatures, and they were well-versed in the works of such philosophers as John Locke and Baron de Montesquieu. Many were lawyers. When Thomas Jefferson, then in Paris, read the names of the delegates, he described them as "an assembly of demi-gods."[3]

George Washington was designated as the Convention's presiding officer, although he contributed very little to the discussions. Commentators have speculated that Washington feared his opinions would carry too much weight with the other men due to his celebrated status as a war hero—even at that early date he was already being regarded as "the Father of the Country."[4] Or maybe his nature made him more prone to reflect than speak during debates, as Jefferson once observed of his former colleague's demeanor in the Virginia legislature. Either way, Washington never rose to speak until the last day of the Convention, although it was known that he was generally in favor of a stronger national government.

The delegates worked through the sweltering summer with the windows and blinds in Philadelphia's State Hall closed. They considered it imperative that the discussions be conducted secretly, so all delegates would feel free to speak their mind. Throughout the debates, the 36-year-old James Madison took comprehensive notes. He said later that his labor in that hot room throughout the summer nearly killed him. "I was not absent a single day, nor more than a casual fraction of an hour in any day, so that I could not have lost a single speech, unless a very short one," he later confirmed.[5] His notes remain the single best source on the debates in the Constitutional Convention.

The mode for electing the Executive was discussed early and often that summer in Philadelphia. The delegates considered it one of the hardest questions that they would be asked to address. They eventually discussed the election of the President on 21 separate days; the issue provoked more than 30 distinct votes.[6]

As with other issues at the Convention, much of the disagreement on the matter of presidential selection reflected the tension between the large and the small states.[7] The friction among the states was perhaps unavoidable. Each state had operated independently for decades—first as a colony, then as a state under the Articles of Confederation. Despite their drastic differences in size and population, these states were accustomed to acting essentially as sovereign nations. It would be no easy matter at this late date for the states, especially the small states, to sacrifice their sovereignty to a new union of states.

The matter came to a head as the delegates sought to finalize a structure for the legislature. The large and small states could not agree, and discussions nearly fell apart. The Convention was saved when a compromise—the "Great Compromise"—was proposed and accepted. One house of Congress would operate on the principle of equal state representation, while representatives in the second house would be elected based upon population. This compromise over the composition of the legislature shaped future discussions on presidential selection. The delegates eventually devised a manner whereby the principles of the Great Compromise could be reflected in the presidential election process. The result was the Electoral College system.

Discussions in the Convention

The presidential selection process was first discussed almost immediately after the Convention opened and established its standing rules. The delegates spent much of these early discussions debating the merits of legislative selection of the President versus those of other modes of appointment, such as a national, direct popular election.[8] Early on, a few delegates suggested the use of electors, as when Luther Martin, delegate from Maryland, advised that they could be "appointed by the several Legislatures of the individual States."[9] These early elector proposals, however, were usually variations on the legislative versus popular election schemes already being discussed. The legislative and direct election proposals remained the primary methods under consideration for much of the Convention.

The small states were concerned about the prospect of direct popular elections. They felt that they would be outnumbered, which made them wary of agreeing to such a plan. Roger Sherman, delegate from Connecticut, stated that the "sense of the Nation would be better expressed by the Legislature, than by the people at large. . . . [The people] will generally vote for some man in their own State, and the largest State will have the best chance for the appointment."[10] Charles Pinckney of South Carolina concurred: "An Election by the people [is] liable to the most obvious & striking objections. They will be led by a few active & designing men. The most populous States by combining in favor of the same individual will be able to carry their points."[11] Moreover, these delegates noted, the size of the country would make it difficult for the populace to be informed about all candidates in a direct election.

The alternative, legislative selection, could not gain steam either, as it was also believed to have crippling disadvantages. Many delegates worried that such a method of appointment would rob the President of his independence from the legislature. Gouverneur Morris, of Pennsylvania, declared that such an executive would be the "mere creature of the [Legislature]: if appointed & impeachable by that body."[12] Instead, Morris continued, the President "ought to be elected by the people at large, by the freeholders of the Country. . . . If the Legislature elect, it will be the work of intrigue, of cabal, and of faction."[13] James Madison concurred:

> If it be a fundamental principle of free [Government] that the Legislative, Executive & Judiciary powers should be *separately* exercised, it is equally so that they be *independently* exercised. There is the same & perhaps greater reason why the Executive [should] be independent of the Legislature, than why the Judiciary should: A coalition of the two former powers would be more immediately & certainly dangerous to public liberty. It is essential then that the appointment of the Executive should either be drawn from some source, or held by some tenure, that will give him a free agency with regard to the Legislature.[14]

The legislative selection proposal was bogged down by yet another problem: the concern over the composition of the legislature. After all, if the small states were not equally represented in the legislature, then they would not have equal representation in selecting the Executive.

Before the election issue could be resolved, these latter discussions regarding the composition of the legislature threatened to tear the Convention apart. The large and small states could not reach an agreement. Luther Martin later described the atmosphere at this juncture, stating that the Convention was "on the verge of dissolution, scarce held together by the strength of a hair."[15] The division among the delegates was resolved when an agreement was forged between the small states and the large states: it was decided that the small states would have equal representation in one of the two legislative houses. From that point on, the discussions surrounding the election of the President changed. The question was no longer *whether* to incorporate the principle of equal state representation into the election process. Instead, the question became *how* to implement it.

The Electoral College mechanism, when it was eventually proposed, made concessions both to the large and the small states. The large states would get more electoral votes in the college, reflecting their greater populations. The small states, however, were guaranteed at least three votes, regardless of population.[16] One further concession was made to the small states: In the event of a contingent election in the House, each state delegation would have one vote, regardless of size.[17] The compromise was quite an important gesture by the large states, as many delegates believed that most elections would be resolved in the House.

Each side, then, made sacrifices to the other at different stages in the election process. James Madison expressed this sentiment when he described the presidential election process as the "result of a compromise between the larger & smaller States, giving to the latter the advantage in selecting a president from the Candidates, in consideration of the advantage possessed by the former in selecting the Candidates from the people."[18]

Evaluating the Final Results

Some have argued that the creation of the Electoral College was not so much a carefully thought out compromise as it was a hasty conclusion to the Constitutional Convention. The delegates, they contend, were tired and under pressure to complete the proposed Constitution. Because they could not come to an agreement on direct election versus legislative selection, they simply drew up a scheme that would be easily accepted by a public that was certain to elect George Washington as President anyway. Two vocal opponents of the Electoral College, Professor

Lawrence Longley and journalist Neal Peirce have stated: "[T]he most basic reason that the electoral college was invented was that the Convention was deadlocked on simpler schemes like direct election and choice by Congress, and thus invented a system that could be 'sold' in the immediate context of 1787."[19]

The delegates were doubtless tired and ready to go home. James Madison admitted as much when he stated, "'[T]he final arrangement took place in the latter stages of the session, [and] it was not exempt from a degree of the hurrying influence produced by fatigue and impatience in all such bodies.'"[20] However, he concluded, "'the degree [of hurrying influence] was much less than usually prevails in [such bodies].'"[21] The fatigue described by Madison was real, but it is unfair to dismiss the quality of the delegates' work based upon this one factor. To do so underestimates the importance of this task to the delegates.

The states were ceding sovereignty to a central, national government. Why would they cede this sovereignty without some assurance that they would be treated fairly in the new government? They had long been abused by a distant, powerful monarch, and they had won independence from that power at great cost. They would be unlikely to give up power to a new, centralized Executive without extensive deliberation into how that Executive would be selected and how his powers would be contained. To the contrary, James Wilson, delegate from Pennsylvania, deemed the presidential election process to be among the hardest issues faced by the Convention. He stated, "This subject has greatly divided the House, and will also divide people out of doors. It is in truth the most difficult of all on which we have had to decide."[22]

Hence, the Electoral College is more than a hasty conclusion to a long summer in Philadelphia. It is a carefully considered and thought-out solution to the problem facing the Convention: In a nation composed of both large and small states that have ceded some, but not all, of their sovereignty to a central government, how should an Executive be selected?

The Electoral College solved the problem by creating a federalist system that incorporated the principles of the "Great Compromise" struck earlier in the Convention. The presidential election process settled upon by the Founders is both a national and a local process. The states determine how to appoint their own electors, but these electors are required to vote for at least one national candidate in addition to the local candidate for whom they would presumably vote. (Recall that electors initially cast two ballots for President. The Convention delegates assumed one ballot would be cast for a local candidate. The modern variation of this rule is that the President and Vice President may not be from the same state.)[23] The President is elected through a series of local election processes, yet he is a national President dependent upon a national people. The election requires the active involvement of each state, yet support from a regional constituency alone is insufficient to win the Electoral College. The President must win local support across the nation to be elected. "'[T]he genius of the present [Electoral College] system,'" a Senate report concluded in 1970, "'is the genius of a popular democracy organized on the federal principle.'"[24]

Early Supreme Court decisions recognized and upheld the federalist nature of American presidential elections. In 1892, the Court held that the Constitution "recognizes that the people act through their representatives in the legislature, and leaves it to the legislature exclusively to define the method of effecting the object. . . . In short, the appointment and mode of appointment of electors belong exclusively to the States under the Constitution of the United States."[25] Today, the Court still recognizes the critical role of the states, as states, in the presidential election process.[26] Most recently, in *Bush v. Gore*, the Supreme Court concluded that the "individual citizen has no federal constitutional right to vote for electors for the President of the United States unless and until the state legislature chooses a statewide election as the means to implement its power to appoint members of the Electoral College."[27] The election, Justice Marshall once noted, is not one "by the Nation as such, but rather by the individual States."[28]

The solution devised by the Founders recognized that, in a federalist republic, the states would and should have a voice in determining the identity of the next President. This state participation was valued at least as highly as the voting rights of individuals in the presidential election process. After all, a federalist system would not easily be maintained in the absence of a federalist election method. And the Founders considered it imperative for the federalist republic to remain intact.

A Federalist Republic

The Constitutional Convention was called based upon the conviction of many early Americans that the United States needed an energetic, central, federal government. After the Revolution, the states struggled for several years under the system of government created by the Articles of Confederation. This government was rather weak and failed to bring the states together as a unified whole. Instead, states' treaties sometimes clashed with each other, commerce suffered, and the country was in debt because the national government could not force the states to contribute to the national treasury. Washington strongly felt that a more powerful national government was needed; he had spent many years struggling to lead the Continental Army under a Congress that did not have sufficient authority to fund and maintain a military. He observed of the Confederation, "Thirteen sovereignties pulling against each other, and all tugging at the [federal] head, will soon bring ruin on the whole."[29] The Constitutional Convention was called in response to the recognition by many that only by creating a central, national government could the states effectively work together.

Yet this need for a strong central government clashed with other sentiments strongly felt by many in the founding generation. Many refused to support the creation of a central government. They had just won their freedom from England in the Revolutionary War. After fighting so hard and sacrificing so many lives, why, then, would these early Patriots create a strong United States Congress to enslave them once again? They might as well have stayed under the thumb of the British Parliament and King.

The clashing sentiments of pro-nationalists and anti-nationalists were exacerbated by another issue: The Founders' review of history showed them that a republic could not successfully extend across a large nation. Large republics could not ensure that every district or segment of society had representation in its own government. Inevitably, someone would not be fairly represented. Republican principles could work well only when the representatives were close to the people.

The solution, the Founders proposed, was to create a federalist republic. Those matters requiring national attention would be left at the national level. Every other matter would be handled by state authorities. In this manner, every person would be adequately represented by his government, particularly on the issues that are closest to home and most impact daily life. Charles Pinckney praised this unique combination of national and state power during the South Carolina ratification debates. The records of the debates summarize his views:

> It had been an opinion long established, that a republican form of government suited only the affairs of a small state; which opinion is founded in the consideration, that unless the people in every district of the empire be admitted to a share in the national representation, the government is not to them as a republic . . . . [Much of the objection] would be done away by the continuance of a federal republic, which, distributing the country into districts, or states, of a commodious extent, and leaving to each state its internal legislation, reserves unto a superintending government the adjustment of their general claims, the complete direction of the common force and treasure of the empire.[30]

American federalism, in its simplest form, is the distribution of power between the federal and state governments. Each government is a sovereign in its own right. Each has a sphere in which its authority trumps the others. Such a system recognizes that larger and smaller governmental authorities may each be better at different tasks. National tasks are handled nationally, but other tasks are handled locally. The country is able to function together on issues requiring cooperation, such as defense, interstate commerce, and foreign affairs. On other issues, freedom is protected by leaving the decision-making process close to where the people live, thereby granting them the greatest influence on the outcome.

Federalism has benefits that were well-recognized by the Founders, who preferred local laws to national laws for several reasons. They knew that it is often easier to influence the content of local laws. Local officials represent fewer people and are therefore more directly accountable to the public. For example, as of the 2000 Census, Texas' 20,851,820 people[31] are represented by 32 Congressmen.[32] Each Congressman, in other words, represents about 650,000 constituents, on average. By contrast, Texas' 150 state representatives[33] represent an average of 139,000 constituents. If a voter or group of voters in Texas wished to influence policy, it would have a greater likelihood of success at the state level, rather than the federal level.

For example, assume that Joe Citizen, residing in Temple, Texas, has been told that his private property is being taken by the government, through its exercise of eminent domain. The government wants to build a highway where his house now stands. Joe wants to fight this process. He has found an alternate path for the highway—one that does not require the government to purchase and demolish his home, or the home of any other citizen. The question is: Would Joe prefer to take this argument to the federal government or to the state government? Most people would prefer arguing before a state legislature, rather than a federal bureaucracy. Joe is more likely to be heard and to have an impact on the process if it is closer to home.

Now take the example a step further. Rather than the state level, wouldn't he really prefer to argue before the county or city authorities? He can certainly have more influence on his local city council members than he can a member of his state legislature—let alone a member of Congress. City council members have small constituencies and would more likely be influenced by a crowd of, say, 50 protesters than would a Senate or House Committee, which is flooded with hundreds of requests even on a slow day. Local lawmaking protects freedom because it allows the people themselves to have the most direct and powerful influence possible on the laws and regulations that affect them on a daily basis.

Another benefit of local lawmaking is that it allows the diversity of subcultures across the country to be reflected in different states and their statutes. Californians, for instance, may be more concerned about environmental care than about creating inexpensive energy sources. America's federalist system allows California to pass legislation accordingly, and it may do so without negotiating with Texans who may care more about saving money on energy. Each state's laws will reflect the differing priorities of its voters. Voters are free to live in a state that reflects their priorities—or to argue for change in their state's laws, as applicable.[34]

Moreover, federalist principles encourage state legislatures to act responsibly. If one state's legislature goes too far in one direction, residents may leave the state for other states, thus encouraging the state legislature to adjust its laws. As an example, residents may leave if a state's tax rates get too high, encouraging lawmakers to restrain spending and bring taxes back to more reasonable levels. California's high taxes and spending rates have caused many companies to move to California's lower-tax neighbor, Nevada. Many people move to Nevada,

Florida, or Texas, because these states do not have state income taxes.[35]

If a state is having difficulty addressing a particular issue, it can look to what has or has not worked in other states and adjust its laws accordingly. During California's 2003 gubernatorial recall election, then-candidate Arnold Schwarzenegger argued that, if elected, he would "[c]reate a working wholesale power market based on the lessons learned from other states . . . . It is time to learn from other successful restructurings enacted by Texas, the New England states, and the Mid-Atlantic states of Pennsylvania, New Jersey and Maryland."[36] States can experiment with new solutions without affecting the rest of the country, as when Ohio experimented with school vouchers in the Cleveland school system. Justice Brandeis once stated, "It is one of the happy incidents of the federal system that a single courageous State may, if its citizens choose, serve as a laboratory; and try novel social and economic experiments without risk to the rest of the country."[37]

The federalist system, in many ways, creates the same incentives and restraints as a free market system. Americans may live and vote and work in the state that best reflects their needs and principles. This freedom to pick up stakes and start afresh encourages lawmakers to create a climate that brings residents to their state.

Professor Judith Best of the State University of New York has explained one last benefit of federalism—a benefit that has particular importance in a presidential election process. A federalist presidential election system, she explains, allows the country to reap the benefits of "safe" factions (or special interest groups) without succumbing to the hazards of "dangerous" factions.[38] Special interest groups in America are based on such public policy issues as gun control, racial preferences, or other social and family issues. These groups, of course, should and do have a voice in America's republican democracy; however, they are best able to contribute to society when they check and control each other. Left to their own devices, these factions could tend toward the extremes of their public policy positions and endanger the freedoms of those who disagree with them.[39]

States are safe factions upon which to rely in the presidential election process. They may act as cohesive units because they share common interests such as environmental, transportation, and local economy concerns. In this capacity, the states are able to play against each other, providing the helpful check-and-balance function that may be provided by special-interest factions. However, because states are also heterogeneous entities composed of individuals with a wide variety of interests, the danger of extremism that often accompanies other special interest groups is muted. Professor Best explains this dynamic:

> The federal principle keeps dangerous factions within bounds by penning them up in multiple small societies. If dangerous factions cannot directly combine their votes across state lines, their destructive potential is reduced. If they are confined within the boundaries of a state, the necessity to compromise in order to achieve national representation can instill moderation.[40]

The country's federalist system prevents local needs from being ignored, controls dangerous factions, and requires a balancing of interests. The Founders recognized that the President should have the same motivation as the Congress, with its House and Senate, to consider local as well as national needs. He should represent the people as a whole, not a bare majority of individuals who may represent only certain regions or special interest groups. Removing states from the presidential election process would undermine the federalist nature of the American republic.

The degree to which the system is valued today will depend upon the degree to which the states, as states, are valued as participants in the process. Those that value the votes of individuals over the influence of states as the *sine qua non* of a modern democracy will downplay the importance of the Electoral College as an institution. Yet many reasons exist to emphasize state participation in the presidential election process, as the Framers of the Constitution understood from their reading of history.

◇

The Framers deliberately created a federalist republic, rather than a pure democracy, because they believed that, ultimately, such a form of government would be the best protection for individual freedom. Moreover, many of the original 13 states would not have consented to being governed by the new American government were it not for the federalist protections in the new Constitution. Delaware's delegates to the Constitutional Convention, for instance, were not authorized to vote in favor of a Constitution that violated the principle of "one state, one vote."[41] Rhode Island refused to participate in the Convention, as it believed that the rights of the small states would not be respected.[42]

Although some modern-day Americans may value individual voting rights more than the rights of the states, it is important to remember that consent of the governed is an equally important component of freedom. This consent would not have been obtained without the protections that the Constitution provides for small states and other minorities. In all likelihood, such consent still could not be obtained today without such minority protections as the Electoral College and equal representation for all states in the Senate.[43]

PART TWO

AN 18TH CENTURY SOLUTION FOR THE 21ST CENTURY

CHAPTER FOUR

A RAPIDLY CHANGING SOCIETY

M UCH HAS CHANGED since 1787. The Founders could not have foreseen the rapid technological advancements that have facilitated national and global communications. They lived in a world that included a healthy fear of tyranny, whereas many Americans today have not been exposed to tyranny except as a theoretical matter. States were then reluctant to give up their sovereignty to a central national government, preferring to handle most matters themselves. Today, states instead often run to the federal government, hat in hand, asking for more funding for roads or schools or medical care. Moreover, Americans increasingly believe that they live in a democracy, rather than a republic; many schools do not teach the republican principles upon which America was founded.

Some academics have predicted for years that these changes could lead to a constitutional crisis. Particularly before the 2000 election, critics often warned that election of a "runner-up" President would throw the country into turmoil. Somewhat pessimistically, they imagined a future election in which Americans would find themselves unable to accept their new President: a popular vote loser. Today's Americans, these critics predicted, are too closely wed to the principle of "one person, one vote" to accept such a President.[1] A book by well-known Electoral College critics Neal Peirce and Lawrence Longley told the story of a hypothetical 1996 presidential election that ended in electoral deadlock and disaster.[2] Professor Akhil Reed Amar of Yale University echoed their warnings, telling a House committee in 1997 that the Electoral College is a "brilliant 18th century device that cleverly solved a cluster of 18th century problems," but "this once brilliant device has become a constitutional accident waiting to happen."[3]

Are these critics right? Could it be that the Electoral College, although once an ingenious solution to many 18th century problems, has today become merely an anachronism—and a potentially dangerous one at that? Or does it still serve the protective purposes intended by the Framers, despite the fact that it sometimes functions a bit differently than originally expected? Are detractors right in saying that our country has changed so much that the benefits of the Electoral College, important in 1787, no longer outweigh any detriments?

These critics have a valid point, worth considering. If the Electoral College is to be kept, it must either serve new, useful purposes in our 21st century world, or it must serve the goals of the Framers in new ways.

Losing Appreciation for States' Rights

Modern Americans cherish their own rights more than the rights of the state in which they live. They may not understand why so many in the founding generation valued their federalist system, in which states have their own areas of total sovereignty. Today's Americans may not know why the founding generation considered adoption of the Tenth Amendment so important—if indeed they know what it says: "The powers not delegated to the United States by the Constitution, nor prohibited by it to the States, are reserved to the States respectively, or to the people."[4]

Yet the problem is still more serious. Many Americans do not always know (or question) upon what basis their federal government claims authority to act. As a result, they do not realize the extent to which one of the federal government's powers, found in the Constitution's Commerce Clause, has been grossly expanded to justify the federal government's intrusion into many matters that should remain the responsibility of individuals or the states. This constitutional provision simply authorizes Congress "[t]o regulate Commerce with foreign Nations, and among the several States, and with the Indian Tribes."[5] The Clause does not authorize governance in matters that are purely *intra*state (as opposed to *inter*state) in nature, yet Congress nevertheless uses the Clause as a pretext to interfere in local matters. Unfortunately, modern American schools do not teach their students about these restrictions upon the federal government. As a result, many Americans remain unaware of the numerous ways in which the federal government illegitimately stretches its power beyond the parameters originally granted to it.

In 1787, the Founders deliberately avoided granting the federal government a general police power; instead, they severely limited federal power, giving the government only certain powers that were enumerated in the Constitution. The Founders considered the concept of limited, enumerated powers an important protection for their hard-won freedom. In modern-day America, by contrast, many Americans seem to have adopted the reverse attitude: They want a governmental solution for every woe. These Americans do not always stop first to evaluate whether the federal government has the authority to provide the solution that they want, nor does it occur to them that their deferral of responsibility may have an unwanted side effect: They may inadvertently undermine their own freedom.

Instead, when the Supreme Court knocks down (for instance) legislation such as the Gun-Free School Zones Act,[6] such Americans wonder why the Supreme Court would declare such a "good" or "useful" law unconstitutional. When the Court strikes down the Violence Against Women Act,[7] the decision is met with similar complaints. Teachers rarely instruct students on the constitutional principle of federalism, which prohibits the federal government from legislating on certain purely intrastate matters. Without this background, it does not occur to many Americans that a federal law may contain a good statement of policy, but still be unconstitutional. Perhaps the good statement of policy is more appropriately enacted by a state government, rather than the federal government.

The Civil War was among the first major events to undermine the value of state decision-making in the eyes of Americans. In the mid-1800s, many southern states opted to continue slavery, citing states' rights as a defense for their actions. Slavery was an appropriate casualty of the war, but the legitimate principle of states' rights unfortunately also took a beating during this time. Later, during the Great Depression, states and individuals lost even more of their independence. Franklin Delano Roosevelt's New Deal offered national, governmental solutions to those in economic hardship. Americans at the time did not dwell on the loss of these states' rights; instead, they were glad for any financial relief.

The Supreme Court initially struck down many of FDR's New Deal measures, arguing that these laws encroached upon purely *intra*state matters. These decisions followed both the Constitution and the Court's own precedents, and they correctly held that Congress may regulate only *inter*state matters when it is relying upon its Commerce Clause power. Congressional power is limited to those powers enumerated in the Constitution, and the Court found that many of FDR's New Deal measures exceeded this federal authority.

FDR, however, was determined not to have his programs thwarted so easily. He was fresh from a landslide victory in the 1936 presidential election, and he resolved to implement his New Deal programs in spite of the Court. He firmly believed that his programs were a necessary component of economic recovery. FDR used his post-election momentum to support a "court-packing" plan, in which the appointment of up to six new Justices was proposed.[8] At the time, he explained that his intent was not to threaten the Justices or influence the Court's rulings— but one would be excused for doubting his claims of innocence in this regard.

The court-packing plan became unnecessary. Justice Owen Roberts buckled under the pressure and switched his vote on a 14th Amendment issue in *West Coast Hotel v. Parrish*, a case that upheld the constitutionality of minimum wage legislation enacted by the State of Washington.[9] The Justice's decision became known as "the switch in time that saved nine" because FDR dropped his court-packing plan soon thereafter.[10]

Following the *West Coast Hotel* decision, the Justice continued his downward spiral, switching his vote on Commerce Clause issues as well. A few weeks later, he joined the majority in *NLRB v. Jones & Laughlin Steel Corp.*, a decision that upheld the National Labor Relations Act (NLRA).[11] This Act gave the National Labor Relations Board expansive power over the country's labor practices. Chief Justice Hughes wrote for the majority: "The authority of the federal government may not be pushed to such an extreme as to destroy the distinction . . . between commerce 'among the several States' and the internal concerns of a State. That distinction . . . is vital to the maintenance of our federal system."[12] In previous cases, similar logic had led the Court to strike down far-reaching federal programs such as the NLRA; however, in *Jones & Laughlin Steel Corp.*, the Court added a big "But." Chief Justice Hughes concluded:

> The cardinal principle of statutory construction is to save and not to destroy. . . . [If there are] two possible interpretations of a statute, by one of which it would be unconstitutional and by the other valid, our plain duty is to adopt that which will save the act. . . . We think it clear that the National Labor Relations Act

may be construed so as to operate within the sphere of constitutional authority.[13]

Following this decision, the Supreme Court embarked on a journey in which it allowed virtually any act of Congress to stand, even when it infringed on matters that were purely local in nature.

In 1942, this stance reached a somewhat ridiculous extreme. The Court upheld the Agricultural Adjustment Act, which set production quotas for farmers. A small wheat farmer in Ohio had been fined for growing more wheat than the Department of Agriculture wanted him to grow. This excess wheat was used on his own farm (as was most of the wheat that he grew), but the Court determined that his wheat use affected interstate commerce anyway. After all, the Court reasoned, had the farmer not grown and used his own wheat, he would have been forced to purchase wheat from others who *are* involved in interstate commerce.[14]

Had FDR's government programs been temporary, or had FDR been less stubborn in pushing his programs past the Supreme Court, perhaps the damage to states' rights could have been lessened. Unfortunately, FDR's actions upset the balance of power between the state and federal governments, perhaps permanently. His New Deal programs became predecessors for many national welfare programs that remain in effect today. The modern Court rarely questions the federal government's authority to legislate in an area. Congress exacerbates the problem by assuming authority to legislate in any area that will score political points in the next election.

Between 1937 and 1994, the list of matters upon which Congress felt justified in legislating grew rapidly. The Court let these federal laws go by, mostly unquestioned, and it did not strike down so much as one law based upon Commerce Clause concerns. Instead, the Court's 1995 decision invalidating the Gun-Free School Zones Act became the first decision in almost 60 years to strike down a law based upon federalism issues. Such a decision is still the exception, rather than the rule, when the Supreme Court reviews a case. As Congress and the Courts have become more accepting of these federal measures, so have Americans become accustomed to congressional action that encroaches upon state and local matters. In fact, many have come to expect and want such federal action. Modern-day Americans increasingly default upon federal action before they seek local solutions. Their attitude directly contradicts that of the Founders.

The early generations of our country understood the need for national action, but they tended to default upon local action first. They understood, of course, that some issues can be addressed only at the national level. This need for national cooperation spurred early Americans to call for a Constitutional Convention. They knew that a centralized government would be necessary to handle certain interstate commerce and national defense matters. Yet they tempered this recognition that national action would be beneficial in certain circumstances with a second belief: They assumed that states and towns could handle a matter until a sufficient argument was made to the contrary.

Many 21st-century Americans do not rely primarily upon their state or local governments to provide a framework for public policy issues. They instead often presume the need for a national solution and consider the possibility of local action only as a last resort. As they have devalued the importance of federalism, so have they changed their views on institutions such as the Electoral College.

Developing a Populist Mentality

Compounding Americans' decreased understanding of federalist principles, their perceptions regarding their form of government have changed as well. The Founders distrusted unchecked democracies, with their historic propensity to degenerate into mob rule, and they instead sought to establish a republic in which the people's voice would be expressed in a tempered fashion. Today's Americans, by contrast, overwhelmingly believe that they live in a pure democracy. They cherish individual expression and populist ideals and seem to view other forms of government as "thwarting" the will of the people.

The founding generation established republican safeguards as a protection against tyranny, but modern Americans have never been exposed to such tyranny (or mob anarchy for that matter) and such a threat seems more hypothetical than real.[15] Instead, they are more likely to view republican safeguards as a hindrance to the principle of "one person, one vote." Why should this sacred democratic principle be less important in presidential elections, they might ask? To the contrary, shouldn't it be even more important than in other elections? George C. Edwards, III, director of the Center for Presidential Studies at Texas A&M University expressed this frustration that many seem to feel:

> There's no justification for the Electoral College—none. We have invested so much in this nation in the principle of "one person, one vote." We've expanded the franchise to make sure that everyone votes. And for someone—no matter who wins the popular vote—to quite legally take the presidency, entirely contrary to democratic principles, is very hard to justify.[16]

Some have argued that the forces nudging the American republic towards such undiluted democratic ideals were present early in the nation's history—as early as 1824. That year, Andrew Jackson lost the election to John Quincy Adams in the House of Representatives, despite winning a plurality both of the popular vote and the Electoral College vote. Jackson won 99 electoral votes and 41.3 percent of the recorded popular vote. John Quincy Adams, in contrast, won 84 Electoral College votes and 30.9 percent of the recorded popular vote.[17] The remainder of the vote was split between William H. Crawford and Henry Clay. The value of this popular vote tally is questionable because many states at that time still selected electors through their state legislatures. Nevertheless, Jackson spent the next four years claiming that the will of the people had been thwarted and that the election had been stolen from him in the House.

Adams won in the House contingent election with the help of Henry Clay, who threw his support behind Adams and was instrumental in obtaining state delegations' votes on Adams' behalf. Adams subsequently made Clay Secretary of State, and Jackson supporters wasted little time in arguing that a "corrupt bargain" had been struck between the two men. Allegedly, Clay initially sought to strike a deal with Jackson, but Jackson refused to "'go to that chair'" except "'with clean hands.'"[18] Of these events, historian Paul Johnson states, "We shall probably never know whether there *was* a 'corrupt bargain.' Most likely not. But most Americans thought so. And the phrase made a superb slogan."[19] Jackson used the issue, in combination with his plurality win in the popular vote totals, to generate public dissatisfaction with the results. Eventually, he was able to win the 1828 campaign, based in part on this issue.

In reality, up until that time, there had been no perception among the electorate that the winner of a direct popular vote should win the presidency; presidential candidates had no reason, therefore, to run their campaigns with such a goal in mind. Nevertheless, the election of 1824 was one of the first events leading to a belief among Americans that popular vote winners should be elected to the White House.

The constitutional amendments after 1824 mirrored the increasingly populist mentality in America. The Civil War resulted in passage of the 15th Amendment, which prevents states from denying minorities the right to vote "on account of race, color, or previous condition of servitude."[20] The 17th Amendment soon followed, removing the election of Senators from the state legislatures and placing that responsibility in the hands of the people.[21] In 1920, the 19th Amendment was ratified, ensuring that women could not be denied the right to vote based on their gender.[22] Other changes to government were less formal, but reflected the growing populist forces nonetheless. For instance, although many state legislatures initially selected electors on behalf of their citizens, today all states hold a direct popular election for the state's electoral votes.

Many critics of the Electoral College maintain that the country's presidential election process has become outdated in a society that increasingly believes itself to be democratic. They discount the ability of the American people to accept Presidents who were not elected with a majority of the popular vote. During the 2000 election, one journalist claimed that the results of that election were "a mess" because "democratic principles count for more" than they did in the early years of our country.[23]

Nevertheless, as the end of President Bush's first term comes to a close without any great constitutional crisis, the claims of these critics ring a bit hollow. The American public, although increasingly democratic, by and large seems to have accepted the outcome of the 2000 election, governed by republican principles.

Evolving into a Global Society

It doesn't take a genius to realize that the ability to communicate, even over distances, has improved dramatically since 1787. Access to news and information was once slow and sporadic. Today, it is instantaneous and practically unavoidable. Presidential candidates can make themselves known to the entire nation through debates, media outlets, and the Internet. Americans can easily educate themselves as to the names, background and policy positions of each candidate, whereas such a task was difficult to impossible in 1787. Traditional journalists no longer have a monopoly on the news. Instead, they compete with weblogs that pour out information (and, sometimes, misinformation), commentary, and humor—all from bloggers' home laptops. An American doesn't have to take the word of the network news anchors regarding the War in Iraq. Instead, he can read the thoughts of Iraqis, directly, by visiting their Internet weblogs.

Americans' ability to communicate with each other has changed dramatically as well. Cell phones and pagers have made users available to each other virtually anywhere in the world. High school students use these phones to text message each other—gone are the days of passing physical notes in class. Blackberrys carry email to users, regardless of where they may be. The Internet is available at the touch of a button from one of these devices, even in the middle of the grocery store check-out line. Technology is available that will allow a person to sit in the middle of Central Park, laptop in hand, surfing the Internet via wireless technology, while he drinks a four-dollar iced frappuccino. Using this technology, he could Instant Message his best friend in Australia from the comfort of his picnic blanket, if he so desires.

Global communication has become so easy and fast that some people even claim that massive self-rule is now possible. Perhaps voters can jump on the Internet and vote for or against legislation. What's the point of voting for representatives in Congress with such technology at the nation's disposal? (One can only imagine the horror of the Framers at such a system, totally bereft of safeguards against majority tyranny and faction.)

Along with the improvement in communications has come a similar change in the nature of commerce. The economy has increasingly become, not just more national, but also more global. Furniture purchased from the store down the street may be made in China. Dialing a technical support center often connects customers to service representatives in India. Opening an email inbox could deliver spam email from all around the world. Wireless technology allows stores to perform instant inventories: Taking a widget off a shelf at the local store could automatically notify a distribution center several states away that more widgets are needed in stock.

At first glance, these changes would seem to undermine the purposes of the Electoral College. The Framers implemented the system based partly on the assumption that the electorate could not be fully informed about each candidate. They could not foresee a world in which truly national candidates would not only be possible, but common. They certainly never predicted that technology would exist allowing their great-great-great grandchildren to vote, simultaneously, via the Internet, if they so desire. Further, some academics contend that federalist principles count for less in today's increasingly global society. State boundaries no longer define the most relevant or meaningful political communities, they argue. The economy is more global than local these days.

◇

The Electoral College undoubtedly operates in a different society from the one that existed in 1787. Global communications and the rise of national political parties have facilitated the rise of national candidates. They have enabled the average voter to be as informed as he would like to be regarding public policy issues and candidates. He can easily debate these issues with those in other states and countries.

Moreover, the Electoral College, in practice, operates differently than it did in 1787. Electors no longer operate as independently as they once did, but they usually merely rubber-stamp the decision of the states' electorates. State legislatures no longer select the electors; instead, electors are selected based on a popular election within each state. Over time, these elections have changed so that all states' electors (except Maine and Nebraska) are now awarded on a "winner-take-all" basis. Confounding the Founders' expectations, the contingent election is a rarity in this day and age.

Despite these changes, the Electoral College has not become an out-of-date electoral tool obstructing the American electorate. It has instead shown an amazing ability to adapt to modern-day America. It operates differently than expected, but still serves the political goals it was intended to serve.

CHAPTER FIVE

THE BENEFITS OF FEDERALISM

P RIOR TO HIS PRESIDENCY, Ronald Reagan discussed the principle of federalism as it relates to the Electoral College. In a 1977 radio broadcast, he described the security the system affords to all states, but especially to small states:

> The very basis for our freedom is that we are a Federation of Sovereign States. Our Constitution recognizes that certain rights belong to the state and cannot be infringed upon by the National government. This is the guaranty that small states or rural, sparsely populated areas will have a proportionate voice in national affairs.
>
> Those who want to do away with the electoral college really mean they want the President elected in a national referendum with no reference as to how each state votes. Thus a half dozen rural states could show a majority for one candidate and be outvoted by one big industrial state opting for his opponent.[1]

His words ring true in any century. Federalism remains important, even in the midst of the Information Age. Americans may operate in a global economy, but, as one columnist recently opined, this globalism has not caused the country to become "one undifferentiated national mass."[2] To the contrary, modern-day American states retain unique interests that should be protected in a free society, and the federalist nature of America's constitutional system provides this indispensable protection.

Separating power between the state and federal governments still protects freedom. Local governance is still preferable on issues that do not require national cooperation. Governance close to home keeps elected officials more directly accountable to enact good policies, as discussed in Chapter Three. Joe Citizen will still have an easier time affecting policy if he brings his concerns to local government officials, rather than to national ones. His vote is more likely to change the outcome of one of these local elections than a national election—and those campaigning for office are always keenly aware of this fact.

The presidential election process devised by the Founders is a cornerstone of America's constitutional system. The Electoral College provides a vehicle whereby this nation of states can elect a President who is truly representative of the diverse interests of the various states. The federalist nature of the presidential election requires candidates to hear and address the unique interests of the various states. The alternative, a direct national election, would most likely produce a President who represents narrower special-interest groups, such as those based on region, state, or ideology.

Critics of the Electoral College allege that the country's presidential election process does less to protect federalism than it does to trample the rights of individuals. Implementation of a direct popular election system, they argue, would not undermine the federalist system. Instead, they contend that the primary consequence of a direct election system is to protect democratic principles. These principles, they argue, should be applied to the nation's most important election: the election of the President of the United States.

The "Wasted Vote" Theory

Critics of the Electoral College often claim that the state-by-state presidential election is unfair and causes some votes to be "wasted."[3] The culprit, they say, is the "winner-take-all" method employed by most states. In perhaps a bit of hyperbole, critics Lawrence Longley and Neal Peirce have alleged that "[t]he operation of the winner-take-all system results in effective massive disenfranchisement of voters supporting losing candidates."[4] They argue for a reform that would eliminate the possibility that a citizen's vote might be wasted simply because he happens to reside in a state where the majority of citizens hold views antithetical to his own.

As this argument goes, a Texan who voted for Gore in the 2000 election wasted his vote, because Bush was awarded the state's entire slate of electors under the winner-take-all method. Then-Governor Bush won his home state with a popular vote total of 3,799,639, but Gore won a fair number of votes, too: 2,433,746.[5] Despite the nearly 2.5 million popular votes cast for Gore, he did not win so much as one electoral vote from Texas. Bush was awarded the entire slate of 32 electors.[6]

Critics condemn this situation as intolerable. After all, in a direct popular election, Gore votes could have instead been included in the final national tally for Gore, and they would not have been wasted simply because they were cast in Texas. Alternatively, critics continue, if Texas were to apportion its electoral votes by district, then this effect of wasted votes would at least be greatly reduced, because some of Texas' electoral votes could have been awarded to Gore in the 2000 election.

These criticisms are unconvincing for two reasons. First, the critics forget that the winner-take-all system is not mandated by the Constitution. To the contrary, any state may change its method of allocating electoral votes at any time.[7] The Constitution mandates that each state, through its state legislature, decide for itself how to allocate its votes.[8] States may cast their electoral votes as a bloc, divide them among multiple candidates, or even cast them according to a lottery system (if they really want to do so). Each state has complete discretion in allocating its electoral votes—and it does not have to agree with its neighboring states on the best method. Each state legislature determines how its state and citizens can best be served in the electoral vote and adopts a method accordingly. If a state's citizens disagree with the chosen method, then they simply need to appeal to their state legislators to change the rules. Texans are free to elect state representatives who are willing to make this change—if, in fact, they feel that such a change would serve the state's best interests.

Some might dismiss this point, arguing instead that the small states are essentially bullied into adopting a "winner-take-all" system once large states, such as California and Texas, have already done so. Arguably, small states have great incentive to cast their votes in a bloc, regardless of what the larger states do. Nevertheless, two small states have apparently determined otherwise. Maine and Nebraska, with four and five votes, respectively, have each adopted a different system. Their elections do not follow the winner-take-all rule; instead, votes are allocated based upon congressional district. The freedom of states to do exactly as they wish is one of the great benefits of federalism.

The wasted vote theory is a bit disingenuous for a second reason. These votes aren't wasted. They were simply cast on the losing side of a popular vote within the state. If the 2000 election had been conducted based on nationwide popular vote totals only, would people claim that any vote for George Bush was "wasted" because Al Gore won the popular vote? Of course not. The votes for Bush were cast in an effort to win. In the event of a loss, they would simply have been votes for the losing candidate—just like any other election.

The nation does conduct democratic, popular elections—but they are conducted at the state level, rather than the national level. Professor Charles R. Kesler of Claremont McKenna College puts it this way: "In truth, the issue is democracy with federalism (the Electoral College) versus democracy without federalism (a national popular vote). Either is democratic. Only the Electoral College preserves federalism, moderates ideological differences, and promotes national consensus in our choice of a chief executive."[9]

Comparing Election Systems

Perhaps the best method of demonstrating the benefits of a federalist presidential election process is to expose the evils suffered without it. As it stands today, presidential candidates have no incentive to poll large margins in any one state. Winning 50.1 percent of the votes in a state is as effective as winning 100 percent of the votes. Either way, the winner is awarded the entire slate of electors for that state—except, of course, in Maine and Nebraska. Presidential candidates therefore tour the nation, campaigning in all states and seeking to build a national coalition of voters that will enable them to win in a majority of states. They cannot focus on one or a handful of states to the exclusion of others. Doing so causes them to risk losing a majority of states in the election. Polling large margins in isolated regions of the country will not help their cause. Instead, their support must have a national component if they are to win a majority of the states' votes in the election.

Presidential biographer James MacGregor Burns has described this phenomenon as "the immense widening of the electorate."[10] Presidential candidates are motivated "to widen and 'flatten out' their vote, [and] to win states by dependable but not wasteful popular majorities."[11] The campaigns of presidential candidates stand in sharp contrast to the campaigns of congressional candidates, who are often campaigning in a district that has been specifically drawn to be "safe" for one of the parties.[12] The different campaign strategies required causes many Congressmen (particularly those in safe districts) to be more ideological than the typical Senator or President, who instead tend to be (or must at least appear to be) more moderate. The former are often able to aim their campaigns at individuals who are similar to themselves; the latter must build coalitions, either at the state or national level. Without coalitions, Presidents and Senators are unable to win. The Electoral College serves the nation well to the extent that it encourages presidential candidates to build coalitions, rather than to aim their campaign solely at one group of voters.

Now imagine an America in which Presidents are elected by direct popular election. Some scholars have claimed that elections would not be significantly different in this new world. Campaign strategies, they claim, would remain essentially the same, even if the Electoral College system were eliminated.[13] It is difficult to see how this could be true. Rule changes impact strategy all the time.

Consider a hypothetical rule change for baseball.[14] If the two teams that scored the most runs during the year were able to go to the World Series, would not the strategies of all the teams change accordingly? In this new baseball world, amassing high run totals against weak opponents would be extraordinarily beneficial. Playing good hitters against an especially talented pitcher is probably a waste of time; perhaps it is better to leave hitters on the bench, where they can rest for the next game against a vulnerable opponent. The coaches' decisions on these and other issues would be greatly impacted by the changed incentives inherent in the new rules of the game.

Presidential campaign strategies, too, would be significantly adjusted if the incentives for various behaviors were changed. The Electoral College, together with the winner-take-all system, treats candidates who win 50.1 percent of a state's votes identically to candidates who win 100 percent of a state's votes. A direct popular vote procedure would reverse this situation. Winning 100 percent of the votes in a state would be infinitely preferable to winning 50.1 percent of the votes. In fact, it may be easier to rack up votes in a friendly state than to gain 50.1 percent of votes in each of two states of similar size, although the pay-off would be essentially the same.

The result? Ronald Reagan concluded his radio broadcast in 1977 by describing the likely consequences of such a change: "Presidential candidates would be tempted to aim their campaigns and their promises at a *cluster of metropolitan areas in a few states* and the smaller states would be without a voice."[15]

Democrats would almost certainly spend most of their time in the large population centers in California and New York. Republicans would campaign in the South and Midwest. Each candidate would promise anything and everything to the regions in which he is strong, ignoring the needs of the rest of the country. Large cities would be focused on almost exclusively as the candidates seek to turn-out as many votes as possible in "their" region of the country. Small states, rural areas and sparsely populated regions would find themselves with little to no voice in presidential selection.[16] The parties would not be able to risk selecting candidates from small states.

By the time a President got himself elected under such a system, he would be indebted to—and would essentially represent—isolated regions, not the country as a whole. In this scenario, a handful of states (or heavily populated cities) win, while the remaining states suffer significantly.

Many critics argue that this description of the two types of elections is not entirely accurate. They contend that the current system does not encourage presidential candidates to tour the nation so much as it encourages them to focus their time and energy on the mid-sized "swing" states. "Safe" states and small states do not receive nearly as much attention on this national tour.

There is, obviously, an element of truth in this. Presidential candidates do not focus as much of their efforts on the safe states that they already feel certain of winning. This is, after all, one of the major goals of the Electoral College. Presidential candidates should not camp out in "friendly" states, ignoring and failing to learn about the needs of the remaining states.

To the degree that safe states don't receive a proportionate amount of attention during campaigns, the logical conclusion is that those states, by and large, must already feel that one of the two presidential candidates represents their interests pretty well. When a candidate ceases to adequately understand and represent one of "his" state's interests, the discontent in that state is usually expressed pretty quickly, forcing both candidates to again focus energy on understanding and gaining the support of constituents in that state.

Consider, for example, the status of West Virginia's electoral votes in 2004. Democrats have considered West Virginia a safe state for years; thus, West Virginia has probably seen less campaign time in many recent elections than it would have had it been more evenly divided. But in 2000, the Bush campaign recognized an opportunity to gain a foothold in the state. Voters in West Virginia perceived that Gore's environmental policies would be harmful to the coal-mining industry in their state.[17] Bush took advantage of this discontent, and he spent more than $2 million communicating his message to voters in that state (compared to $830,000 spent by Gore).[18] When election results were tallied, Bush became the first Republican to win an open race for the presidency in West Virginia since 1928.[19]

In 2004, West Virginia is no longer considered a safe state for Democrats. Because party loyalties are in question, both parties are already spending increased time and energy on winning the state's electoral votes.[20] If party loyalties were to fully shift in 2004 or a future election, then West Virginia would follow in the steps of states such as Texas, which used to be a safe state for Democrats, but now consistently votes Republican.[21]

A second argument made by critics is similarly flawed. True, the winner-take-all system causes large states (especially large swing states) to elicit more attention than small states. However, these critics erroneously compare the amount of campaigning in small states under the current system against the amount of campaigning in large states, also under the current system. Instead, they should compare the amount of campaigning in small states under the current system with the amount of campaigning that would occur in small states under a new one.

As the system stands today, states with small numbers of electoral votes undoubtedly receive less attention than those states with large electoral vote allocations (unless, of course, the large state is considered a safe state). However, a direct vote system would magnify, not improve, this problem. Small states will likely never receive as much attention as large states, but the Electoral College allows them to receive as much attention as possible—enough to keep them from being the victims of tyranny by the majority.

At the time of the 2000 census, California had a population of 33,871,648 people,[22] and it was allocated 55 electoral votes.[23] Wyoming, by contrast, had a population of 493,782 people,[24] and it was allocated three electoral votes.[25] California has more than 68 times as many people as Wyoming, but only 18 times as many electoral votes. If, as critics contend, Wyoming receives a disproportionately small amount of attention now, when the difference is three to 55 electoral votes, how much greater would the problem be if the relevant difference were half a million people to nearly 34 million people?

Wyoming will never receive as much attention as California during a presidential campaign, but such will be the case under any election system. The relevant issue is not to eliminate this disparity, but to minimize its severity. Under the Electoral College, the states are as evenly represented as possible, given that they are not all the same size. The majority, often localized in the big states, may still clearly wield its influence as the majority. The protections of America's federalist republic allow this majority influence to stand, as they should in any self-governing society, but they also give the minority enough leverage to keep itself from being tyrannized by the majority in the other, larger states.

Last, opponents of the Electoral College dispute that a presidential candidate in a direct election system would have the luxury of relying upon one or two regions of the country to get elected. After all, there are simply not enough votes in one or two regions to deliver an election to a candidate. This observation may be true, but only if it is assumed that the general election is held between two, or perhaps three, main candidates, as it usually is today. Neither California nor Texas has a large enough population to deliver an election under this scenario. Similarly, relying upon one special interest group will not be sufficient to obtain election—none of these groups can guarantee that enough of their supporters will cast ballots on one issue alone. Under a direct election system, however, the situation changes.

The likely consequence of a change to a direct popular vote is the breakdown of the two-party system (discussed more in the next chapter) and a general election among many candidates. Electoral College proponent Judith Best has hypothesized that direct popular elections at the national level would result in multi-candidate races and the constant necessity for runoff elections.[26] Candidates would crop up for every special interest conceivable: the "feminist candidate, the Hispanic candidate, the moral majority candidate, the environmental candidate, the gay rights candidate, the military candidate."[27] These candidates won't garner many votes, but they will each obtain some. The more divided the vote, the fewer votes are needed to get into a runoff election.

California may not have the ability to deliver 40 percent of the nationwide vote (the minimum plurality that has been suggested for a direct popular election), but it does have the ability to help a candidate win the 15 to 20 percent of the vote potentially needed to qualify for a nationwide runoff. Absent the two-party system, a special interest group such as a union or the National Rifle Association may also find itself able to deliver enough votes to get a candidate into a runoff. As multi-candidate races become the norm, presidential candidates would find themselves with more and more incentive to promise "their" voters anything and everything to get this much smaller percent of the vote needed to win.

Individuals v. States

An interesting twist to the prior arguments raised by Electoral College critics focuses on the reality that even if *small states* benefit from the Electoral College, they do so at the expense of the *individuals* who reside in small states. The Electoral College, its detractors argue, violates the principle of "one person, one vote" and creates a disparity in individual voting power. Worse, from their point of view, the disparity in individual voting power sways in favor of voters who happen to reside in large states.

This complaint can be confusing at first because it sounds like the opposite of another complaint—that the two vote add-on for small states (giving all a "guaranteed minimum" of three electoral votes) creates a bias in their favor. The two extra electoral votes given to all states, regardless of population, do create an advantage for those states. As a statistical matter, however, the advantage plays in favor of the *state as a whole*, rather than the *individual voter*. By contrast, the mathematical advantage granted by the winner-take-all system plays in favor of individual voters in the larger states. These voters have a statistically higher probability of materially affecting the outcome of the election. An example may help to explain this phenomenon.

If a citizen resides in California, with its electoral bloc of 55 votes, then the mathematical probability that his vote will affect the outcome of the election is greater than if he lived in Montana, which has more citizens than some of the smallest states, but only three electoral votes.[28] Electoral College critics Lawrence Longley and Neal Peirce conclude that citizens in California during the 2000 election had "2.663 times the potential for determining the outcome of the presidential election of a citizen voting in the most disadvantaged state—Montana."[29]

Most of the time, one vote by one citizen will not determine which way the state's popular vote comes out. However, in the event that it does so, this mathematical model says that voters in large states have more power than those in small states. If a California citizen votes for Kerry in the 2004 election and that one vote determines that Kerry, not Bush, wins the state's slate of electors, then that one voter's ballot has determined the outcome of 55 electoral votes. A voter faced with the same situation in Montana does not have this much power. If his one vote determines that Bush, not Kerry, gets Montana's vote, he has determined the outcome of only three electoral votes, compared to the 55 swayed by the California voter.

As a mathematical matter, perhaps voters in larger states have a disproportionately larger chance of changing the outcome of the election. Yet the odds of any one voter providing the "tipping point" in an election are still exceedingly small. Further, any individual disadvantage for those who reside in small states is outweighed by the larger advantage given to the state as a whole. The advantage given to small states is more than a theoretical mathematical advantage. Indeed, it has very real practical effects and should not be dismissed easily. Moreover, individual voters within small states benefit when their states benefit—and they will do so in *every* election, as opposed to the infinitesimal odds of "hitting the jackpot" and being the one voter who changes the outcome of one election in one year.

Residents living in the same state often share similar concerns. For instance, in Midwest states, voters may share opinions about agricultural policy. Voters in Alaska may share the same attitude about drilling for oil on their land. Nevada voters may band together against those who wish to dump nuclear material on their soil. Without the Electoral College, presidential candidates would likely never take the time to visit these smaller states and learn about the concerns of these residents. Without the Electoral College, candidates would not need votes from at least some of these small states to win the presidency.

The Electoral College, then, accomplishes an important goal: It ensures that the voices of small states are not drowned out altogether, as they otherwise could be. It ensures that the large states will not rule as majority tyrants over their smaller neighbors. As the small states are protected, so are the voters that reside within them.

Preserving Federalism

A direct popular election would probably cause some people to *feel* like they are better protected. After all, the principle of "one person, one vote" ensures that everyone is treated equally—right? In the presidential election process, this sentiment may feel true, but it is not. Individuals are best protected in the presidential election system when they can combine with others in their state and make their voices heard as a bloc. Obviously, voters will lose in their states sometimes (just as they would sometimes lose in a national direct popular election); however, they are protected even in their loss. No presidential candidate can afford to ignore any segment of the country.

To be logically consistent, Electoral College opponents should criticize other federalist features of our government as they have the Electoral College. After all, disparaging the Electoral College as "unfair" requires that similar criticisms be directed at the Senate or at other, similar features of our government that were created as protections for the small states. No one, however, is seriously questioning the right of the Senate to exist. The Electoral College is simply one of several constitutional devices created by the Framers to protect the diverse interests of the states.

The Electoral College protects the interests of the states, and thus their voters today, just as it did in 1787. It forces presidential candidates to build a support base that is national in character. A focus on any one area or special interest—urban or rural, east or west, coastal or interior—will cause the candidacy to fail. Solutions must be proposed that appeal to as many states' interests as possible, as at least some of the small states will be needed to win the presidency.

The truth of the matter is that many of the people who complain about the Electoral College are more concerned about their own individual votes than about how their states can best be served. They are entitled to this opinion, of course, and they may fight in their own state legislatures to have the rules for their states changed. However, they might be better served to remember the important safeguards provided in a federalist system and then apply themselves towards thinking how their states can best represent themselves within this structure. These protections still serve the states today.

CHAPTER SIX

MODERATION AND COMPROMISE

C URRENTLY, presidential candidates must build a national base among the states before they can be elected. They cannot target any one interest group or regional minority. Instead, they must achieve a consensus among enough groups, spread out over many states, to create a broad-based following among the voters. Any other course of action will prevent a candidate from gaining the strong base he needs to win the election.

The necessity of building such a national base has led to moderation and a strong two-party system in American politics. Third parties are not usually able to achieve more than a minimal base of power, particularly because they tend to target narrower or special-interest groups. Third parties or special interest groups can wield influence only by working toward consensus with one of the major parties. On their own, they cannot usually win more than a fraction of the electoral vote—if they even manage to win that much.

Some see this trend toward moderation and a two-party system as a liability. They argue that certain points of view on the far left or right do not have representation. Perhaps voters identify with a third party more than they identify with one of the two major parties. The two-party system, however, has a definite benefit: Hand in hand with the Electoral College, it tends to prevent the rise to power of extremist groups and radical minorities.

Maintaining a Two-Party System

A major third-party candidate has entered each of the past three elections. In 1992, Ross Perot of the Reform Party ran against Republican George H.W. Bush and Democrat Bill Clinton. Clinton won the election, but he won by a plurality rather than a majority of the vote. Perot ran again in 1996 against Clinton and Republican Bob Dole, with the same result. In 2000, Perot was replaced on the Reform Party ticket by Patrick Buchanan; Ralph Nader of the Green Party also joined the field, running against George W. Bush and Al Gore.[1] Neither Bush nor Gore was able to achieve more than a plurality of the vote.

Political operatives and pundits chastised these third-party candidates, arguing that they would upset the election results. The candidates were encouraged to drop from the race, and voters were told that a vote for a third-party candidate is a wasted vote. Prior to the 1992 election, conventional wisdom held that a vote for Perot was a vote for Clinton, because it wasn't a vote for George H.W. Bush.[2] In the same way, many believe that Gore would have won in 2000 if Nader had not taken so many votes from him.

In American politics, third-party candidates are not usually successful in their bid for the presidency. Any success that they do have comes from grabbing the attention of a major party and influencing that party's platform, at least at the edges. The Reform Party was unsuccessful in its bid for the presidency in 1992, but its voters arguably did capture the attention of the major parties that year. One of the major campaign platforms for the Reform Party in 1992 was fiscal responsibility. Reform Party supporters, by and large, argued for a balanced budget and restraints on spending.[3]

Is it any coincidence that both parties made a push for fiscal responsibility before and during the 1994 mid-term elections? Democrats supported a 1993 budget reconciliation bill that raised taxes,[4] arguing that increased taxes were necessary to bring the budget back into balance. As the election neared, Republicans countered with their "Contract with America," which promised an "audit of Congress for waste, fraud or abuse," cuts in "the number of House committees . . . [and] committee staff," and an "honest accounting of our Federal Budget by implementing zero base-line budgeting."[5]

Third parties usually form when one of the two major parties is either unable or unwilling to work with a bloc of minority voters. This third party, if it is big enough, may be able to impact an election in one of two ways: It can focus on a state or states and win a handful of electoral votes there, or it may be able to win enough votes in a swing state to shift the outcome. In either event, if it demonstrates its ability to affect an election, it usually encourages one of the two major parties to work with it. The result is compromise and moderation because it is unproductive for either the third party or the major party to refuse to do so. Refusing to work together basically guarantees that both will go down in defeat.

Bucking the two-party system is an exercise in futility in American presidential politics. The election of 1912 is perhaps the prototypical example of why this is so.[6] That election featured a three-way race among the incumbent, Republican William Howard Taft, Democrat Woodrow Wilson, and third-party candidate (and former President) Theodore Roosevelt. During the 1908 election, Roosevelt had chosen Taft to succeed him as President; however, he became disappointed with the decisions that Taft made as President, and he was determined to re-enter the political arena and win the Republican Party nomination.

Roosevelt's campaigning won him the support of many Republican voters nationwide; however, the leaders of the Party chose to ignore the voters' preferences. When the party convention was held, they announced that the incumbent Taft would be the Republican Party nominee. Upon hearing this announcement, many backers of Roosevelt marched out of the convention. The Bull Moose Party, led by Roosevelt, was born.

Roosevelt campaigned hard in his attempts to re-win the presidency. He worked so hard that his campaign took a near-tragic turn. As Roosevelt prepared to attend an October rally in Milwaukee, he was shot in the chest by a gunman. Roosevelt resolved to give his speech anyway. He spoke to the crowd at a level barely above a whisper, explaining that he would need absolute silence, as he had just been shot. The crowd was able to see a bullet hole in the notes for his speech, which Roosevelt had carried in his breast pocket. Roosevelt claimed, at the time, that the thick speech may have saved his life. He spoke for more than an hour before he was taken to the hospital and treated.

Results: Election of 1912

	Party	Electoral Vote	Popular Vote
Woodrow Wilson	Democrat	435	6,293,152
Theodore Roosevelt	Bull Moose (Progressive) Party	88	4,119,207
William Howard Taft	Republican Party	8	3,486,333

Despite Roosevelt's gallant campaign efforts, he could not win the presidency. When the election totals came in, the Republican vote was badly split between Taft and Roosevelt. Although Roosevelt and Taft earned a combined 7.6 million popular votes to Wilson's 6.2 million popular votes, they were able to win only a combined 96 electoral votes. Wilson was elected with 435 electoral votes, although he would likely have been defeated by a unified Republican Party.

The Republican Party would have done well to learn the lessons of earlier presidential elections, such as the election of 1836.[7] In that election, the Whigs could not agree on a nominee. In its defense, the party was still relatively new and was not well-organized. Instead, the party deliberately decided to fracture its vote among several regional candidates. Its hope was not to win, but to keep the Democratic candidate, Martin Van Buren, from obtaining a majority of electoral votes. They hoped to send the decision to the House of Representatives. Van Buren, however, benefited from the Whig strategy and defeated his nearest opponent in the Electoral College by 97 votes.

Results: Election of 1836

	Party	Electoral Vote	Popular Vote
Martin Van Buren	Democrat	170	764,176
William H. Harrison	Whig	73	550,816
Hugh L. White	Whig	26	146,107
Daniel Webster	Whig	14	41,201
W.P. Mangum	Indep. Democrat	11	-0-

The Whigs quickly learned their lesson. In 1840, they united behind William Henry Harrison of Ohio.[8] They ran a fierce national campaign and took the presidency back from Van Buren, 234 electoral votes to 60, although Harrison won the popular vote by a much smaller margin: 1,275,390 to 1,128,854.

The lesson of these and other, similar presidential elections? Cooperate and compromise.[9] The electoral vote cannot be won if voters split into various, marginal groups. Neither third parties nor major parties succeed when they insist on going it alone, ignoring others who may have differing viewpoints. The result is that American public policy tends to remain in the middle: not too far left, not too far right. This moderation can be admittedly frustrating when one's personal views might tend a little to the left or the right on a particular issue or issues, but as a general rule, the requirement for moderation protects Americans' freedom. Extremists cannot obtain power when moderation rules.

The Solar System of Governmental Power

Some proponents of a direct election system argue that the Electoral College is a divisive, not a moderating, factor in American politics. They further dispute that the Electoral College is responsible for the two-party system.[10] Of course, these proponents may acknowledge, America's system of checks and balances is the foundation upon which moderation and compromise has been built. However, they argue that changing the presidential election system, alone, would not undermine these protections or enable "rigid ideologies and inflammatory class appeals" to gain too much power.[11]

Electoral College opponents Neal Peirce and Lawrence Longley argue that a direct popular vote is "hardly a risky, untried governmental principle . . . . It is the tried and true way of electing every nonappointive government official in the United States today."[12] Moreover, they argue, other defenses against immoderation and factionalism still exist. Legislation, for instance, must pass both houses of Congress. The Bill of Rights and the judiciary serve as a check on unrestrained power. A variety of checks and balances still remain on the President, even without the Electoral College.[13] Changing the presidential election process, they contend, will not suddenly undermine the entire political system.

These arguments are not completely without merit. The American form of government contains multiple safeguards, and it does not rely exclusively upon one particular mechanism to protect citizens. If an "extremist" President were elected, he would not have absolute power, and the harm to the nation could potentially be somewhat mitigated by Congress or the judiciary. However, it is also important to remember the degree to which presidential power has grown in recent years.

Presidents act through executive orders more often than they did in the past,[14] and they have significant power in the area of judicial and other government appointments.[15] Moreover, they act as Commander-in-Chief of the armed forces and serve the country as its foremost ambassador in foreign countries.[16] During national emergencies, the scope of presidential power expands even more.[17] While the other two branches of government act as checks on the executive branch, the President may take many significant actions before these checks come into play. The check placed on the President by the Electoral College, along with the two-party system, should not be written off too quickly.

Speaking in support of the Electoral College, John F. Kennedy once referred to the checks and balances in the Constitution as a "solar system" of power:

> [I]t is not only the unit vote for the Presidency we are talking about, but a whole solar system of governmental power. If it is proposed to change the balance of power of one of the elements of the solar system, it is necessary to consider all the others.[18]

The system of checks and balances works as a whole, taken together. Eliminating the Electoral College would get rid of only one of several protective devices. Perhaps the impact would be minimal, as anticipated by many direct election proponents. On the other hand, it could throw the physics of the entire solar system (as JFK would say) out of balance.

Proponents of a direct election system often make the mistake of assuming that they can change one factor but leave all other dynamics unchanged. For instance, critics Neal Peirce and Lawrence Longley suggest that runoffs in a presidential election would not happen often.[19] To support their contention, they cite the fact that all but one President was elected with at least 40 percent of the popular vote. Gubernatorial races, they note, usually show similar results.[20] None of the races they cite, however, has ever been held in the absence of a two-party system; therefore, these campaigns cannot provide evidence for what would happen without it.

Electoral College proponent Judith Best makes a similar point, contending: "Many of the proponents of the direct nonfederal election with a 40 percent plurality rule assume that they can make such a major change in the rules without changing the way the game is played and without changing the nature of the winning team. That is nonsense."[21] Her opinion is shared by Professor Michael Glennon of Tufts University, who compares the American political system to a Rubik's Cube:

> One may not like the appearance of one side, and may wish to change that side, but one must remember that the other sides will then change as well. . . . [No one] is far-sighted enough to know how the political cube will look after we finish twisting it to eliminate the Electoral College.[22]

It is a known quantity that JFK's solar system, with the Electoral College in it, moderates political campaigns, contributes to the stability of the two-party system, and controls the rise of extremism, as the Founders expected. What is the point of spoiling a system that has proven itself in such a way?

The Solar System, Without the Two Major Parties

Predictions of what would happen in a direct election system should assume that it is at least possible that changing the rules of the presidential election game will cause more than one aspect of the political process to change. Indeed, a relatively quick deterioration of the two-party system is quite likely under such a set of changed incentives. Runoffs would become not only possible, but probable. These runoffs cannot prevent the rise of factions; instead, they are likely to encourage them.

Some proponents of direct election seem to understand that runoffs are not beneficial to the stability of America's political system and should be avoided if possible. They believe that adjustments to the direct election plan could keep the two national parties from being undermined. Most often, they propose to control the demise of the two-party system through a requirement that the President gain at least 40 percent of the vote before he can be elected.[23]

This proposal sounds plausible at first glance, until one real-izes that there is a lack of historical or anecdotal evidence supporting it. Instead, the most likely result is that this system, too, will eventually undermine the two-party system. Even with the 40-percent rule, voters no longer have the same disincentives to vote for a third party. One has only to look to history to see how easily such a system could disintegrate into multi-candidate races, which would, in turn, devolve into a system of regular runoffs.

Consider the election of 1992. One of the primary factors that prevented some people from voting for Perot was that they felt their vote would be "wasted." A vote for Perot is a vote for Clinton, voters were told. Now imagine the 1992 election without an Electoral College. Suddenly, the incentives change. Clinton no longer has to be beaten; he just needs to be held under the 40-percent mark. To get in the runoff, Perot voters do not need to win, they simply need to overtake George H.W. Bush. If they can accomplish these two goals, a runoff between Clinton and Perot will follow. A vote for Perot is no longer wasted. The Reform Party has a specific, achievable goal with which to motivate its supporters.

In the actual 1992 election—even with all the disincentives inherent in the Electoral College system—Perot received 18.9 percent of the popular vote. Bush received 37.4 percent of the vote, and Clinton received 43.0 percent. Had this election been a direct popular election, it would have been only 3 percent away from triggering a runoff. With such incentives, would not Perot supporters have had a much easier time getting voters to switch their vote? Dissatisfied Bush and Clinton supporters risk very little if they vote for Perot. After all, they would always have a second chance to vote for one of the major parties during the runoff. Is a strong third party showing, triggering a runoff, really so unbelievable? Once one runoff has been triggered, why would multiple third parties not jump into the race in 1996?

The country already hosts at least 56 political parties with differing levels of activity.[24] Some of these political parties represent precisely the kind of extremist factions that most Americans do not want to find as one of their two choices in a runoff: the American Nazi Party,[25] the Prohibition Party,[26] the Knights (a.k.a. Ku Klux Klan) Party,[27] and the Pansexual Peace Party, which is based on Wiccan principles.[28] Most of these alternative political parties obviously do not achieve a significant amount of public support, at least in part because the Electoral College makes it more beneficial for voters to work toward compromise with one of the two major parties. However, the fact that so many alternative political parties exist, even in the face of every conceivable disincentive, indicates that they could grow larger and magnify if those disincentives were removed.

At least five political parties have ample reason to believe that they could get a significant percentage of the popular vote in the absence of an Electoral College system: the Republican Party, the Democrat Party, the Reform Party, the Libertarian Party, and the Green Party. If the Electoral College were removed today, each of these parties could make credible runs for the presidency. Indeed, each of these parties is already running a candidate for President in 2004, even with the presence of the Electoral College. In a world in which five parties could make strong runs for the presidency, a runoff is almost certain. Moreover, the runoff would be between two candidates who had attained some small percent of the vote—no more than 39 percent, but perhaps as little as 20 or 25 percent apiece. A runoff would then be held between these two minority candidates so that one of them could be deemed the winner.

As such a situation became the norm, more and more candidates would be motivated to enter presidential contests over the years. Support from a smaller and smaller percentage of the population would be needed to qualify for the runoff. Over time, candidates would become more and more extreme and uncompromising. Professor Judith Best explains this dynamic:

> [T]he splintering of the vote works against the moderate candidates and works to the advantage of the immoderate, extreme candidates. It does this because the middle is where the inclusive coalitions can be built. By undermining coalition building prior to the general election, a runoff fragments the middle, not the extremes; the extremes are rarely fragmented—fanatics have solidarity. Coalition building seeks to spotlight most people's second choice, which is a satisfactory and inclusive choice.[29]

Direct popular election proponents sound plausible when they argue for election of the President by a "majority" of the people. In reality, however, a President elected by the majority of citizens will rarely be achievable, except in an idyllic world. A majority, after all, will never agree on their ideal candidate. Individuals' opinions vary too widely. Instead, runoffs will proliferate, and Presidents will essentially be elected by the initial 20 or 25 percent of voters who got them into the runoff. Presidents will know that at least 75 to 80 percent of the people originally voted for someone else.

Given the general inability to obtain majority consensus, the Electoral College provides the country with the next best alternative. Electing Presidents by states' votes, rather than individuals' votes, creates a method of electing a President who is a good compromise candidate for the majority of Americans. The Electoral College requires moderation, compromise, and coalition-building from any candidate before he can be successful.

Direct elections and a system of runoffs discourage such behavior.

Other electoral systems utilizing a direct popular vote have seen increased influence by extremist, radical groups due to the fractured nature of the popular vote. Professor Robert Hardaway of the University of Denver has noted the results of a December 14, 1993 Russian election in this context. In that election, the top three candidates were the "liberal Democratic" (or Fascist) Party (23 percent), the People's Choice Party (13 percent) and the Communist Party (11 percent). In other words, Russia was two percent away from having a runoff between Fascists and Communists, even with a democratic election and 66 percent of the population voting for other candidates.[30] Historical evidence in other historical systems, Professor Hardaway notes, reveals similar results.

Granted, America is a long way away from such a multiparty, fractured political system. Psychologically, if nothing else, the electorate is used to thinking in terms of a two-party system. It could take a while before the system deteriorated. However, if the Electoral College facilitated the growth of the two-party system that has brought so much stability to American elections, would it not be natural to assume that eliminating the Electoral College would eventually lead to the end of the nation's stable two-party system? Even if the danger of an American election featuring Fascists and Communists is somewhat remote, why remove one of the safeguards that have kept such a scenario exactly that—remote?

CHAPTER SEVEN

STABILITY AND CERTAINTY IN ELECTIONS

M ANY ELECTORAL COLLEGE proponents argue that fraud will increase under a direct election system. Any vote stolen in any part of the country would have some impact on the final outcome. Stolen votes can have an impact under the Electoral College system—but the only realistic way to impact the election is to somehow predict in advance where stolen votes will matter. No such predictive power is needed with respect to direct elections. Moreover, the Electoral College tends to magnify the margin of victory and promote finality in elections.

Opponents of the Electoral College disagree, arguing that fears of fraud under a direct election are "probably exaggerated," and "fraud in a closely contested state with a large bloc of electoral votes may already be enough to swing the entire national election."[1] These opponents emphasize the unequal weight given to votes from state to state, thus placing a premium on stealing votes in certain parts of the country. Fewer stolen votes are needed to change the outcome of a state election than are needed to change the outcome of a national election. As the reasoning goes, in a nationwide election, one stolen vote does not have much of an impact; therefore, the incentive to steal votes is reduced.

Opponents further dispute that the Electoral College makes election outcomes more certain. To the contrary, they argue, if the electoral vote is close or one candidate does not receive a majority of electoral votes, the potential for more chaotic proceedings follows. An ambitious elector could choose to swing the election. Deal-making in the contingent election could leave the election result uncertain for weeks.

In a few, limited circumstances, the arguments of Electoral College opponents could ring true. These circumstances are the exception, rather than the rule, however. As a historical matter, the Electoral College has generally served to promote certainty in election outcomes and to reduce the incentive for fraud.

Magnifying the Margin of Victory

The 2000 election was an unusual election in many ways: The popular vote was remarkably close, but, amazingly, the electoral vote margin was razor thin, too. Historically, most elections have not been as close in the Electoral College, even when the popular vote is close. The Electoral College system, when combined with the winner-take-all rule, tends to magnify the margin of victory, giving the victor a certain and demonstrable election outcome.[2]

The election of 1960 was one such close election. John Kennedy won only 49.7 percent of the popular vote, compared to Nixon's 49.5 percent; however, Kennedy won 56.4 percent of the electoral vote, compared to Nixon's 40.8 percent. Eight years later, this magnification effect worked in favor of Nixon. Although he won the popular vote by less than one percent, he won 55.9 percent of the electoral vote to Hubert Humphrey's 35.5 percent. Jimmy Carter was the beneficiary of the magnification effect in the close election of 1976. Carter won 40,830,763 popular votes compared to Gerald Ford's 39,147,793 popular votes. The margin between the two numbers was only two percent of the total number of votes cast for both men. Yet, the Electoral College magnified the victory. With 297 votes, Carter won a solid 55.2 percent of electoral votes.

This magnification effect is not a recent phenomenon. The Electoral College produced a similar lop-sided effect in the 1888 election. That election resulted in a popular vote winner who lost in the Electoral College. Grover Cleveland won the popular vote by 0.8 percent; however, Benjamin Harrison won the electoral vote by a much larger margin: 65 votes.

Results: Close Elections

		Electoral Vote		Popular Vote	
		Actual	Percent	Actual	Percent
1888	Benjamin Harrison	233	58.1%	5,443,892	47.8%
	Grover Cleveland	168	41.9%	5,534,488	48.6%
1960	John Kennedy	303	56.4%	34,226,731	49.7%
	Richard Nixon	219	40.8%	34,108,157	49.5%
1968	Richard Nixon	301	55.9%	31,785,480	43.4%
	Hubert Humphrey	191	35.5%	31,275,166	42.7%
1976	Jimmy Carter	297	55.2%	40,830,763	50.1%
	Gerald Ford	240	44.6%	39,147,793	48.0%

Indeed, as popular vote totals start to spread apart, the magnification effect increases dramatically. For instance, in 1952, the winning candidate won 55.1 percent of the popular vote, but a much larger 83.2 percent of the Electoral College vote. In 1956, the difference was 57.4 percent (popular vote) to 86.1 percent (electoral vote); and 1964 was 61.1 percent (popular vote) to 90.3 percent (electoral vote). The magnification of the electoral vote can work to solidify the country behind the new President by bestowing an aura of legitimacy.

The presidential elections since 1804 (the year that the 12th Amendment was passed) have generally seen wide margins of victory in the Electoral College. These margins have gotten wider, on average, through the years as the winner-take-all rule has been adopted by more states and the two-party system has solidified. Since 1804, only two elections—those in 1876 and 2000—were won by fewer than 20 electoral votes. Only six elections were won by fewer than 50 electoral votes. Four of these six elections were held in the 1800s. Of the 26 elections held between 1900 and 2000, 17 Presidents have been elected after winning the electoral vote by a margin of 200 votes or more.

Margin of Victory in the Electoral College:
1804 to present

	1804 – 1896 elections	1900 – 2000 elections	Total
N/A—Decided in contingent election	1	0	1
1-50 electoral votes	4	2	6
51-100 electoral votes	8	2	10
101-200 electoral votes	8	5	13
200 or more electoral votes	3	17	20
TOTAL	24	26	50

These consistently wide margins of victory in the Electoral College have come about despite the fact that the margin between the top two candidates in the popular vote was less than

10 percent in 14 of the 26 elections held since 1900. This margin exceeded 20 percent only five times since 1900.

A direct popular election, by contrast, would not grant certainty nearly as often. Close popular votes such as those discussed above could easily result in demands for recounts on a national scale. America rarely has close Electoral College votes; it does, however, have close popular votes fairly consistently. Do Americans really want a presidential election system that could result in hotly contested recounts once every several elections?

A direct popular election would compound matters in a second manner. As discussed in Chapter Six, the likely outcome of such an election system is that presidential elections will devolve into multi-candidate races. As more candidates enter presidential races, individual votes will be divided among an ever-increasing number of candidates. The result will be lower vote totals per candidate and an increased likelihood that two or more candidates will have close popular vote totals. Recounts could be held simply to determine who is entering the runoff; then they could be held again to determine who won the runoff. Certain, immediate election outcomes under this scenario will be a thing of the past.

Arguably, the picture that has just been painted is a worst-case scenario; however, it should not be dismissed lightly. Many pundits have noted that the American President is the most powerful man in the world in many respects. Americans should assume that ambitious men will come along who will use every means at their disposal to obtain the position. The Electoral College provides a buffer against the uncertainty and turmoil of constant recounts and election disputes. This buffer is even more important when ambitious candidates lack the will or the inclination to concede for the good of the country.[3]

Bush's 2000 win by a mere five electoral votes is unusual and should not be used as a reason to condemn the Electoral College. When reviewing the historical record as a whole, the general impact of the Electoral College, when combined with the winner-take-all system, is to magnify the margin of victory for the winning candidate. The magnified electoral vote count generally makes outcomes certain and close elections a rarity. A direct election system would not produce this certainty nearly as often.

Reducing Fraud and Error

The Electoral College provides yet another benefit: It reduces the incidence of fraud and error. Obviously, no system can completely eliminate the element of human error. Neither can any system eradicate the tendency of some dishonest individuals to cheat. An election system can, however, minimize the extent to which these human errors or fraudulent behavior impact elections. The Electoral College minimizes the impact of fraud and error by isolating problems to one state or a handful of states.[4]

Electoral College opponents disagree with this analysis, pointing to elections such as the 2000 presidential election in which the election could have been changed by just a handful of stolen votes. In 2000, Bush won the election without a state to spare. He won one state, Florida, by only 537 votes.[5] Six hundred stolen votes in Florida in the 2000 election would have changed the outcome and crowned Gore the winner. Another election similarly referenced in this regard is the 1960 election. Nixon lost the election by only two states: Texas and Illinois.[6] A shift of 4,430 votes in Illinois and 23,129 votes in Texas would have swung the election in Nixon's favor.[7] Moreover, many believe that fraud was rampant in these two critical states during the election. The fraudulent voting may or may not have been enough to swing the election. The extent of the fraud may always remain a matter of disagreement.

While these two examples of close elections do suggest that fraud and error could impact the Electoral College outcome, they do not indicate, in and of themselves, that American presidential elections are highly susceptible to fraud or that an alternative system would ameliorate this impact. Electoral College opponents have once again made the mistake of assuming that infrequent problems in the current system damn the entire system. Instead, they should compare the current system with the likely outcome in a changed system. No system is perfect, but one will prove better than the alternatives in the long run.

The Electoral College defends against fraudulent behavior and human error in two ways: First, the system makes it difficult to predict where stolen votes will make a difference. Not impossible, obviously, but more difficult. In a direct election system, any stolen vote matters, but under the Electoral College system, stolen votes impact the election only if they are stolen in the right location. Second, to the degree that fraud and errors do occur, the Electoral College makes it possible to isolate the problem to one state or a handful of states.[8]

The 1960 election provides an illustration of the ability of the Electoral College to control a situation that could otherwise degenerate into chaos and uncertainty. Nixon had ample reason to demand a recount in Illinois and Texas, particularly given the expressions of concern regarding voter fraud in these states. A few examples of this alleged fraud have been cited by Richard Reeves, author of *President Kennedy: Profile of Power*. For example, Reeves reports that 6,138 votes appear to have been cast by 4,895 voters in Fannin County, Texas. In Chicago's sixth ward, 43 voters apparently cast 121 votes in one hour.[9] Nixon could not have been blamed had he challenged the votes in these two states, although he chose not to do so.

In his memoirs, Nixon explains the reason that he conceded the election, rather than demand a recount in Texas and Illinois. He explained, "A presidential recount would require up to half a year, during which time the legitimacy of Kennedy's election would be in question. The effect could be devastating to America's foreign relations."[10] He was right, and his actions saved the country from a difficult situation. A recount, with or without the Electoral College, would have created a fair amount of disorder and confusion. Nevertheless, the chaos created under a direct election system would be far greater than the lesser disarray that Nixon sought to avoid under the Electoral College system.

The overall official results of the 1960 election revealed a difference of only 118,574 votes between the two men.[11] Under a direct election system, such an extraordinarily close vote could easily have been used to justify a demand for nationwide recounts by Nixon. The Electoral College system, however, made the close popular vote irrelevant. Instead, had Nixon demanded recounts, these disputes would have been isolated to the two states that really mattered: Illinois and Texas. Moreover, the allegations of fraud have focused on these two states for a reason. Even if votes were stolen somewhere else in the country on that Election Day in 1960, the other stolen votes were not remarked upon because they would not have affected the election one way or another. The Electoral College successfully isolates problems of fraud and error to one or a handful of states. The remaining electoral votes, in other states, can remain above the fray, as they are undisputed. The country is given a clear set of problems to resolve one way or another before moving on to a definitive election outcome.

The Electoral College served a similar purpose during the 2000 election. Yes, of course, 600 stolen votes in Florida would have changed the election. But stealing these votes would have required knowing in advance that such a small number of votes in Florida could swing the outcome of the election. Even if someone had successfully guessed that a handful of votes in Florida would change the election, surely this guess would have been the exception, rather than the rule. Moreover, the Electoral College made it possible for the nation to isolate the problem to Florida. The nation was in suspense for weeks at the end of 2000, waiting to see how the election would come out. However, the situation could have been much worse. Recounts could have ensued in virtually every state of the Union; instead, the focus was on a handful of counties in Florida.[12]

Under a direct election scheme, a national recount (complete with lawsuits in many states, not just Florida) could easily have occurred and left the country in suspense for months. Today, some might question whether Bush "really" won Florida's vote; however, the votes in other states are not questioned. The broad national coalition that Bush pieced together outside Florida is undeniable. Under a direct vote system, even this certainty would be absent. Instead, given the close popular vote in 2000, many today would likely be questioning whether Bush or Gore "really" won the national popular vote. There would have been no certain point at which the country could have stopped the legal wrangling over recounts.

The 2000 and 1960 elections exhibited the amazing ability of the Electoral College to control situations that could very easily degenerate into chaos. In each instance, the country was given a certain and definite election outcome, even in the midst of dispute.

Imperfect World, Optimal Solution

Today, both the electoral and the popular votes must be extremely close before voting disputes and recounts are threatened. By contrast, a direct popular election would require only a close popular vote before these scenarios became possible. National recounts and legal challenges would be a constant possibility, particularly because the likelihood of multiple candidacies, lower individual vote totals, and smaller margins among candidates would increase. Confusion would reign while cities, counties and states across the nation attempt to tabulate and re-tabulate votes. Imagine Florida in 2000, but on a national scale.

The current system makes it possible to be certain as to the precise number of electoral votes for each candidate. Human fraud or error is less likely to impact the outcome, and, if all else fails, state legislatures are constitutionally empowered to take action and resolve uncertainty. It is not possible, however, to be certain as to the precise number of popular votes for a candidate. Human error can not be driven out of the equation—and human errors across the country could easily combine to influence the outcome of a close election.

Moreover, a direct popular vote system would increase, rather than decrease, the incentive for fraud. After all, any stolen vote would have at least some affect, regardless of its location. Today, if fraud is suspected in one state, it may not trigger a recount if the vote in the state was not close. The Electoral College minimizes the impact of fraud, isolating it to the one or two states where the vote was close and disputed. Under a direct election, any stolen vote in any location could matter. When taken together with the increased possibility of close popular vote margins, the potential for national challenges and recounts would be greatly increased under a direct election system.

The Electoral College system cannot be said to completely eliminate the incentive for fraud. Where people are vying for power, there will always be motivation to cheat. That is human nature. A successful electoral system can hope only to isolate the incidents of dishonesty and provide controls on situations that would otherwise get completely out of hand. The Electoral College system isolates fraud to the state in which it occurred. In most elections, the national election cannot be changed without a concerted plan of action, spanning several states. Recounts, when necessary to ferret out illegal votes, can be isolated in a state or two. The country is given a definite election outcome, even in the face of electoral challenges.

PART THREE

REFUTING REMAINING CRITICISMS

CHAPTER EIGHT

THE FAITHLESS ELECTOR PROBLEM

T HE TUMULTUOUS 2000 election highlighted a feature of the Electoral College system that has doubtless gone unnoticed by many Americans for decades. Following certification by Florida's Secretary of State of her state's slate of electors, Bush had 271 electors pledged to vote for him, while Gore had 267 pledged electors—but these pledges, alone, did not seal the outcome of the election. Bush was the presumed winner because he had a majority of the pledged electors; however, these electors had not yet officially voted and their votes had not been counted by Congress. When push comes to shove, the electors are individuals with the ability to cast votes contrary to the expectations of voters, although some electors take pledges (of dubious enforceability) not to do so.

Given the unusually close election, faithless votes by only three electors could have thrown the election to Gore. A switch by two electors could have prevented either candidate from obtaining a majority of electoral votes, thus triggering a contingent election and leaving Congressmen to decide which of the two men would be the nation's next President. At least one group, calling itself "Citizens for True Democracy," devoted a website to this effort.[1] Despite the intense political pressure, most electors remained faithful to their party during the December 18, 2000, meetings of the Electoral College. Only one elector—a Gore elector—chose to abstain, rather than cast her vote. (Even her vote, however, was merely cast in symbolic protest. Presumably, she would not have abstained if her vote would have swung the election for Gore.) The final vote tally was thus 271 to 266. Bush won, but his victory was not guaranteed until these votes were officially cast and counted by Congress.

At the time the Electoral College was created, some early Americans may have believed that electors would serve as representatives for a citizenry that would be unable to keep abreast of all the presidential candidates' platforms and activities, particularly those of non-local candidates. The electors would act as representatives for the people, learn about candidates, and decide which candidates might deserve a vote for the presidency. Today, the situation is reversed: Voters are more familiar with the positions of presidential candidates than the qualifications of electors. As a result, many argue, the role of elector as an independent decision-maker has become outdated in modern-day America. In this day and age, why should an individual elector have the ability to cast a vote that does not follow the outcome of the popular vote within his state? The possibility of an elector exercising autonomy in decision-making is enough to make most voters cringe.

America has changed much in the past 200 years. As this book has argued, these changes have not undermined the usefulness of the Electoral College in many respects, but it is hard to see what positive purpose the role of elector plays in today's society. As discussed below, the fear of a "faithless elector" swinging an election outcome has proven groundless in practice; however, the possibility of such faithlessness coming into play in the future is real. If any change is to be made to the presidential election system, it should be to eliminate the role of elector and automate the process of casting the states' electoral votes.

Independent Deliberators or Mere Formality

Communications in early America were slow, erratic, and unreliable. Most American voters would have found it difficult to be informed regarding each and every presidential candidate. It is more likely that voters would have known local candidates and maybe a handful of the more widely known national candidates. The Founders included at least one provision in the Constitution that would balance out this possibility of local bias. Article II of the Constitution provides that electors "[shall] vote by Ballot for two Persons, of whom one at least shall not be an Inhabitant of the same State with themselves."[2] The 12th Amendment contains a similar provision, requiring that either the vote for President or the vote for Vice President be for an out-of-state candidate.[3]

Some academics argue that the Founders created the role of elector, at least in part, because they knew that voters would be handicapped by slow communications and unable to know all the candidates. The Founders probably anticipated that electors would be "distinguished citizens" who would act as representatives for the people in the presidential election process.[4] At the time the system was created, such a solution would certainly have been understandable as a logistical matter. Some academics, however, dispute this reading of history. They argue that the Founders never intended the electors to be completely independent.[5] Perhaps the role of elector instead evolved primarily because the drafters of the Constitution did not want to decide for the states how they should go about casting their electoral votes. Either way, any expectation that electors would act independently did not last long.

In the early 1800s, many electors were already being chosen for their party loyalty and other similar factors.[6] By the 1830s, voters in all states except one had been given the power to choose their electors directly.[7] Afterwards, the instances in which state legislatures selected the electors were few and scattered.

South Carolina was one exception: Its legislature continued to select electors until 1860. Florida's legislature selected electors in 1868, and Colorado selected its electors in 1876.[8] Today, however, electors are most commonly nominated at state party conventions.[9] The outcome of the state's popular election determines which slate—Republican or Democrat—will be appointed the official slate for the state.

The electors themselves are typically party loyalists who are committed, either by state law or party rules, to vote for the candidate nominated by their party.[10] Some of these state statutes are arguably not enforceable under the Constitution. The Supreme Court has heard only one case on the subject, and the opinion it issued in this 1952 case was somewhat limited in scope.[11] In that case, the Alabama chapter of the Democratic Party refused to certify an individual as a candidate for presidential elector.[12] This individual was qualified for the office of elector, except that he refused to take the Democratic Party pledge to support the Democratic nominee for President.[13] Individual electors may vote as they please once they get to an Electoral College meeting, the Court observed, but a political party may require a pledge of loyalty before supporting an individual as candidate for elector.[14] The Court did not take a position on other types of pledges, such as those required by *states*, rather than *political parties*. It therefore remains unclear whether a state can force an elector to vote in a particular way.[15] Also unclear is what would happen if the elector violated a pledge. Could a law punishing such a violation be enforced? Even if punishment could be handed down for the elector's action, the vote probably could not be retracted. Further questions exist regarding whether Congress must accept the vote of a faithless elector.

Despite these unanswered legal questions, the problem of unfaithful electors has proven more of a theoretical problem than a real one. Between 1796 and 1996, Neal Peirce and Lawrence Longley report that no more than 17 of 21,291 electoral votes were "indisputably cast 'against instructions.'"[16] Moreover, eight of these votes, cast during the 1824 election, may or may not have been "faithless," depending upon one's reading of the facts.

Faithless Electors Since 1796[17]

Year	Name of Elector	Pledged to:	Cast Ballot For:
2000	Barbara Lett-Simmons, D. C.	Al Gore, Democrat	Abstained
1988	Margaret Leach, West Virginia	Michael Dukakis, Democrat	Lloyd Bentsen, Democrat
1976	Mike Padden, Washington	Gerald Ford, Republican	Ronald Reagan, Republican
1972	Roger MacBride, Virginia	Richard Nixon, Republican	John Hospers, Libertarian
1968	Lloyd W. Bailey, North Carolina	Richard Nixon, Republican	George Wallace, Am. Indep.
1960	Henry D. Irwin, Okalahoma	Richard Nixon, Republican	Harry F. Byrd, Democrat
1956	W.F. Turner, Alabama	Adlai Stevenson, Democrat	Walter E. Jones, Democrat
1948	Preston Parks, Tennessee	Harry Truman, Democrat	Strom Thurmond, States Rights
1824	Five of 15 electors, North Carolina	John Q. Adams, Dem.-Repub.	Andrew Jackson, Dem.-Repub.
1824	Three of 36 electors, New York	Henry Clay, Dem.-Repub.	J.Q. Adams (DR) W.H. Crawford (DR) A. Jackson (DR)
1820	William Plumer, New Hampshire	James Monroe, Dem.-Repub.	John Q. Adams, Ind. Dem.-Repub.
1796	Samuel Miles, Pennsylvania	John Adams, Federalist	Thomas Jefferson, Dem.-Repub.

In 1824, the North Carolina slate of 15 electors voted en bloc for Andrew Jackson, despite the fact that as many as five of them may have been pledged to vote for John Quincy Adams. In New York, three electors pledged to Henry Clay defected, but they did not do so until it was already clear that Clay would not qualify for the tie-breaking contingent election in the House.

The next electors to defect were in 1948 through 1968. Each of these electors broke their pledges in an effort to make a statement regarding civil rights issues. Three defectors were, oddly, all Nixon electors. One elector defected in each of his three presidential races. Three more electors have broken their pledges since the Nixon races, one each in 1976, 1988, and 2000. None of these faithless votes changed the outcome of an election. Two faithless electors in 2000, however, easily could have. The 2000 election, more than any election in recent memory, tested the durability of the elector system.

After Gore's concession to Bush on December 13, 2000, much discussion centered on the possibility that "only three" faithless electors could throw the election to Gore. Some Gore supporters publicized the names and telephone numbers of Republican electors and instigated campaigns to encourage some Bush electors to change their vote to Gore. Despite the week of speculation and pressure, most electors remained faithful to their party during the Electoral College vote on December 18, 2000. As previously noted, only one elector—a Gore elector—chose to abstain, rather than cast her vote. She reportedly abstained to make a statement about the lack of congressional representation for the District of Columbia.

The 2000 election was one of the most emotionally and politically charged in recent memory, yet only one elector changed her vote during this election—and she did so for symbolic purposes, rather than to affect the election's outcome. This result provides good anecdotal evidence that the danger of a faithless elector changing the outcome of an election is not great. Most electors are extremely reluctant to break the trust placed in them, even when placed under great pressure. Moreover, most of these electors are chosen precisely because of their loyalty to the party. The combination of loyalty and trust makes the electors unlikely to exercise independence.

As a result, the role of elector has become a formality. By and large, neither the populace nor state legislatures—nor the electors themselves—expect electors to act independently. Instead, electors are universally expected to cast votes in accordance with the popular vote outcome in their states. If an elector were to suddenly decide to exercise independence, after all, the state's citizens would likely revolt.

This state of affairs is confirmed by the fact that the names of the electors do not appear on the ballots in most states. In 1940, 15 states used the presidential short ballot, on which the names of the electors do not appear. By 1980, this number had jumped to 38.[18] Today, all but eight states list the name of only the presidential candidate himself on the ballot, although his name may be preceded by the words "electors for."[19] Some ballots include a disclaimer at the top of the ballot announcing that "[a] vote for the candidates will actually be a vote for their electors."[20] As a result of this system, most voters have no reason to know the name of the elector for whom they have voted, unless they take time to investigate. In other words, we now have the exact opposite situation as contemplated at the Founding: the candidates themselves are well-known, but the electors are completely unknown to the average voter.

It is hard to see how independent deliberation by electors in this day and age will do anything to advance the goals of the Electoral College, as described above. To the contrary, the public is more informed about the character and policies of presidential candidates than they are about those of the electors. In many cases, they may not even know the names of the electors. The advent of mass communication and other changes to American society have not impacted the usefulness of the Electoral College in most respects; however, it is fair to say that they have nullified the role of the elector.

The Automatic Plan

Many political commentators and academics have come to the conclusion that the role of elector serves no significant purpose in modern-day America. Therefore, a potential reform proposal, usually referred to as the "Automatic Plan," is often discussed as a potential modification to the current Electoral College system.

In all likelihood, the present system can continue to function successfully without thwarting the will of the people as it is expressed in the state-level democratic elections held during American presidential elections. The role of elector will remain simply a formality and a tradition, as it has been for decades. However, the probability that a faithless elector could change the course of an election, while remote, is not zero. If any change is to be made to the presidential election process, it should be to abolish the role of the elector. Electoral votes should be cast automatically based upon the popular vote in the state.

Of the reforms that have been proposed to the Electoral College, the Automatic Plan is one that would remove the possibility of faithless electors from the system, while leaving the framework of the system largely untouched. Implementation of the Automatic Plan would require a constitutional amendment to eliminate the provision that allows states, through their legislatures, to decide for themselves how to select their electors. Instead, the new constitutional provision would provide for the automatic allocation of electoral votes based on the popular vote outcome in each state. These votes would be awarded on a winner-take-all basis within each state, precisely as they are awarded today in all states except Maine and Nebraska.

Most critics of the Electoral College feel that the Automatic Plan does not go far enough, as it leaves the bulk of the system unchanged. Worse, they shudder at the thought of the winner-take-all system and other perceived inequities being officially incorporated into the Constitution. As they see it, the Automatic Plan does nothing more than to ensure that the principle of "one person, one vote" will never be honored at the national level.[21]

These critics are right in saying that inequality in individual voting will be further solidified in the presidential election process as a result of such an amendment, but they downplay the benefits that will also be solidified, including federalism and protection for minority groups. As this book has observed, the Electoral College will likely never be appreciated fully by those who do not value principles of federalism and who continue to value individual votes over the good of the states and their voters as a whole.

If any reform is to be adopted to the Electoral College, it should be to award the electoral votes automatically, based upon certified election returns within each state. Such a solution would preserve the benefits of the current system. It would continue to keep the large states from trampling on the smaller states, and it would support continued stability and moderation in American politics. Moreover, it may aid in the unraveling of several logistical tangles that exist in the current system.

Unraveling Logistical Tangles

The death of a presidential candidate either immediately before or after Election Day would create a series of complications, and each state would handle these complications differently due to their differing statutory schemes. For instance, the method by which presidential candidates can or cannot get on the ballot varies by state; thus, the death of a candidate before Election Day would be addressed in a variety of ways nationwide. Additionally, the political parties each have their own rules regarding replacement of the party nominee in the event of death, thus, they would individually work with the states once they have settled upon a replacement nominee.

Death of a candidate prior to Election Day could be extraordinarily complicated, regardless of whether the country is relying upon direct election or the Electoral College; however, most of these matters are issues of state or federal law that are beyond the scope of this book.[22] This book will address only one aspect of these matters: How the Automatic Plan might help to solve some potential logistical problems if a candidate passes away during the latter part of an election year.

The Constitution does not provide a contingency plan if a winning presidential candidate passes away either between the general election and the meetings of the Electoral College or between the meetings of the Electoral College and the counting of the electoral votes by Congress in January. It does, however, provide for presidential succession if the winning candidate passes away after congressional counting of the electoral votes, but before Inauguration Day. The 20th Amendment applies to this latter period, providing that the Vice President-elect succeeds the President-elect if the President-elect passes away before he is inaugurated.[23] The 20th Amendment may not be applied before this time because the winning presidential candidate is not officially the President-elect until he has been formally declared the winner after the congressional counting of votes in January. The country has not yet been faced with the death of a winning presidential candidate at the end of an election year, but it came close twice: once in 1872 and once in 1912.

In 1872, Republican Ulysses S. Grant ran for re-election against Democratic-Liberal Republican candidate Horace Greeley.[24] The November 5, 1872, election revealed that Grant would soundly defeat Greeley in the electoral vote. Greeley had gained only 66 pledged electors to Grant's 286 during the general election. Greeley, however, passed away on November 29, 1872,[25] a mere five days before the Electoral College vote on December 4. The situation threw his electors into a bit of a quandary. Who were they to vote for? Three electors decided to vote for Greeley, even though he had passed away. (Congress later refused to count these votes, determining that votes could not be cast for a deceased candidate.) Sixty-three other Greeley electors split their votes among several alternative Democratic candidates. No crisis ensued in 1872, mostly because Grant clearly would win the vote regardless of what the Greeley electors decided.

Several elections later, in 1912, confusion among electors became possible yet again. President Taft's running mate, James S. Sherman, passed away on October 30, mere days before the election. Individuals who voted for the Republican slate on Election Day did so without knowing who the replacement candidate would be. The Republican Party eventually selected a replacement, but did not do so until after the general election. The potential for confusion among electors was mitigated that year by two factors: First, Taft placed third in the election, so the actions of his electors were not as important as if a winning candidate had died. Second, the Republican Party had plenty of time between Election Day and the Electoral College vote during which to settle upon a replacement, in sharp contrast to Greeley's last-minute death in 1872.

These elections were uneventful, but difficulties could arise in the event that a *winning* presidential candidate passed away with mere days to go before the electoral vote could be officially cast. If the presidential and vice presidential candidates both died during the same event (perhaps a terrorist attack), then the potential for confusion escalates. In that event, for whom should the electors vote? What if Grant, not Greeley, had passed away on November 29, 1872? What would his electors have done? In 1912, the Republican electors had plenty of time to come up with a concerted plan of action, but what if they had no time to do so? Would their confused and fractured vote help a losing presidential candidate to default into office, despite a low number of electoral votes? In the 1872 election, with no time for planning, the Greeley electors exhibited precisely this kind of confusion, as their votes were scattered among several men.

In November 2001, Professor Akhil Reed Amar discussed this problem in conjunction with issues of terrorism.[26] His concerns continue to resonate today, particularly following such events as the March 11, 2004 terrorist attack in Madrid, Spain, which some have credited with changing the outcome of that country's elections. Terrorists could not only try to change the direction of a presidential vote through their attacks, as they did in Spain, but they could take advantage of logistical loopholes in the presidential election system to throw the country into turmoil as it sorts out who should be its next President.

The political parties have power to designate replacement candidates in the event of the death of one candidate; however, if a candidate passed away shortly before the Electoral College vote, parties may not have time to designate alternative candidates and electors may not have time to coordinate their efforts. Moreover, death of a presidential candidate immediately before the counting of the electoral votes by Congress could cause a fair amount of confusion.

Given the increasing threat of terrorism, these logistical tangles should be unraveled immediately. Many timing issues can and should be addressed by state and federal statutes; however, a constitutional amendment would be needed for passage of the Automatic Plan. The plan can solve at least a portion of these logistical issues through several rather simple provisions: First, the amendment should provide that electoral votes be automatically cast for the winning presidential candidate, eliminating the interim period between the general election and the Electoral College vote. The potential for confused and fractured voting by electors if a candidate passes away too close to the meetings of the Electoral College would be eliminated.

Second, the amendment should provide that electoral votes won by a presidential candidate should be deemed automatically cast for the vice presidential candidate if the presidential candidate passes away between Election Day and the counting of the electoral votes by Congress.[27] (It should also make provision for the death of a vice presidential candidate, perhaps by deeming the votes automatically cast for the next in line for the presidency under already-existing constitutional and statutory presidential succession provisions.) The Congress might even consider moving up the day on which it counts these votes to ensure that the winning presidential candidate is formally designated President-elect as quickly as possible.

A provision such as the Automatic Plan would make it possible to know for sure who the President-elect will be based upon the votes that are cast on Election Day.[28] Once a President-elect is designated, the presidential succession mechanisms in federal law and the 20th Amendment can take effect.

CHAPTER NINE

THE CONTINGENT ELECTION

T HE CONTINGENT election is a little-understood and much-disparaged component of America's presidential election system. Critics observe that the contingent election procedure could result in one person casting the deciding vote in an election, a situation that is "distasteful in a democracy."[1] Even Electoral College proponents are likely to hesitate at the prospect of a contingent election. One Electoral College proponent, for instance, labeled the prospect of a contingent election a "horror."[2]

These critics note that many prospective problems could arise if a contingent election were ever needed. A President and Vice President of different parties could be elected. The election procedure could degenerate into self-interested deal-making among representatives. In a worst case scenario, the President-elect could find himself feeling indebted to the Congressmen who secured his election. Such sentiments could damage our system, which values separation of powers among the branches.

The potential for these problems is real, but also more remote than it appears on the surface. Further, the solutions that have been proposed do not remedy the problem. Most make matters worse. One possible solution that has not been proposed (to this author's knowledge) is an automated secondary election process. This automated process would operate in a manner similar to the automated processes that have been proposed for elimination of the role of elector. Yet even this new potential solution is probably unnecessary.

Without reform, the contingent election would most likely continue to function as it has over the course of the past 200 years, without causing any serious upheaval to America's political system. America rarely uses its secondary election process. The Electoral College, combined with the winner-take-all system, usually magnifies the margin of victory for one candidate and grants certain election outcomes. Nearly 200 years have passed since the country last witnessed a contingent election for the presidency. In all likelihood, the election process will not provoke more than one secondary election in the next 200 years—if it provokes that many.

Allowing the contingent election to stand "as is" would grant one additional—and important—side benefit: It would prevent unnecessary tinkering with the governmental solar system of power. As JFK observed, unanticipated consequences easily may result if one portion of the solar system is altered. Because the dangers of a contingent election are more theoretical than real, it may be better simply to leave the system unchanged.

Understanding the Process

The original Article II election procedure did not provide for separate voting for the President and Vice President. Its contingent election procedure, therefore, could be triggered in either of two situations: First, if no candidate won at least one vote from a majority of the electors, or, second, if two candidates obtained votes from a majority of electors (remember that each elector could cast two ballots), but each candidate had an equal number of votes.[3] In the first situation, the House chose a President from the top five candidates. In the latter situation, the House chose from the two candidates who had tied. In all cases, the person who placed second in this House election would be Vice President.

Following the confused election of 1800, Congress enacted the 12th Amendment to separate the voting for President and Vice President, both in the Electoral College voting and in the secondary contingent election procedure. The 12th Amendment provides for a contingent election in the event that no presidential candidate receives a majority of the electoral vote.[4] In such a situation, the House chooses the President from the top three presidential candidates. A similar procedure exists in the Senate, but the Senate may choose a Vice President from only the top two vice presidential contenders. In the House election for President, each state delegation has one vote. In the Senate election for Vice President, each Senator has one vote. If the House of Representatives fails to make a choice before Inauguration Day, then the Vice President acts as President until such time as a choice is made.[5] If the Vice President has not yet been chosen, then the Presidential Succession Act kicks in,[6] making the Speaker of the House of Representatives acting President until a choice can be made.

Critics raise three main complaints about this system.[7] First, the Senate and House may elect candidates from different parties. The House considers three presidential candidates, while the Senate considers only two vice presidential candidates. By definition, one presidential candidate will not have the option of working with his preferred Vice President if he is elected. Second, many predict that a future contingent election would degenerate into political, partisan, or self-interested deal-making. For example, a representative from an evenly-divided state delegation would be tempted to cut deals in exchange for switching his vote (and thus his state's vote) to a different presidential candidate. Third, many complain that all states, large or small, each get one vote in this special election—regardless of the size of the state or the number of voters who cast votes in each state's general election.

The first two concerns are reasonable. Arguably, the contingent election process should guarantee that a President and Vice President from the same party are elected. Imagine what could have happened in a hypothetical contingent election in 1992. This secondary election procedure would have resulted in House consideration of Ross Perot, George H.W. Bush, and Bill Clinton as presidential candidates. Dan Quayle and Al Gore would have been considered as candidates for Vice President in the Senate, but the Senate would not have the option of selecting Ross Perot's preferred vice presidential candidate, Reform Party candidate Admiral James Stockdale. Moreover, the Senate can choose a Vice President from a different political party than that of the President chosen in the House. Perhaps the contingent election process would better serve the country if it endorsed either the Clinton-Gore, Bush-Quayle, or Perot-Stockdale ticket. It may be unproductive for the country to end up with, say, President Clinton and Vice President Quayle.

Moreover, critics have genuine worries about deal-making in the House. These issues, in fact, plagued the contingent election in 1824 when Andrew Jackson lost the election to John Quincy Adams in the House of Representatives. Adams won in the House with the help of Henry Clay, who was subsequently made Secretary of State in the Adams administration. Jackson claimed that a "corrupt bargain" in the House stole the election from him, and he eventually went on to win the 1828 election.[8]

Despite the country's experiences in 1824, a reasonable argument can be made that the danger from deal-making is not quite as great today as it was during the country's early years. Improved communications have increased the ability of voters to quickly discover which way their Congressmen voted. Presumably, voter attention to the actions of Congressmen would act as a disincentive to deal-making because congressional members must seek reelection if they are to continue in office. Those who wish to act for political or selfish advantage cannot do all their deal-making behind closed doors. They must be able to explain their actions to the public, particularly on an issue that is as high profile as a vote for President. In all likelihood, Congressmen will probably vote fairly predictably: for their party candidate, the popular vote winner, or the state's popular vote winner. Voters can act in reliance upon this expectation when they vote for their congressional candidate—an election that will always occur at the same time as presidential elections because Congressmen run for re-election every two years.

Finally, the objection regarding the contingent election, that states vote in delegations rather than as individuals, is simply a variation on the argument that Electoral College opponents have made to the current presidential election system. Votes are cast by state delegation in the Electoral College for the same reason that states are given two extra electoral votes, regardless of population. These devices ensure that small states are not forgotten in the process of selecting a chief executive. They buttress federalist principles and reinforce the need of presidential candidates to build a national coalition as they campaign for the presidency.

The procedure of casting votes by state delegations is in accordance with the federalist goals of the Electoral College system. Arguably, the divided voting between the House and Senate, together with the possibility of deal-making in the House, makes the contingent election an imperfect procedure. Finding an alternative, however, is more difficult than it may appear at first glance. Critics' proposed solutions typically lead to more problems than they solve.

Runoff Election

Some have proposed holding a runoff between the two leading candidates (along with their running mates) if neither presidential candidate wins a majority of the electoral vote.[9]

Other proposals dispense with the majority requirement, arguing that a candidate can win the presidency with a plurality of electoral votes, as long as he passes the 40 percent mark. (The proposals do not bother to explain what is magical about the 40 percent mark. Why not 39, 30, or 25 percent?) The runoff, once triggered, could be conducted either by electoral or popular vote. One advantage of this proposal is that the President and Vice President who are eventually elected would both be from the same party. However, many problems accompany this proposal.

Creation of a runoff system would undermine the certainty, stability, and moderation that have generally characterized American presidential elections.[10] Certainly, a runoff system, combined with the Electoral College vote, would not deteriorate into multi-candidate races as quickly as a pure direct election system would. Obviously, it remains harder to siphon off electoral votes from candidates than to shave a few percentage points from their national popular vote total. However, the harmful effect of introducing a "second chance" to vote into the presidential election system should not be underestimated.[11] Critics who wish to replace the contingent election procedure with a national runoff have yet to address the fact that their system has the potential to create many of the problems already discussed in connection with a direct election system, including deterioration of the two-party system, multi-candidate races, and difficulty in controlling factions.

The American electorate generally has confidence that the votes cast on Election Day are the votes that will determine, with finality, the winner of the presidency. They don't get a second chance to express a different opinion. In what might be dubbed the "Perot" or "Nader effect," they can't vote for their favorite (but unelectable) candidate the first time, knowing that they can vote for the candidate that they actually expect to win on the second try. Runoffs contain the potential to change this situation. Voters are given a second chance to vote. Psychologically, they may feel more comfortable voting for third-party candidates during the general election. As multiple candidacies accrue, each candidate, again, needs a smaller and smaller percent of the electoral vote to make a runoff.

Local races commonly result in runoffs, but local races differ from the presidential contest in a few important respects. First, certainty and finality in a presidential election are more important than certainty in an election for mayor or governor. If a mayoral contest is undecided for a few weeks, any harm is likely to be minimal. The presidency, by contrast, is the top executive office in the nation. Certainty, finality, and quick transitions between administrations are essential, particularly for national security reasons. Second, runoffs can be conducted more quickly and efficiently in local races than they can across 50 states. Last, runoffs or third-party candidates in local races do not undermine the national two-party system as multi-candidate presidential races could. When independent candidate and professional wrestler Jesse "The Body" Ventura is elected Governor of Minnesota, it is viewed as a novelty. Absent further incentives at the national level, no one seriously expects to suddenly start running serious independent or third-party candidates for national office based solely upon Ventura's success.

Selection by a Joint Session of Congress

A second proposal would send the presidential election to a joint session of Congress in the event that no candidate wins a majority of the electoral vote. Each member of Congress would have one vote. Voting for the President and Vice President would be combined, rather than separated as they are today. The small states would still retain a slight advantage because they have two Senators and one Congressman, regardless of population.

Some object to this plan because it would allow the winner of the popular vote plurality to lose the election if his party is in the congressional minority.[12] Some congressional members might vote for the popular vote winner (or the popular vote winner in their state), but they would doubtless be under great pressure to vote along party lines. In all likelihood, most congressional members would vote with their party, making it difficult for a President of the minority party to be elected, regardless of the amount of support that he carries among the populace.

Although this proposal cures the problem of separate voting for President and Vice President, it otherwise seems subject to many of the same defects already inherent in the contingent plan. Congressional members would still be under great political pressure to vote along lines not dictated by the popular vote. Deal-making could still result if congressional membership is evenly divided between the two parties. No great advantage results from a switch to this plan, except to the degree that some might prefer to allow individual members of Congress to vote, rather than state delegations. In both plans, the small states retain a slight edge, although this advantage is undoubtedly greater in the current contingent system.

Neither the current contingency plan nor the joint session plan is perfect. Both carry the potential for deal-making among politicians, although the incentive to cut deals on high-profile issues may be reduced in an era of mass communication. Deal-making is a potential danger in either of these systems, but it is not the greatest downfall. The greater weakness is the permanent advantage given to the presidential candidate from the majority party.

Given that voting by a joint session of Congress does not have overwhelming advantages in comparison to the contingency plan, it seems best to maintain the status quo. Constitutional amendments should be rare, enacted only as a last resort. The solar system of governmental power certainly should not be altered without a strong argument in favor of changing it.

Potential Solutions

The Electoral College, by design, prevents the need for secondary election procedures most of the time.[13] It instead tends to magnify the margin of victory, giving the country a certain winner even when popular vote totals are close. As a result, the contingent election has not been used to select a President since 1824. Secondary election procedures are extremely rare in the United States. In all likelihood, America could continue with its current system without any great harm—which is, in and of itself, a good argument for leaving the current system largely as it stands. A few remedies, however, may be considered as further precautionary measures.

First, the procedures for the contingent election should be clarified. If a contingent election were suddenly needed today, the only available precedent for the logistical details surrounding the House election would be the rules adopted by the House in 1801 and 1825. These rules, however, leave some unresolved questions, many of which were discussed in Chapter One.[14] Are votes within each state determined by a plurality or a majority? Are votes by open or secret ballot? Which House conducts the election—the House existing at the time of the presidential election or the new House, which will be sworn in the following January?

These procedural issues should be established before the contingent election is actually needed. Of course, any discussion on these matters will be fraught with partisanship, but at least where the event is a mere hypothetical, there can likely be a relatively unbiased committee discussion. Before the time of need, it is unclear which procedure will give which party in the future an advantage. In the midst of an undecided election, any debate over logistics could (and most likely would) quickly devolve into partisan bickering.

Second, recombining the separated voting for President and Vice President could be beneficial, as it would prevent the election of two candidates from different parties. It is hard to see any benefit if Presidents and Vice Presidents from different parties are elected. As early as 1796, when President John Adams (Federalist Party) was required to work with Thomas Jefferson (Democratic-Republican Party) as his Vice President, the two had difficulty working together productively. To the contrary, the relationship between Jefferson and Adams broke down soon after the two men had been inaugurated. Afterwards, Jefferson recalled, Adams never again "consulted me as to any measures of the government."[15]

Last, a system could be considered that would eliminate the possibility of partisan or self-interested deal-making. This system, however, should retain the federalist principle and leave the small and large states on a relatively even playing field. Finding a solution that serves both purposes is more challenging than it may appear.

One solution could be considered as a resolution for both of these problems. Just as the role of elector can be automated to resolve the problem of deal-making or faithlessness by electors, so could the voting in the House be automated. In this new procedure, each state would still get one vote in the secondary election. However, rather than leaving it to legislators to determine how to cast this vote, the outcome of the state's popular election would determine which candidate will receive the state's one vote. Essentially, Congressmen would be deemed to have voted for the winner of the popular vote in their states. Both the presidential and vice presidential elections could be resolved through this single procedure. The District of Columbia could also be given one vote, as if it were a state. The total current number of state votes awarded in this secondary election procedure would thus be 51.

For example, had the 2000 election resulted in a contingent election, these new procedures would give the Bush/Cheney ticket 30 state votes and the Gore/Lieberman ticket 21 state votes (20 states, plus the District of Columbia). Bush and Cheney would be deemed the winners of the presidency and vice presidency, respectively, because they won a majority of these secondary state votes. Another close race, caused by the third party candidacy of George Wallace in 1968, would be resolved in a similarly easy manner: Richard Nixon (32 state votes); Hubert Humphrey (14 state votes—13, plus the District of Columbia), and George Wallace (5 state votes). Nixon would be deemed the winner.

This alternate procedure would accomplish several important goals: First, it would allow Presidents and Vice Presidents to be elected together, with their running mates. Second, it would automate the process and eliminate the possibility of deal-making among congressional members in the event that a secondary election procedure is needed. Third, it provides a certain and immediate answer to the question of who won the election. Last, it avoids the dangers of a runoff election, which encourages multiple candidacies and the "second-chance psychology" of the electorate.

The primary drawback of this new contingent procedure is that there is no way to automate the process in the event that no candidate receives 26 state votes. If, for instance, two candidates each received 25 state votes and a third-party candidate won one state vote, a back-up plan would be needed. In that case, there is no real alternative except to go to voting by the House or a joint session of Congress. As a mathematical and practical matter, however, the likelihood that no candidate would win either the electoral vote or the automated state vote is slim to none. After all, the Electoral College discourages third parties, inflates margins of victory, and encourages candidates to build national coalitions. In the event that a contingent election was needed, one of the candidates would almost certainly have obtained a majority of state votes through this automated procedure.

On the other hand, a strong argument exists that JFK's principle applies even to the generally unpopular contingent election. Perhaps Americans should not tinker too much with the solar system of governmental power, particularly when they do so merely to avoid remote or rare problems such as those that could occur in a contingent election.[16] The nation's presidential election process, with the contingent election in it, has served the nation well for more than 200 years. Perhaps it is best to leave the election process untouched. As the saying goes, "If it ain't broke, don't fix it."

Perhaps the specter of a contingent election, in and of itself, has done its part to uphold and maintain our stable, two-party system in America. If one election a century ends in political deal-making in the House, that may be a small price to pay for an otherwise stable and certain system.

CHAPTER TEN

CONCERNS ABOUT LEGITIMACY

T WO DAYS after the 2000 election, a Knight Ridder/Tribune columnist wrote that George Bush's Electoral College win, combined with a popular vote loss, "could trigger a crisis of legitimacy."[1] The circumstances under which Bush won, the columnist concluded, constitute the "kind of electrifying election finish that would surprise—and even enrage—many Americans, particularly those who voted for Gore only to find that the majority doesn't necessarily rule."[2] A *New York Daily News* editorial echoed his words. In an age of "one person, one vote," this journalist opined, an electoral vote win combined with a popular vote loss "would rob Bush of the legitimacy he needs to govern effectively."[3]

Electoral College critics have warned the country for years that such sentiments would arise in the event that a popular vote winner failed to win the presidency. In any given year the potential for such a legitimacy crisis exists, these critics lament, because in any given year America's presidential election system could allow a "wrong winner" or a "runner-up President" to win the election. The perpetual possibility of runner-up Presidents, one detractor grumbled, is "the great anomaly in the American democratic order."[4]

These legitimacy arguments are perhaps the silliest raised by Electoral College opponents. If a President is elected by a majority of electoral votes but a minority of popular votes, why should he be considered less legitimate than a President who won a runoff election, but squeaked his way into that runoff by earning, say, 30 percent of the vote in a general election? Neither President would govern with a majority of the individual popular vote. At least the former President would have been forced to obtain the support of the majority of states before being declared the winner. The latter could easily be a default winner who was opposed by the majority of Americans in the general election.

The rules that govern the presidential election process exist for a strong and valid reason: to ensure that Presidents represent national coalitions, rather than isolated segments of the country. A President is legitimately elected if he campaigned and won under these rules. To the small degree that voters do not perceive the election outcome as legitimate, this minor problem can and should be cured by educating voters on the important rationales underlying our Electoral College system.

Playing by the Rules of the Game

In any game, rules are established for a certain purpose. As discussed earlier, one example is America's traditional pastime, baseball.[5] Any baseball fan knows that teams do not get to the World Series by scoring the most runs throughout the course of the season. Instead, teams earn their spot in the playoffs by winning the most games in their league. Naturally, rules *could* be established that would allow the two teams that score the most runs to play in the World Series, but such rules would not accomplish the stated objective of a championship game: Allowing the two best overall teams to face off at the end of the year.

A revised set of rules might allow a team, for instance, to earn a spot in the World Series by having one great month and several poor months. Or perhaps a team that is great at taking advantage of weak opponents (but rather poor at facing off against good opponents) would win a berth in the World Series. Excellent performances throughout the baseball season would not be required to earn the championship. Occasional, stellar performances could be sufficient.

The rules for the presidential election contest are established with a similar purpose. They seek to identify the best national candidate, overall. The system leans in favor of candidates whose strengths play out evenly, rather than those who perform brilliantly in one part of the country but terribly in other regions.

Once these presidential election rules have been proposed and established as the best method of achieving the country's stated objectives, is not a winning candidate legitimate any time that he plays by and wins under the rules in effect? Indeed, a President is unfairly labeled "illegitimate" when he simply followed the rules of the game.

Some academics cannot accept this reasoning simply because they cannot accept the legitimacy of any election procedure that allows a presidential candidate to win, despite losing the nationwide popular vote. Other commentators accept the reasoning to some extent, but they are afraid to accept it fully. They may agree that the Electoral College is beneficial to the degree that it produces winners of "federal pluralit[ies]"; however, if a candidate were to ever win a "large majority of the popular vote" while losing the electoral vote, they claim it would be evidence that reform of the system is necessary.[6] After all, a President should have the "support of the people."[7]

Either stance demonstrates a lack of understanding of the Electoral College. Assume, for argument's sake, that a presidential candidate wins the election, but the final vote totals reflect a rather large discrepancy between the outcome of the popular vote and the electoral vote. Perhaps the losing candidate won the popular vote by a landslide, while the winning candidate hand-ily won the electoral vote. Such a situation has never come about, but if it were to occur, the benefits and legitimacy of the Electoral College remain unchanged. The discrepancy between vote totals is not evidence that the electoral system has failed the American people.

The Electoral College was devised to ensure that a President will have the "support of the people"; however, this support must be broad-based. It would be mathematically difficult for two candidates to create a large gap between the popular and electoral votes; however, if they did, the most likely explanation is that the losing candidate spent too much time camped out in one region of the country—precisely the type of behavior that the Electoral College is designed to prevent. Such a candidate would deserve to lose. He might technically have the support of the majority of individuals, but this majority would be in danger of being a tyrannical or regional majority. The Constitution dictates that the other candidate, who successfully obtained the *federal* majority, wins.

Electoral College critics cannot accept the legitimacy of popu-lar vote loser Presidents, partly because they have assumed the need for the very matter in question.[8] Must a presidential election process require presidential candidates to obtain support from a majority of individuals? Or can the process legitimately require that candidates obtain support from a majority of some other aggregate of individuals, such as states, counties, or families? Many today may avoid these questions, but the Framers evalu-ated them at length. They concluded that freedom would best be protected if presidential candidates were required to win a majority of state votes. Such a system, they believed, would be successful because it combines the best elements of federalism and democracy.

All that can be expected of a presidential election system is that the rules are fair and lead to their stated objectives. The Electoral College has succeeded in this regard for over 200 years.

Similarly, all that can be expected of a presidential candidate is that he play by the rules of the game then in effect. If he wins under the existing set of rules, then he is the legitimate winner.

Voters' Perceptions

Some argue, however that the crux of the problem is not whether candidates are or are not playing by the rules—or even whether those rules are fair. Instead, they contend that the problem centers on voters with negative perceptions. Pursuant to this focus, voters are predisposed to value democratic outcomes and will not accept a President who did not win the popular vote as legitimate. Electoral College critics Neal Peirce and Lawrence Longley stated prior to the 2000 election that people may "find a way to live with" a popular vote loser, but the "authority of the presidency and the quality of American democracy would certainly be undermined" by such an outcome.[9]

The degree to which voters question the legitimacy of Presidents who gained the majority of states' votes, but not the majority of individuals' votes, must be questioned in the aftermath of the 2000 election. Despite dire predictions, the election of George W. Bush seems to have been accepted by Americans with relative ease. What is perhaps most striking about the weeks of uncertainty in 2000 is the readiness with which voters accepted that the winner of Florida would be the winner of the Electoral College and, hence, the presidential election. Most of the unrest that occurred revolved around the recounts in Florida, rather than the nationwide popular vote totals. Once the election was decided, calls for Electoral College reform did not last for more than a few weeks. Indeed, as early as February 2001, one columnist remarked,

> Before the election, I wrote in this column that "several possible squeaker scenarios could produce some strange political dynamics after November 7." . . . But where I really went wrong was in saying that if the popular vote went one way and the elec-

toral college another, there could be a "crisis of presidential legitimacy."

Perhaps the strangest aspect of the election's aftermath is
that none of what happened, nationally or in Florida, seems to
make any difference now.[10]

The electorate has accepted Bush so easily that a *L.A. Times* book
review declared in the Spring of 2003 that the "significance of the
election . . . now seems diminished to a level inconceivable two
years ago. The legitimacy of George W. Bush's reign as President
has rarely been questioned; the election reform laws passed by
Congress were so slight as to barely merit notice; the electoral
college is still with us."[11]

Obviously, a handful of people still vehemently object to the
outcome of the 2000 election. Yet this bitterness is not directed
primarily at the Electoral College. Many protestors instead
emphasize the fact that recounting of Florida votes was stopped;
they claim that Gore really won Florida. The implication of such
complaints seems to be that the Electoral College is legitimate,
but Gore, not Bush, should have won the electoral vote.[12]

Of course, some protestors do complain about the legitimacy
of the Electoral College itself. It is fair to say that at least some of
these people have political, rather than philosophical, motiva-
tions. Al Gore's campaign passionately defended the sanctity of
the popular vote during November and December of 2000;
however, this position was at least partially one of convenience.
Prior to the election, predictions abounded that Gore, not Bush,
would win the election without winning the popular vote.[13] As
discussed in the Introduction, Gore's campaign reportedly
sought in advance to prepare itself for a public relations battle to
convince the American public that the winner of the Electoral
College, rather than the popular vote, is the legitimate President.[14]

Voters' perceptions are certainly important as a public relations matter. However, Electoral College opponents have once
again failed to acknowledge the full spectrum of consequences

that could result from a modification to the presidential election system. Perhaps some Americans are so predisposed to value democratic outcomes that they do have a problem with a President who did not win the national popular vote. Would this situation really improve under a direct election system? Are direct elections really the best cure for any perception problems, or is not education a more direct and effective manner of curing any problems that may exist?

Under a direct election system, as has been discussed in other chapters, the likely result is that general elections will devolve into races among multiple candidates. Multiple candidacies mean that one of two situations will likely occur each election year. First, one contender will win the bare minimum of votes necessary to gain the presidency without a runoff—40 percent, as proposed by many direct election advocates. What makes this candidate more legitimate than a President elected under the Electoral College system? This candidate, although democratically elected, did not win a majority of votes, nor did he win a majority of states. He won a bare plurality of votes. Sixty percent of the populace could easily complain that the majority of voters did not vote for the winning candidate.

A second situation is perhaps more likely to occur. Multiple candidacies will become the norm, and candidates will achieve fewer and fewer votes in the general election. Instead, most candidates will simply strive to gain enough votes to make it into a runoff. Perhaps two candidates will win 15 or 25 percent of the vote apiece, guaranteeing themselves a spot in the runoff. Sure, one of these two candidates will then win "a majority" of votes in the runoff, but they will do so only because there are no other options available. These candidates will not be the first choice of as many as 75 to 85 percent of the population, who voted for a different candidate in the general election. What would make this President legitimate, while the candidate elected through the Electoral College is not? Voters who once complained about "popular vote loser" Presidents may suddenly find themselves wishing for the days when presidential candidates had to at least obtain the support of a majority of the states.

Those who back direct popular elections have a good sound bite to throw at a public that, by and large, does not know much about the origins of its presidential election system. Naturally, these critics' arguments sound irrefutable when they call for election of a President by "the majority of the people." The reality, however, is that (absent a two-party system) election systems are unlikely to produce presidential candidates who are able to gain support from 50.1 percent of the people. Voters' opinions vary too widely. Given the opportunity for a purely democratic vote, the most likely result is a fracturing of the electorate into many groups. The Electoral College system seeks a better method. It produces a candidate who has gained the support of a majority of voters in a majority of states.

Voters obviously can be satisfied with candidates who have not gained majority support. Electoral College proponent Judith Best points out that 15 "minority" Presidents governed the country from 1824 through 1971.[15] (Two more minority Presidents have been elected since Professor Best's observation: Bill Clinton and George W. Bush.) Included among these minority Presidents is Abraham Lincoln, who was elected to the presidency with the lowest popular vote percentage in the nation's history.[16] Lincoln is not today considered illegitimate; instead, he is generally regarded as one of the nation's greatest Presidents.[17]

High vote totals do not guarantee success. Although George Washington, Ronald Reagan, and FDR were elected with overwhelming support and are often treated favorably by historians, a handful of other Presidents who were elected with high popular vote totals, including Richard Nixon, Warren Harding, Ulysses Grant, and Lyndon Johnson, are not generally regarded as having had successful presidencies.[18]

<>

The winner of the presidency has legitimacy if he played under the rules then in effect. These rules, in turn, can have legitimacy even if they require winning candidates to obtain a majority of something besides individual votes. Requiring a majority of states' votes serves several purposes that uphold the federalist nature of America's republican democracy.

Moreover, in any given election, no one can say with certainty what the outcome would have been under a different set of rules. Candidates strategize differently when the rules are changed. Had a direct popular vote system been in effect in 2000, maybe Bush would have won that election, too. He probably would have spent more time racking up votes in Texas and other southern states. Bush, however, was not trying to win the popular vote in 2000. Both Bush and Gore were striving to win the most electoral votes. Bush succeeded. Gore did not. The truth of this observation was confirmed by former Clinton Solicitor General Walter Dellinger while the 2000 election was being decided. He observed, "There's no real legitimacy argument. If the presidency was decided by the popular vote, the two candidates would have run different races. We simply don't know who would have won."[19]

Americans accept the winner of the World Series, even when the winner does not score the most runs during the baseball season. They accept the winner because they understand and accept the validity of the rules. Similarly, voters will accept the legitimacy of the Electoral College winner, even when he loses the popular vote, if they understand the rules of the game. Education is the key to any legitimacy problem that may exist.

The Electoral College has a history of more than 200 years of electoral stability and success. Lack of understanding alone, on the part of some of the populace, is an insufficient reason for abolishing the system. A better solution is to educate voters as to the importance and benefits of a federal election system.

CHAPTER ELEVEN

ALTERNATIVE PROPOSALS

D IRECT POPULAR election is not the only alternative to the Electoral College that has been proposed. Critics of the Electoral College argue that any one of several other alternatives would be an improvement upon the current system: (1) The "Bonus Plan" would retain the Electoral College, but award a large electoral bonus to the popular vote winner; (2) The "District Plan" would award electoral votes by congressional district, rather than by state; (3) The "Proportional Plan" would divide states' electoral votes proportionally, according to the popular vote outcome within the state; and (4) The "De Facto Direct Election" plan, a fairly recent proposal, would attempt to sidestep the constitutional amendment process altogether and implement a direct election system in practice, if not in legal reality.

Some of these plans sound plausible at first glance, but a deeper analysis shows that none truly constitutes an improvement upon the country's existing federalist presidential election process.

Bonus Plan

Some academics acknowledge that the Electoral College, with its state-by-state voting, has encouraged stability and a two-party system in American politics. They seek an alternative that will maintain this stability and prevent the rise to power of extremist factions, yet which will nevertheless award the presidency to the popular vote winner. They propose that the presidential election system remain more or less as it is, but that a 102-electoral vote "bonus" (two votes per state, plus the District of Columbia) be awarded to the popular vote winner.[1] The Bonus Plan could still technically allow a candidate to win the presidency without winning the popular vote, but that possibility would be exceedingly remote.

The Bonus Plan might sound appealing at first, but it is likely that America's stable presidential election system would deteriorate under such a plan, just as surely as it would under a direct election system. One major problem with the Bonus Plan is that it lowers the total number of (pre-bonus) electoral votes needed for victory. Presidential candidates would no longer need 270 electoral votes to win; 219 plus the 102-vote bonus would be sufficient.[2] Under the current system, as few as 11 states can deliver the presidency to a candidate (if the 11 most populous states vote for the same candidate, which admittedly rarely happens). Under the Bonus Plan, as few as *eight of 50 states* could deliver the presidency to a candidate. When candidates need the support of fewer states to win, then they also have less incentive to build national coalitions.

The primary focus of candidates under the Bonus Plan would be on popular vote totals: The biggest prize goes to the candidate who wins the popular vote, regardless of where the votes are captured. Campaigning in California could not only garner 55 electoral votes for a candidate, but it could also make a significant contribution toward collecting the 102-vote bonus. What hope does Wyoming have under such a system? Once the focus turns to popular vote totals, rather than coalition-building, the delicate balance of the American presidential system is thrown out of whack.

The Founding Fathers created a presidential election plan that would deliberately inflate the voting power of small states. The Bonus Plan instead dilutes the importance of small states, leaving them in essentially the same position that they would be in if the country implemented a direct election system. If the 2004 or 2008 elections were held under the Bonus Plan, the results would be reasonably predictable, just as they would be with direct election. Democratic candidates would run up their popular vote totals in California and New York, and Republicans would camp out in the South, so as to run up their popular vote totals there.

Over time, the Bonus Plan would lead to a deterioration of America's otherwise stable political system. In a "best case" scenario, the Bonus Plan allows the two-party system to be maintained, but at great cost: Large regions of the country feel neglected as the two major parties focus on the large population centers along the coasts and in the South. Hardly a good state of affairs. In a "worst case" scenario, these sparsely populated regions feel so neglected that they throw their support behind a regional third-party candidate or candidates. If enough third-party candidates are motivated to jump into the fray, the danger of multi-candidate races, runoffs, and a fractured electorate arise, just as they would under a simple direct popular election plan. In either situation, the possibility of nationwide recounts is heightened. After all, a 102-electoral vote bonus is quite a prize for any candidate.

The Bonus Plan appears to maintain federalist principles at first glance, given that it maintains state-by-state voting. But, in practice, it would be unlikely to do so. Professor Paul Schumaker summarizes the problems inherent in this presidential election alternative: "[The Bonus Plan] would be susceptible to the flaws of a popular-vote-plurality system because its outcome would always hinge on the national popular vote."[3]

District Plan

A second alternative to the Electoral College would award electoral votes based upon congressional district. The candidate with the most votes in any congressional district would win that district's one electoral vote. The two Senate "add-on" votes in each state would then be treated as "at-large" votes and awarded to the state's popular vote winner. Maine and Nebraska already operate under this system; the proposal would require other states to join them.

Proponents of the plan argue that the District Plan will preserve the small state advantage, while allowing diversity within the states to be reflected in the national election totals.[4] Moreover, they add, campaigning would no longer focus on "swing states"; instead, candidates would be encouraged to campaign in states previously considered "safe." As this argument goes, the District Plan would not only encourage presidential candidates to campaign more widely, but it would also promote greater voter participation, because every voter would feel that his vote counts. Other Electoral College critics dismiss the District Plan, however, arguing that inequality of individual votes remain and the plan fails to address the "problem" of a popular vote winner failing to win the presidency.[5] Indeed, Bush's margin of victory in the Electoral College would have been *greater* under the District Plan, despite his popular vote loss.[6]

In a perfect world, the District Plan could be a good idea. America's presidential election system should encourage national coalition-building, and campaigning by districts would certainly work toward this goal.[7] But the plan has one serious flaw: The primary incentive created by the District Plan is an increased motivation to draw congressional boundaries in such a way as to benefit one political party. (Partisan drawing of congressional lines is a political tactic often referred to as "gerry-mandering.") Congressional districts are already seriously gerrymandered today, when only the outcome of congressional elections hinges on the drawing of the boundaries. Imagine the ferocity that would accompany redistricting battles every ten years if presidential elections also turned on where these boundaries lie. To the extent that districts' boundaries can be contrived and controlled by those in power, election outcomes will always be influenced as well. State boundaries have one significant advantage over congressional district boundaries: They are permanent and cannot be changed by an incumbent class of officials.[8]

Despite these arguments against the District Plan, the current system allows a state (acting through its state legislature) to switch to the District Plan if it decides that doing so would be beneficial within its borders—and it may do so without the necessity of passing a constitutional amendment. Moreover, the state can switch back to a winner-take-all system if implementing the District Plan causes more problems than it solved (as it is likely to do). Constitutional amendments are not completed—or undone—nearly as easily. Today, states are free to change their election system every year, if they choose. No reason exists to pass a constitutional amendment requiring all states to permanently implement the District Plan.

Proportional Plan

Under the Proportional Plan, the Electoral College would be retained, but the electoral votes in each state would be allocated based upon the percentage of the popular vote won. If implemented nationwide via constitutional amendment, some versions of the Plan call for whole electoral votes to be divided in the interest of accuracy.[9] Others also propose that the total number of electoral votes needed to win should be lowered to a 40 percent threshold.[10]

Proponents argue that the plan would preserve the states' Electoral College strength, but that the results would be closer to the national popular vote outcome.[11] Further, they argue, the voices of minority voting groups would be reflected in the final election tally because even ballots cast for third-party candidates could be reflected in the national results. Presidents could be elected without winning the popular vote, but such an outcome would be less likely than under the current system. Many Electoral College opponents consider the Proportional Plan to be an improvement, but others deem even the small remaining possibility of a "popular vote loser" President to be unacceptable.[12]

The Proportional Plan is yet another option that sounds good on the surface, but that creates problems in practice. First, constant fighting would erupt over election tallies. After all, a swing of a mere decimal point or two in one or several states could change the outcome of the election. In her book, *The Choice of the People? Debating the Electoral College*, Electoral College proponent Judith Best discusses the multiple difficulties with calculating election tallies under such a system. Should electoral votes be rounded to a tenth of a vote? A hundredth or a thousandth of a vote?[13] In any of these circumstances, the potential exists for at least one electoral vote in each of the 50 states to be open to dispute. Even small differences in the popular vote could determine how that electoral vote is divided or whether it is awarded to one candidate or another.[14]

Worse, because this type of election is so similar to a direct popular election system, it contains many of the downfalls that have been reiterated throughout this book: Multiple candidacies, close elections, runoffs, and few disincentives for extremist candidates who wish to join the fray. Definitive election outcomes are discouraged. Close vote totals and challenges to election outcomes become the norm.

One last point should be made about implementation of the Proportional Plan because at least one state is considering this option as a replacement for its winner-take-all system as this book goes to press. A Colorado citizens' organization—financed by a liberal nonprofit group from San Francisco[15]—recently collected enough signatures to place a referendum on its November 2004 ballot. If passed, this referendum would supposedly replace Colorado's winner-take-all system of casting electoral votes with a system of proportional allocation, making Colorado the only state to enact such a method in presidential elections.[16]

The referendum, however, has one glaring flaw. It purports to let Colorado voters decide the method of allocating the state's electoral votes, despite the fact that the Constitution gives this power to state *legislatures*, not state *citizens*.[17] For constitutional purposes, the difference is very real. If the referendum passes, the most likely result is a series of court challenges in Colorado.

Proponents of the referendum disagree. They argue that state statutory and constitutional provisions make the people equivalent to the legislature when they act through referendum or initiative. Therefore, they conclude, passage of a referendum or other citizen initiative is a perfectly legal and valid manner of changing electoral vote allocations in the state.

These proponents, however, have forgotten the most basic tenet of constitutional law: State laws and constitutions may not trump the federal Constitution. The U.S. Constitution is the supreme law of the land and preempts all other laws. That same Constitution explicitly designates each state's legislature as the entity with authority to decide the manner of appointing electors. State legislatures may certainly delegate legislative power to citizens for purposes of state law, but they may not delegate their constitutionally mandated duties in the national presidential election process.

This principle has been upheld by the Supreme Court. Speaking to an Ohio plan that would allow the people to act in place of the legislature for certain purposes related to constitutional amendments, the Court observed that the Founders wrote the constitutional language based upon their wish to "secur[e]" deliberation and consideration before any change [to the Constitution] can be proposed."[18] It continued:

> The framers of the Constitution might have adopted a different method. Ratification might have been left to a vote of the people, or to some authority of government other than that selected. The language of the article is plain, and admits of no doubt in its interpretation. It is not the function of courts or legislative bodies, national or state, to alter the method which the Constitution has fixed.[19]

In short, the Court held, when the Constitution says "the legislature," it means "the legislature." This principle applies to the constitutional process for electing a President, just as it applies to the constitutional amendment process.

As this book has discussed, state *legislatures* certainly may choose a proportional method of electoral vote allocation if they deem such a method to be in the best interest of their state. However, if one state acting on its own (particularly a small state) were to enact a proportional method of allocating electoral votes, the primary effect of its action would be to significantly dilute its voting strength as compared to the other states. State legislatures are authorized to change their methods of electoral vote allocation, but they will better serve their citizens if they leave the winner-take-all system in place.

De Facto Direct Election

Several academics have recently floated a plan that would effectively implement a direct popular election without amending the Constitution.[20] This plan is floated, one professor argues, because public discussion regarding a direct popular vote is likely to be "stifled" by the difficulty of effecting a constitutional amendment.[21] After all, a constitutional amendment essentially requires the support of two-thirds of the House, the Senate, and 38 state legislatures.[22] Quite an uphill battle. This alternative plan would allow a handful of states to do an end-run around the amendment requirements, implementing a "De Facto Direct Election" until such time as support for a constitutional amendment can be found.[23]

To date, this plan has not been widely discussed as an option for amending the country's presidential election system. It has, however, been discussed by more than one academic,[24] and the arguments for and against such a plan are worth discussing in the event that the idea gains more steam in future years.

Proponents of the De Facto Direct Election argue that at least 11 states should take advantage of their ability to appoint their presidential electors in any manner that they so choose. Currently, 270 electoral votes are needed to win an election; the 11 most populous states have a combined total of 271 electoral votes following the 2000 Census. Therefore, if these 11 states were to choose to award their electors in accordance with the national popular vote total, then they could determine the outcome of the election.[25] (If one state bowed out, then it would need to be replaced by a handful of other states.) Their decision would hold even if the other 39 states and the District of Columbia voted for the other presidential candidate.[26]

Proponents of the De Facto Direct Election fail to address several issues: Why should 11 states automatically overrule 39 other states in each and every presidential election? Why do these 11 states not abuse their power if they attempt to effect a constitutional amendment without bothering to get the consent of at least 27 additional states? Surely their actions violate the spirit of the Constitution, if not the letter of it.

The Constitution is set up as a system of checks and balances. The constitutional amendment process requires the approval of two-thirds of the states so the large states cannot bully the small states, yet that is exactly what the De Facto Direct Election proposal attempts to do. Eleven populous states would implement change with or without the approval of their smaller neighbors. True, the amendment process is an uphill battle. *It was intended as such.* Constitutional principles should be changed only after great thought and approval from the vast majority of the country. Difficulty in changing the Constitution protects the freedom of Americans.

Interestingly, those professors who have suggested the De Facto Direct Election plan often acknowledge several difficulties that could arise if their proposal were implemented. Not surprisingly, these issues coincide with many factors that complicate direct elections generally, as argued by this book. For instance, would the states award their electoral votes on a principle of majority rule or plurality rule? Would they require runoffs? How would they handle recounts and challenges?

These academics acknowledge one last challenge that confronts this proposal. This challenge results directly from the arrogance of effecting constitutional change without bothering to first obtain the consent of the governed. How, academics wonder, would the states handle "noncooperating states" who refuse to conduct internal state recounts or who otherwise attempt to "sabotage the system"?[27] At least two professors have theorized regarding the possibility of a nongovernmental "National Presidential Vote" system that would essentially bypass the official vote tallies in the small states.

Fortunately, at this stage of their article, the professors who proposed the National Presidential Vote seem to have devolved into a mere intellectual exercise regarding what's *possible*, rather than arguing as active proponents for such a scenario. The Founders would most certainly roll over in their graves if they realized that constitutional provisions were being so badly abused to effect majority tyranny over the small states.

If It Be Not Perfect, It Is at Least Excellent

The Electoral College is not perfect, nor is it realistic to expect perfection out of a presidential election process. A flawless presidential election system is surely impossible in an imperfect world. The Electoral College system, however, is unusually clever. It is certainly better than the other options, which often sound reasonable but work out poorly in practice.

The direct election option, for instance, appears to result in a President who is the choice of the majority of the people. In practice, a majority of people will never agree on one person. The electorate consists of a variety of people with an assortment of opinions. The best that can be hoped for is that the presidential election process will provide a method whereby compromise can be achieved. The President may not be the first choice of the majority, but the majority recognizes and votes for him as a good choice.

The Bonus Plan sounds as if it should uphold federalist principles because the states still cast votes. In reality, the Bonus Plan has all the downfalls of the direct election plan because the single biggest prize in the election is a 102-electoral vote bonus. The focus is on popular votes. Developing a national coalition is merely a secondary goal. The Electoral College, by contrast, requires presidential candidates to create national coalitions.

The District Plan, in an ideal world, would encourage national coalition building. Practically speaking, it will result in even more intense gerrymandering of districts. The Electoral College relies upon permanent state boundaries.

The Proportional Plan appears to retain the small state advantage, while giving greater weight to the popular vote. In reality, it would devolve into constant disputes about who gets the last electoral vote in each state. The Electoral College, by contrast, tends to magnify margins of victory and give certain election outcomes.

Last, the De Facto Direct Election is simply a silly academic proposal that sounds good to those who favored a direct popular election anyway. (Only academics could believe that the eleven most populous states would willingly cede their sovereignty with respect to presidential elections.) In reality, the primary effect of the proposal is to do an end run around the constitutional amendment process. The 11 most populous states would undermine the most basic principle of democracy: Government should operate only on the consent of the governed. The Electoral College remains the only election alternative that has been able to obtain the consent of the majority of states.

Alexander Hamilton was right when he described the Electoral College in *The Federalist No. 68*. Perhaps the Electoral College is imperfect—but a perfect solution is doubtless unachievable. Nevertheless, the presidential election process devised by the Framers is certainly excellent.

PART FOUR

THE ELECTORAL COLLEGE IN ACTION

CHAPTER TWELVE

SUCCESSFUL RESULTS OVER THE YEARS

O PPONENTS of the Electoral College seem to live in constant fear that the next election will be the one that produces a constitutional crisis of astronomical proportions. Apparently, 200 years of a smoothly functioning presidential election system are insufficient to convince these critics that the country is not constantly on the edge of an election "mistake" or disaster.

Instead, detractors of the current system point in horror to the fact that, technically speaking, a candidate could win the 11 largest states, each by a mere plurality, and thus be elected — despite the fact that he was not the preferred candidate of more than 75 percent of the states. Of course, such a situation is unlikely to occur. The 11 most populous states are scattered across different regions of the country. The political concerns expressed by the voters in these states are fairly diverse. A candidate could not obtain the votes of each of these 11 states without first generating some degree of cross-regional and cross-ideological appeal. It is hard to imagine liberal, Democratic California and conservative, Republican Texas voting for the same candidate while the majority of the states vote for someone else.

Electoral College opponents also point out, in dismay, the multiple elections in which a swing of "only" X thousand votes in State A could have caused the election of a "popular vote loser President." It seems the country has been on the brink of disaster multiple times, and nothing but good luck has kept the country running for so long. These claims, however, are mere manipulation of statistical data and do not take other, practical, factors into consideration.

America's election systems have operated smoothly for more than 200 years because the Electoral College accomplishes its intended purposes. America's presidential election process preserves federalism, prevents chaos, grants definitive electoral outcomes, and prevents tyrannical or unreasonable rule. A review of the dynamics in four elections—two resulting in Presidents who did not win the popular vote and two resulting in "electoral landslide winners"—will show that the Electoral College is a well-designed machine serving its purpose well, election after election.

Smooth Operations, Election After Election

In theory, the votes of the 11 largest states, alone, can deliver an election to a presidential candidate—their electoral votes, taken together, currently constitute a majority of the Electoral College.[1] Critics of the current presidential election process find this prospect horrifying. They shudder at the thought of an election decided by 11 states while the other 39 are ignored. Well, at least, they shudder at the thought of a decision made by 11 states under the Electoral College system. If the 11 states want to unilaterally redirect the country toward direct election (a De Facto Direct Election, as discussed in Chapter Eleven), some critics apparently have no problem with *that* decision made on behalf of the other 39 states.

An evaluation of the historical evidence provides a strong indication that the one-sided outcomes pictured by Electoral College opponents are more theoretical than real. The 11 most populous states are composed of voters from various regions of the country. These voters have diverse interests, and they cast their ballots for a wide range of reasons. If a presidential candidate managed to earn the support of these 11 quite different states, then he undoubtedly managed to obtain the support of many other states in the Union as well.

The last candidate to win all 11 of these states was Ronald Reagan. In 1984, Reagan won every state except Walter Mondale's home state of Minnesota. (He also lost the District of Columbia.) Reagan achieved the support of these 11 states because he successfully built a national coalition, a goal that the Electoral College seeks to encourage. A Senate minority report effectively made a similar point in 1970:

> A commonly heard indictment of the electoral college . . . is that the 11 largest states (plus another small State or the District of Columbia) would suffice to carry a candidate into office. The conclusion one is supposed to draw from this argument is that the 11 largest States are therefore in a position to dictate to the other 39. But what those who use this essentially emotional argument always conveniently forget to add is that the very compromises which enable a candidate to carry the 11 largest States also enable him to carry many others as well. And that is precisely why no candidate has ever won with anything like 11 States. In point of fact, only one President in this century (John F. Kennedy) was ever elected with less than a majority of the States supporting him. That exception excluded, no one in this century has ever won with less than 29 States, and the average number carried by the winner has been nearly 37.[2]

Since the time of that Senate report, only one other President has won with less than 29 states. Jimmy Carter won the presidency with the support of 23 states and the District of Columbia in the close election of 1976.

The next argument of Electoral College detractors concerns another "nightmare" scenario, which is also unlikely to occur. They comment on the many elections that have "nearly" ended in the election of a President who lost the popular vote.[3] (An event that would supposedly lead to rioting in the streets.) It would appear that the country has come close to calamity repeatedly, and only the best of luck has kept the country operating smoothly year after year.

Putting aside the fact that the "perfect storm" hit in 2000 without causing any discernible damage, one could find examples of three "near misses" in the last century. The election of 1916 between Charles Evans Hughes and Woodrow Wilson is often cited as one example of an election nearly gone awry. Hughes would have won if an additional 2,000 votes in California had gone his way. Had he gained these extra votes, a Hughes victory would have occurred despite the fact that Wilson led in the popular vote by more than 500,000 votes.[4] In 1948, Thomas Dewey could have won the election with a shift of less than 30,000 votes across three states, despite the fact that Harry Truman received 2.1 million more votes than Dewey nationwide.[5] Jimmy Carter would have been denied victory in 1976 if Gerald Ford had obtained just 9,300 more votes in two states, although Carter received nearly 1.7 million more votes overall.[6]

As a mathematical matter, these observations of Electoral College critics may be true. However, in most of these examples, a candidate could not have gained the extra votes he needed in one state without losing more votes in another state or states. Electoral College proponent Judith Best has completed an analysis of several of these so-called electoral disasters.[7] In discussing each of these elections, she identifies the policy issue that would have, in all likelihood, swung extra votes in one state, obtaining an Electoral College victory for one candidate despite his loss of the popular vote. In each instance, she notes, the "[shift-in-votes argument] fails because it abstracts from political realities."[8]

For example, the election of 1844 is often cited by Electoral College opponents as a near-electoral disaster.[9] In that election, a shift of 2,555 votes in New York would have swung the election in Henry Clay's favor from James Polk. As a purely theoretical matter, this consequence appears accurate. In the real election, obtaining those votes was not quite so easy. Clay might have been able to win New York, but he likely would have had to change his position on the annexation of Texas. Modifying his position on this issue to win New York would probably have caused him to lose Tennessee, a state that approved of his position on annexation. Clay's margin of victory in Tennessee was only 113 votes. Gaining New York but losing Tennessee would still have led to an election loss for Clay.

In sum, the scenarios forecast by Electoral College proponents are possible as a purely abstract matter, but in reality, they are unlikely to occur. Although critics correctly note that, as a mathematical matter, the outcome of this or that election could easily have swung in a different direction, they fail to take into account the practical issues and concerns that would realistically have affected the actual campaigns.

Historical results support an assessment of the Electoral College as a successful election device. The American election system encourages presidential candidates to seek national support and build cross-regional coalitions. Presidents who have lost the popular vote are not elected very often, but when they are, the situation usually comes about because the presidential candidate who won the popular vote simply did not work hard enough to amass the support of individuals across state boundaries. Instead, that presidential candidate spent too much time focusing on one region or one special interest group.[10] These candidates, despite winning the popular vote, did not deserve to win the presidency. The President should be an American President; he should not be a regional one.

Presidents Who Lost the Popular Vote

Some disagreement exists regarding how many American Presidents can be fairly characterized as candidates who were elected with an Electoral College win, but a popular vote loss. Some academics argue that the country has had as many as four such Presidents: John Quincy Adams (1824), Rutherford B. Hayes (1876), Benjamin Harrison (1888), and George W. Bush (2000). None of these men garnered either a majority or a plurality of the recorded individual popular vote before being inaugurated. The elections of 1824 and 1876, however, cannot accurately be described as elections in which the clear winner of the popular vote lost the presidency.[11]

In 1824, Andrew Jackson won a plurality of both the popular and the Electoral College votes.[12] Because he did not win a majority of electoral votes, the election was thrown into the House contingent election, where he lost to John Quincy Adams. Jackson spent the next four years claiming that he should have won the election because he won the popular vote. His arguments scored points with the American people, who elected him to the presidency over Adams in 1828.

Jackson's claims, however, were not entirely accurate. He won a majority of the *recorded* popular vote in 1824, but many individual votes were never recorded. At the time, many states' legislatures were still selecting electors on behalf of citizens. There is no way to know what the popular vote would have been in 1824 if all states had then relied upon a popular vote as their method of elector selection. Adams may or may not have been what Electoral College critics would call a "runner-up" President; it is impossible to know for sure. Either way, the election of 1824 is not representative of today's electoral system, which relies upon popular votes in all the states and a winner-take-all system of appointing electors.

The next election that allegedly produced a President who lost the popular vote is the election of 1876.[13] In that election,

Rutherford B. Hayes received approximately 250,000 fewer popular votes than did his opponent, Samuel J. Tilden. The general election was followed by weeks of doubt as 20 electoral votes in Florida, Louisiana, Oregon, and South Carolina were disputed. Three of the states submitted votes from multiple slates of electors; one electoral vote in Oregon was disputed. Hayes needed all 20 of these contested electoral votes to obtain a majority of 185 electoral votes and the presidency; Tilden needed only one.

The Republican-controlled Senate and the Democrat-controlled House had difficulty determining which slates of electors to accept. They eventually agreed to appoint an Electoral Commission to resolve the challenges. The Commission was composed of 15 individuals: seven Republicans, seven Democrats, and one independent Supreme Court Justice. Unexpectedly, the independent Justice, Justice David Davis, was elected to the Senate by the Illinois state legislature. After his election, he declined to serve on the Commission, and he was replaced by Justice Joseph Bradley, a Republican appointee. Perhaps predictably, the Republican-controlled Commission decided all 20 disputed electoral votes in favor of Hayes, throwing the election to him. A Democratic filibuster nearly sidetracked congressional acceptance of the Commission's findings, but eventually Congress declared Hayes the winner of the presidential election.[14]

The Hayes victory in 1876 cannot accurately be characterized as a definitive popular vote loss for Hayes. Elections in the South were not free and blacks were often not allowed to vote. Fraud and dishonesty pervaded the election as the northern and southern portions of the country struggled to reunite after the Civil War. At least one study has concluded that a "fair and free election" would have resulted in a popular vote victory for Hayes.[15] Under such circumstances, many more ballots would likely have been cast for Hayes in states such as Mississippi, Alabama, and North Carolina.

Only two elections can be properly characterized as ones in which a President lost the popular vote but won the electoral vote: the election of Benjamin Harrison in 1888 and the election of George W. Bush in 2000. These elections, however, are not causes for alarm. Instead, they demonstrate that the Electoral College is working as intended. In each case, the victor was able to succeed only because his opponent did not build the national coalition that is required by the Electoral College. In each case, smaller states were protected from their larger neighbors. In each case, the presidential election system functioned effectively to give the country a President with broad-based support. Perhaps most importantly, in each case the Electoral College winner was accepted by the country as a legitimate President—despite dire predictions that a crisis would ensue.

The elections of Harrison and Bush have been unfairly condemned. Although neither of these men garnered popular vote pluralities, their elections illustrate successful results of the Electoral College. Indeed, the most likely result of these elections will be to encourage future presidential candidates to remember small states as well as large states. Candidates will be reminded of the need to understand all the nation's regions, not just one or two of them.

Electoral Landslide Winners

If the Harrison and Bush elections demonstrate the successes encouraged by the Electoral College, then those elections resulting in electoral landslides do as well. As explained in the next chapter, Cleveland (1888) and Gore (2000) lost their bids for the presidency because they were less successful at building national coalitions than their opponents. The two candidates who won by the biggest electoral landslides exemplify the reverse situation. These two candidates were perhaps more successful than any other men in the country's history at generating nationwide support, even across lines that normally divide the electorate.

The two Presidents winning by the greatest electoral land-slides were Franklin Delano Roosevelt and Ronald Reagan. (Richard Nixon comes in a close third. Prior to Watergate, he defeated George McGovern by an electoral vote of 520 to 17 in the election of 1972.)[16] In 1936, Roosevelt lost two states, beating his opponent Alfred M. Landon by a vote of 523 to 8. Reagan defeated Walter Mondale in 1984 by a similar margin of victory: 525 to 13. Reagan won every state except Mondale's home state of Minnesota and the District of Columbia.

FDR and Reagan won by huge margins because they attained the objectives encouraged by the Electoral College. These two men established support across the country, and they won their electoral victories easily because voters across regions and partisan lines generally felt that FDR and Reagan understood them and would work to represent their interests. Whether by design or by accident, these candidates managed to embody exactly the type of President that the Electoral College is meant to select. The one characteristic that these two men shared, perhaps better than any modern-day President, was their ability to win the confidence of Americans.

Not coincidentally, these two men were in the news, to-gether, a great deal during June 2004, when Reagan passed away after a long battle with Alzheimer's. Repeatedly, reporters remarked upon the two Presidents who reflected the values of Americans throughout the 1900s: Roosevelt during the first half of the century, and Reagan during the last half of the century. Following Reagan's death, one newspaper described him as "perhaps the most seminal figure in 20th century American politics."[17] It concluded that "only FDR could also be considered" for the title.[18] The same day, historian Richard Norton Smith observed: "FDR shattered the political consensus that he found in place in 1933, and he left behind a new consensus and an army of followers who for 50 years really defined American politics. And Ronald Reagan really followed in his footsteps."[19]

Americans from all over the country flooded to California and the Capitol, where Reagan's body lay in state during the week following his death. The outpouring of affection confirmed the degree to which Reagan had won the hearts of voters across state lines during his time in public life. As the first week of the month-long remembrance beat on, former Reagan speechwriter Peggy Noonan wrote for the *Wall Street Journal*:

> By Friday it was no longer a question, as it had been for years, whether he was one of our top 10 presidents. It was a question only whether he was in the very top five or six—up there with Lincoln and Washington. An agreement had been reached: the 20th century came down to FDR and RWR.[20]

These two Presidents, who won by the largest electoral vote margins in U.S. history, exemplify the purpose of the Electoral College system. Each man campaigned for the support of voters across state lines, and each successfully earned the support not merely of a numeric majority, but also a federal majority. These election outcomes should remind candidates that the greatest success comes when they learn about the diverse needs and interests of voters across the nation. Electoral landslides occur when voters feel that one candidate represents *Americans*, not simply Republicans or Democrats.

<>

More than an accident of history has kept America's election systems operating smoothly for two centuries. The Founding Fathers created a stable, well-planned and carefully designed system—and it works. Past elections, even the elections of Presidents who lost the popular vote, are testaments to the ingenuity of the Founding Fathers. Those Presidents who won the electoral vote by landslide victories understood perhaps better than many what the Founders were trying to accomplish as they designed a presidential-election process.

In each instance, the Electoral College brought about the intended result, preserved federalism, prevented chaos and uncertainty, or kept an unreasonable or regional majority from trampling the few. The nation's presidential-election system has served America well for more than two centuries. An evaluation of the historical results of the nations' elections confirms that the Electoral College should be preserved at all costs.

CHAPTER THIRTEEN

HARRISON & BUSH: NARROW VICTORIES

T WO AMERICAN PRESIDENTS have been elected to the Oval Office despite losing the nationwide individual popular vote: Benjamin Harrison and George W. Bush. Although these election victories are criticized by some as instances in which the presidential election process failed the American people, they are precisely the opposite. Each election highlights the unique dynamics of the Electoral College, which successfully encourages candidates to attain federal, rather than individual, majorities.

Benjamin Harrison

In the aftermath of the Civil War and Reconstruction, elections were intensely regional. As a general rule, Republicans had an advantage in the northern and western regions with their 248 electoral votes, while Democrats were generally preferred in the southern region with its 153 electoral votes.[1] At the time, 201 electoral votes were needed for victory. To win an election, then, Democrats needed to pick up at least 48 electoral votes outside the South.

The regional nature of these elections was obviously harmful to the country. Arguably, the Republican advantage during these years had less to do with building national coalitions, and more to do with the fact that Republicans were favored in two regions, while Democrats were favored in only one. Without the Electoral College, however, the country would likely have remained divided along these regional lines for much longer than it did. The incentives inherent in the presidential election process forced candidates to reach out to voters beyond their home base. Democrats could never win without obtaining votes outside the South. Republicans were perhaps less motivated than Democrats to reach out to southern voters; however, their margin of victory when relying upon northern and western voters, alone, was always dangerously narrow.

In 1884, Democrat Grover Cleveland successfully reached out to non-southern regions, and he won the presidency. In the following election, he gained additional support among southern voters, but he lost the votes of many independents in other regions who had stood behind him in the 1884 election. This lost support undermined his re-election bid against Republican Benjamin Harrison. The final election results in 1888 revealed a hefty margin for Harrison in the Electoral College: 233 to 168. Harrison was elected to the presidency, despite the fact that Cleveland had won the popular vote by 0.8 percent.[2]

Cleveland's widest margins of victory were focused in six southern states: Alabama, Georgia, Louisiana, Mississippi, South Carolina, and Texas. In these six states, Cleveland won 72.5 percent of the votes cast for both men with a popular vote tally of 686,303 Cleveland votes to Harrison's 260,771.[3] Harrison's support, by contrast, was less intense but spread across the northern and western portions of the country. His widest margins of victory appeared in multiple regions: Colorado, Kansas, Maine, Minnesota, Nevada, and Vermont gave him 502,261 votes, compared to Cleveland's 317,223 votes. Harrison's vote totals in these six states constituted 61.3 percent of the votes cast for both men.[4]

Overall, Harrison won 20 states across the northern and western regions, while Cleveland's wins were focused in the South. Harrison's win made him the first American President to ascend to the presidency with an undisputed popular vote loss. The victory resulted, in large part, from the manner in which Cleveland alienated voters outside the southern parts of the country during his first term.

Cleveland's initial view of his role as President led to early problems with Congress.[5] Cleveland believed that the legislative and executive powers should be strictly separated. As a result, he began his term by restricting his engagements with Congress. He would make recommendations on issues, but would then simply veto or sign any bills that resulted without making significant efforts to ensure that bills were fashioned in line with his suggestions. His limited involvement caused him to lose influence among members of his party.

The embattled President eventually sought to regain some control by taking a more active stand during the crafting of legislation, but it remained an uphill battle throughout his first term. One Democratic Congressman observed at the time that "[a] President of the United States ought to have great influence with his party, but Mr. Cleveland deliberately threw his away, and he can't now pick it up again."[6] Cleveland's reserve and lost clout among Democrats caused him to miss opportunities to participate in the creation of bills, particularly a tariff bill that would later cause problems for him during his re-election campaign.

Cleveland was further plagued by his inability to curb abuse of the pension system following the Civil War. Congress was generally amenable to requests by Union veterans for pension funds, even when their requests were weak or fraudulent. Cleveland, however, repeatedly vetoed these pension requests, eventually issuing a record number of vetoes during his first term (414).[7] His firm stance earned him the respect of some who were weary of the fraud and waste, but it also increased his unpopularity with Union veterans and others who could not resist the appeal of the "bloody shirt."[8]

Cleveland stumbled again in 1887, committing two political gaffes that caused him to slip even further in the esteem of many northerners and Union veterans. Cleveland had agreed to attend the national encampment of the Grand Army of the Republic (GAR) in St. Louis. He saw the meeting as an opportunity to shake hands with voters and suggested to GAR that his reception there be public, rather than private. Many veterans viewed the request as an inappropriate politicization of their convention, and the *National Tribune* denounced the President's request stating, "Does anyone want the National Encampment running in conjunction with a grand political mass meeting?"[9]

Yet matters continued to worsen. At about the same time as the GAR convention controversy, Cleveland endorsed a proposal to return all Confederate flags captured during the war to their home states. Members of GAR were horrified at the prospect of Confederate flags returned to their southern owners, and they criticized Cleveland harshly for his decision. In the end, Cleveland withdrew his acceptance of the invitation to appear at the GAR encampment, and he stopped the return of Confederate flags to southern states. But the damage was done. The entire series of events contributed to Cleveland's unpopularity among many veterans, particularly those that did not reside in the South.

A last problem that confronted Cleveland during his term eventually led him to propose a tariff reform measure that proved unpopular among the northern states. While Cleveland was in office, the surplus in the government's treasury grew at a rapid clip, to Cleveland's great consternation. At the beginning of his term, the surplus was $17 million. By the end of his term, the surplus had grown to $140 million.[10]

A surplus would doubtless be a welcome asset to many modern Americans, but in the late 1800s, the surplus was a matter of concern. After much investigation, Cleveland determined that tariff reduction was the best method of reducing surpluses. He devoted his entire 1887 annual address to the subject, against the advice of his advisors, who worried that he would alienate the New York vote. His speech was the first annual address to focus exclusively on one subject, and it forced Democrats in the Congress to address the issue.

Unfortunately, the legislation eventually passed by the Democratic House was a watered-down bill that favored the Democratic South over the northern states. True tariff reform was never enacted during Cleveland's term, and many Americans most likely failed to understand the arguments behind his proposal. They thought that he was currying favor with the South, as the Democratic bill appeared to do.

The matter troubled Cleveland, and he attempted a retreat from the issue later in his campaign. He worked to distance himself from discussions of the subject at the Democratic Party Convention, and he appointed anti-tariff reform men to conspicuous positions in his campaign. Yet he remained convinced that he was on the right side of the issue. "My friends," he said, "told me that it would hurt the party; that without it, I was sure to be re-elected . . . . I did not wish to be re-elected without having the people understand just where I stood on the tariff question and then spring the question on them after my re-election."[11] He paused, "Perhaps I made a mistake from the party standpoint; but damn it, it was right. I have at least that satisfaction."[12]

Matters were further complicated for Cleveland when Harrison took advantage of the tariff issue, bringing it up repeatedly even as Cleveland sought an honorable retreat. Harrison's campaign labeled free trade an evil, claiming that it did more to help foreign interests than to help Americans. Those who supported tariffs, then, were pro-American. Those who opposed tariffs were not. "'The policy of the Democratic party,'" Harrison declared in an October 25 speech, "'means a vast and sudden increase of importations. Is there a man here so dull as not to know that this means diminished work in our American shops?'"[13]

As borne out by history, Cleveland was on the right side of the tariff matter. Unfortunately for him, Harrison grabbed the issue, framing it in a way that caused voters to perceive Cleveland as a President who represented only the South. The proposal for tariff reduction served primarily to antagonize those who were already upset regarding Cleveland's pension vetoes and his proposal to return the Confederate battle standards to southern states. The issue added to veterans' antipathy toward Cleveland, who did not serve in the Civil War and who impoliticly went fishing on Memorial Day, causing many to feel that he did not respect veterans. Cleveland led a lackluster and unenergetic campaign and was never able to regain the tariff issue from the Republicans. He failed to show voters that tariff reform could help the entire nation and that the benefits need not be limited to a handful of southern states.

Harrison's campaign, by contrast, was energetic, well-organized, and monitored the sentiments of voters across the states. Harrison gave more than 80 speeches to nearly 300,000 people in 16 weeks—quite an unusual feat in the late 1800s.[14] During the post-war years, many found it easy to support Harrison, a Civil War veteran who had served with distinction in the Union army. Moreover, those in charge of Harrison's campaign understood and capitalized on the increasingly popular nature of the presidential campaign, and they worked hard to build Harrison's image as an everyday American. The Republican Party even went so far as to solicit a book on Harrison's life from General Lew Wallace. Emblazoned on the book's cover was the apt title: *Life of Ben Harrison by the Author of Ben Hur*.[15] His tactics worked well among a populace that was still enamored of the concept of the "log cabin." His supporters often gloated that, even if Harrison wasn't *born* in a log cabin, at least he was *educated* in a log schoolhouse.[16] Harrison's strategy successfully prevailed over Cleveland, who left to others much of the task of campaigning and spent a large portion of the campaign season in isolation.

Cleveland's proposals may have been good for the country as a whole, but he did not present them in a manner that enabled him to obtain strong cross-country support. Instead, his campaign in 1888 represents the type of campaign that should lose under the system devised by the Founders. If Cleveland had won, then six southern states voting on (what was at least perceived as) a regional matter would essentially have out-voted the northern and western portions of the country combined. A candidate would have won an election, not by tailoring and communicating a message with national appeal, but by amassing landslide victories in a few key states.

The Electoral College in this instance effectively sent a message to future presidential candidates: Do not ignore the interests of the many by catering to the few. Cleveland himself successfully learned this lesson and returned to win election to a second term in 1892.

George W. Bush

The 2000 election made George W. Bush the first President since Benjamin Harrison to win the presidency without also winning the popular vote. Bush lost the popular vote by a fairly close margin: only 540,520 votes nationwide, although more than 100 million votes, total, were cast for the two major party candidates. The close election results should not have been surprising. They followed months of polling that showed the two candidates running neck and neck in a national popular vote tally.

The conventional wisdom in 2000 was that the election results reflected a "closely divided" nation. President Bill Clinton observed soon after Gore's concession speech: "In this election, the American people were closely divided. The outcome was decided by a Supreme Court that was closely divided."[17] He was soon echoed by political commentators, such as National Public Radio's Juan Williams who stated, "Never before have we seen the nation so closely divided as this election year. . . . From the vote for president to the Florida Legislature to the courts, decisions are being made by the narrowest of margins in history."[18] Another editorialist similarly observed, "It's eerie how closely divided the nation has become. . . . Five to four court decision. Four to three court decision. Three-hundred thousand margin out of 100 million votes. House and Senate in a virtual tie."[19]

Taken as a whole, the 2000 congressional and presidential elections were, some say, like the perfect storm. They were "the perfect tie."[20] (Assuming, *arguendo*, that the presidential election was essentially a tie, then it could be argued that the Electoral College served as a tiebreaker.) Commentators accurately recognized that *individuals* across state boundaries appeared to be pretty evenly divided; however, *states* were not so evenly divided.

An examination of the vote totals by state or county reflects a nation that leaned heavily toward Bush: Sixty percent of the states favored Bush. He won 2,434 counties nationwide, compared to Gore, who won only 677 counties.[21] The population in the counties won by Bush was 143 million people, compared to the 127 million people who resided in the counties won by Gore.[22] Bush carried the election in 2,427,000 square miles of the country, compared to 580,000 square miles carried by Gore.[23] Bush earned the votes of at least one state in every region of the country. Most of Gore's support was concentrated in several heavily populated regions in the Northeast and on the western seaboard.

Both Bush and Gore won some states by landslides of 15 percent or more, but Bush won 15 of these states, compared to Gore's seven (plus the District of Columbia). Bush's sizeable victories were spread throughout the Midwest and the South.

Gore's largest margins of victory were isolated primarily in the Northeast.

State Landslide Victories Won By Bush[24]

State	Margin of Victory	Bush		Gore	
		Popular Vote	Percent	Popular Vote	Percent
Kentucky	15.1%	872,520	56.4%	638,923	41.3%
Indiana	15.6%	1,245,836	56.6%	901,980	41.0%
South Carolina	16.0%	786,892	56.9%	566,037	40.9%
Mississippi	16.9%	572,844	57.6%	404,614	40.7%
Kansas	20.8%	622,332	58.0%	399,276	37.2%
Texas	21.3%	3,799,639	59.3%	2,433,746	38.0%
Oklahoma	21.9%	744,337	60.3%	474,276	38.4%
South Dakota	22.7%	190,700	60.3%	118,804	37.6%
Montana	25.1%	240,178	58.4%	137,126	33.4%
North Dakota	27.6%	174,852	60.7%	95,284	33.1%
Nebraska	29.0%	433,850	62.2%	231,776	33.2%
Alaska	31.1%	167,398	58.8%	79,004	27.8%
Idaho	39.5%	336,937	67.2%	138,637	27.6%
Utah	40.7%	515,096	67.2%	203,053	26.5%
Wyoming	40.9%	147,947	69.2%	60,481	28.3%
TOTALS		**10,851,358**		**6,883,017**	

Gore won fewer state landslide victories, but he gained nearly as many votes in these highly populated states as Bush did in his 15. In his seven states, Gore earned 10,100,298 votes, while Bush earned 10,851,358 in the 15 states that he won by large margins. Exit polls further reflected the extent to which Gore's support was isolated in certain highly populated regions of the country. Polls showed that 71 percent of voters living in cities with populations of 500,000 or more voted for Gore.[25] By contrast, rural voters went 59 percent for Bush and 37 percent for Gore.[26]

State Landslide Victories Won By Gore

State	Margin of Victory	Bush		Gore	
		Popular Vote	Percent	Popular Vote	Percent
New Jersey	15.8%	1,284,173	40.3%	1,788,850	56.1%
Maryland	16.3%	813,724	40.2%	1,143,888	56.6%
Connecticut	17.5%	561,104	38.4%	816,659	55.9%
Hawaii	18.3%	137,845	37.5%	205,286	55.8%
New York	25.0%	2,403,374	35.2%	4,107,697	60.2%
Massachusetts	27.3%	878,502	32.5%	1,616,487	59.9%
Rhode Island	29.1%	130,555	31.9%	249,508	61.0%
District of Columbia	76.2%	18,073	9.0%	171,923	85.2%
TOTALS		6,227,350		10,100,298	

At the turn of the 20th century, Democrats were strong in the Pacific West and the East, while Republicans had solid support in the South, Mountain West, and Midwest. Political commentators Henry C. Kenski, Brooks Aylor, and Kate Kenski argue that, in 2000, ten states were "core" Democratic states, while 19 "leaned" Democratic.[27] Gore could have won the election if he had obtained the support of all 29 of these states. Unfortunately for his campaign, he lost one of his core states and eight of his "lean Democratic" states. Republicans, by contrast, had 21 Republican and Republican-leaning states, worth about 192 electoral votes. To win the election, Bush would need to win these states and obtain 78 additional electoral votes from Democratic-leaning states. Bush accomplished his task. He won all 21 Republican states, plus he added nine Democratic or Democratic-leaning states to his electoral vote tally. He achieved his goal by creating a cross-regional coalition that supported him on a couple of core issues.

The themes driving the election in 2000 were more nebulous than those driving the 1888 election. The country was doing well economically. This peace and prosperity should have weighed in favor of Vice President Al Gore, the heir-apparent to incumbent President Bill Clinton. Indeed, during the campaign, Gore attempted to capitalize on the economic issue, arguing that a Bush tax cut could endanger the stability of the economy. Exit polls show that 61 percent of those who believed the country to be on the right track voted for Gore.[28] Bush campaign chief strategist Karl Rove later noted that, had Gore been able to take better advantage of the economic issue, he might have won the election.[29] Bush, however, took some wind out of the sails of Gore's economic arguments. He positioned himself as a moderate who would keep prosperity safe. Once he nullified the economic factor (at least to some degree), he was better able to tackle Gore in other areas, in which many perceived that the country was not doing as well.[30]

Perhaps the main issue driving the outcome of the 2000 election concerned "values"—a notoriously hard-to-define concept.[31] Many people felt that the incumbent, Clinton, had performed well in office, but they did not like him personally. His scandal-ridden presidency adversely affected the mood of voters, and Clinton became a political liability for Gore, particularly in many swing states in the South and the Midwest.[32] The Bush campaign capitalized on this discontent surrounding the perceived decline in moral values. Indeed, Bush focused on the morality issue, even as he simultaneously acknowledged one of his opponent's strengths: the country's economic prosperity. Bush's nomination acceptance speech at the Republican Party Convention in Philadelphia opened, "Prosperity can be a tool in our hands—used to build and better our country. Or it can be a drug in our system—dulling our sense of urgency, of empathy, of duty. . . . Our generation has a chance to reclaim some essential values."[33]

Bush's campaign worked to link Gore with the dishonest and unprincipled behavior that voters perceived had intensified during the Clinton administration. Vice presidential candidate Richard Cheney declared, "Mr. Gore will try to separate himself from his leader's shadow. But somehow we will never see one without thinking of the other."[34] Gore further contributed to his own downfall, binding himself to Clinton's failings in the minds of many voters, primarily by his failure to strongly condemn Clinton's actions during the 1998 impeachment proceedings. Diane Wright, a homemaker in Gore's home state of Tennessee, expressed this sentiment. She stated she would likely vote for Bush, "[p]robably because of Clinton. Gore should have been stronger. He could have distanced himself. A lot of people in Tennessee feel that way."[35]

Bush successfully courted voters who were concerned about values, particularly those residing in the conservative South and Midwest. Polls showed that 57 percent of voters believed the country to be on the wrong moral track. Of these people, 62 percent voted for Bush.[36] An additional indicator of the importance placed upon moral issues during the 2000 election is the breakdown of the vote according to religious practice. Of those attending religious services more than weekly, 63 percent voted for Bush. The situation was reversed for those who do not attend religious services: 61 percent voted for Gore.[37] Forty-four percent of voters thought the Clinton scandals were an important issue in the 2000 election.[38] Of those who rated the scandals "very important," 80 percent voted for Bush.[39] Moreover, questions about other moral values, such as stem cell research and abortion, also pulled at the electorate. Many were concerned about judicial nominations, perceiving that liberal, activist judges were leading the nation astray morally. In response, Bush promised to appoint judges who would "strictly interpret the Constitution and not use the bench for writing social policy."[40] Gore instead argued that "[i]t would be likely that [his judges] would uphold *Roe v. Wade*."[41]

In 2000, voters in the majority of states viewed Bush as an honest, sincere man who would strive to do the right thing. They viewed Gore as an experienced candidate, but one who was insincere and too ambitious. These characteristics, whether perceived or real, contributed to his inability to distance himself sufficiently from Clinton's moral failings. Gore made the mistake of thinking that peace and prosperity would carry the day with most of the country. He was right in thinking that it would carry the day with most *individuals*; however, most of these voters resided in the more liberal east and west coasts. Voters in the majority of states, particularly in the more conservative Midwest and South, voted on a different range of issues. To them, honesty, trustworthiness, and other leadership qualities were equally valid issues to consider when casting their votes. Gore was unable to obtain the support of most of these latter individuals.

Bush worked in other ways to broaden his base of support. He deliberately sought to gain the support of many independents by avoiding actions that might be perceived as partisan or solely Republican. Rove notes that Bush gained backing by avoiding the old Republican rhetoric on many issues. Instead, he looked for ways to reach across partisan lines. Rove observed, "When [Bush] talked about welfare, he didn't say, 'Let's get the welfare cheats off the rolls.' He said, 'We're losing some of our best and brightest to dependency on government. How can we help free people to meet their greatest potential in life?'"[42] Moreover, Bush purposely tackled issues that are traditionally considered advantageous for Democrats, such as education, Medicare, and Social Security. He worked to paint a picture of himself as a new kind of Republican, a "compassionate conservative" that could reach across partisan lines. He did not always persuade voters on these issues, but he at least decreased the advantage that Gore had in these areas.[43]

In the end, election results show that Bush succeeded in his efforts to build a cross-regional coalition of voters. Rove notes that Bush made some major (and little discussed) inroads into the Democratic vote. He won a swing of 11.3 million new votes since the 1996 election.[44] New Hispanic voters, alone, grew by 1.5 million. Further, he won a number of traditionally Democratic states, such as West Virginia, that he should not have carried. Gore also increased the number of votes cast for his party since the 1996 election, but these additional votes were from constituencies that consistently vote Democratic anyway.[45] For instance, he gained new votes among labor unions and black voters.

The election of 2000 is a perfect example of why the Electoral College exists. If America operated under a direct election system, Gore would have won despite losing the election in 60 percent of states and more than two-thirds of counties in America. He would have won despite the fact that he had virtually no support in two large regions of the country and the bulk of his support was isolated on the east and west coasts. The rural and less populous states would have been trampled by the will of a few heavily populated regions.

<>

The elections of 1888 and 2000 are illustrations of Electoral College success. In each case, the candidate who did a better job of building a national coalition and generating support nationwide was sent to the White House. Harrison and Bush were the appropriate winners for each of these elections. They proved themselves to be better representatives for a diverse, federalist society than Cleveland and Gore, who would have owed their wins, had they occurred, to landslide victories in a few states.

CHAPTER FOURTEEN

ROOSEVELT & REAGAN: LANDSLIDE VICTORIES

F RANKLIN Delano Roosevelt and Ronald Reagan both came to the presidency during times of economic difficulty, and each conquered the daunting task of uplifting a discouraged country. Both men possessed a unique talent for speaking to people in a manner that restored their hope and made them feel understood. Each President had his detractors; no candidate will ever be supported by *all* voters. However, FDR and Reagan, perhaps better than any other candidate during the 20th Century, attained the goals encouraged by the Electoral College.

The 1936 and 1984 elections proved the ability of these men to achieve support across racial, regional, and ethnic lines. Each President's critics were outnumbered by the great majority of constituents who trusted their President, even if they disagreed with him on the margins. By and large, FDR and Reagan were perceived as *American* Presidents, first and foremost. These two men who obtained such wide cross-country support earned more electoral votes than any other President in U.S. history; they were elected to the White House by electoral landslides.

Franklin Delano Roosevelt

FDR's popularity with the American people cannot be properly appreciated without an understanding of the context in which they first elected him.[1] He assumed the Oval Office during the Great Depression, which began when the New York stock market crashed in 1929. At the time of the crash, Republican President Herbert Hoover was in office and most of the blame for the economic disaster was laid at his feet. During the following presidential campaign between Hoover and FDR, the country was still suffering from the consequences of the economic decline. Thousands of banks had failed, and stock values had dropped to about 20 percent of their previous value.[2] Thirteen million Americans found themselves unemployed by March 1933.[3] Under such circumstances, FDR was elected easily in 1932 on what was essentially an "anti-Hoover" vote.

Almost immediately, FDR proposed sweeping reforms that became known as the New Deal. His package of proposed solutions injected the federal government extensively into many economic and labor matters that had previously remained private. FDR explained his plans to the American public during evening radio talks, called "fireside chats." He also relied upon these chats to give people optimism and a sense of security, despite the nation's economic difficulty.

To many Americans, the New Deal meant relief; they trusted FDR's confident outlook on the future. Others remained worried about FDR's policies, perceiving that government had been inserted too much into private matters; they worried that the end result would be confiscatory taxation and a lack of self-reliance. The J.P. Morgans, for instance, hated FDR, going so far as to forbid the mention of his name in their home.[4] The Morgans and those like them, however, were vastly outnumbered by those who trusted FDR and believed his offer of hope. The gulf between the two groups widened still further between the elections of 1932 and 1936.

Ironically, FDR's New Deal probably prolonged the Depression, due to the greatly increased federal taxes necessary to support the government programs. These new taxes sucked capital out of the private market, making it harder for employers to hire new employees or invest in new businesses. The median unemployment rate was 17 percent throughout the New Deal era.[5] Americans were relying upon a man who was most likely making their economic situation worse. But, for election purposes, it didn't matter. Voters believed in FDR, and they believed his contentions that the New Deal would cure the economy. His appeal to voters in the face of such economic disaster is a huge testament to his ability to make people trust him, even when he may not have deserved it.

FDR was extremely popular by the time the 1936 election rolled around, although the economy was still slow and eight million Americans remained unemployed.[6] Few presidential candidates could have realistically hoped to challenge FDR in his bid for re-election, but Republicans eventually nominated Alfred "Alf" Landon, Governor of Kansas. Landon was the only Republican governor to win reelection during the Democratic landslides of 1934, and he was known for his battles in favor of civil liberties and against the Ku Klux Klan. Of the potential candidates, it seemed that he had the best chance of defeating FDR.[7]

Even Landon, however, was not up to the task. He often seemed to agree with many of FDR's New Deal policies, although he objected that the programs went too far and were "strangling . . . free enterprise."[8] Moreover, Landon was not especially talented at public speaking. His lack of talent may have helped with some voters who viewed his clumsy manner as more sincere than FDR's slick charisma. Nevertheless, Landon's ineptness in public remained mostly a hindrance. Other Republicans labeled him a "'pretty poor specimen'" or no "'world beater'" as the campaign heated up during the summer of 1936.[9] Worse, Landon was a weak campaigner. He stayed at home during much of the campaign and did not participate in the Republican primaries. Instead, most attacks on FDR originated with others in his party.[10]

During the campaign, Republican criticisms focused on allegations that FDR's policies extended the federal government into too many areas of state and private life. Republicans disapproved of FDR's decision to abandon the gold standard and condemned the seemingly permanent federal deficit. Landon won the support of those who were alarmed by ever-increasing federal tax rates, as well as those who felt that FDR's policies undermined such virtues as self-reliance and thriftiness. When all was said and done, though, Landon's supporters were not bound together by any characteristic of Landon or his platform; instead, they were bound together by their dislike of FDR and his programs. Senator Arthur H. Vandenberg stated at the time, "I belong to but one bloc and it has but one slogan—stop Roosevelt."[11] Unfortunately for FDR's detractors, their aversion to the New Deal alone, without some other unifying factor, was not sufficient to stop a President who had much of the country on his side and who was determined to fight.

FDR's campaign turned the election into warfare between the classes. He argued that his New Deal would protect average Americans from Big Business and the wealthy. FDR boasted, "Never before in all our history have these forces been so united against one candidate as they stand today. They are unanimous in their hate for me—and I welcome their hatred."[12] He continued, "[T]he forces of selfishness and of lust for power met their match [during my first term]. I should like to have it said of my second Administration that in it these forces met their master."[13]

Most Americans believed that FDR stood staunchly on their side, opposed to the rich and powerful who would take advantage of them during a time of economic difficulty. Their beliefs were reinforced by FDR's campaign speeches, which often began with FDR's observation: "You look happier today than you did four years ago."[14] As he continued his speech, he would regale the audience with strings of numbers that supposedly indicated how his programs were working and the economy was improving. As FDR campaigned, people often came to hear him speak and would yell their thanks to him as he passed by: "He saved my home," or "He gave me a job."[15] One worker exclaimed in 1936 that FDR was the "'only man we ever had in the White House who would understand that my boss is a son-of-a-bitch.'"[16]

FDR added to his cross-country appeal by putting together his "New Deal Coalition," an alliance of voters from different regional, racial, religious, and ethnic backgrounds.[17] Labor unions, minorities, liberals, and southern Protestants forged a partnership of sorts under this coalition. Catholic voters swung in favor of FDR because he appointed so many Catholics to the bench. During FDR's tenure, one in four judicial appointees was Catholic, as opposed to one in 25 during the previous three administrations.[18] Black voters also began to come to the Democratic side during these years. They appreciated FDR's appointment of blacks to important posts, and they felt that FDR's New Deal programs had offered them relief from economic depression.

On Election Day, the broad-based coalition that FDR put together paid off handsomely. FDR trampled Landon, both in the popular and the electoral votes. He obtained 523 electoral votes to Landon's eight votes and 27,757,333 popular votes to Landon's 16,684,231 votes. FDR won every state in the union except for Maine and Vermont.

FDR's coalition of voters enabled him to obtain the widest margin of victory in the nation's history: 515 electoral votes. Ronald Reagan came closest to beating FDR's record when he defeated Walter Mondale by 512 electoral votes nearly 50 years later.

Ronald Reagan

As with FDR, Reagan's success cannot be fully appreciated without first understanding life in America before his presidency. Reagan initially won the presidency by defeating Jimmy Carter in the election of 1980. Domestically, Carter's administration had been characterized by high inflation, long gas lines, and increasing unemployment. In foreign affairs, voters worried about the proliferation of nuclear arms, the spread of communism, and the possibility of war with the Soviet Union. The nation seemed stuck in despondency. In July 1979, Carter stated on television that the nation was undergoing a "'crisis of confidence.'"[19] Carter had hoped to spur the people to action with his words, but he succeeded only in disheartening them further. His speech became known as the "malaise" speech. Matters degenerated still further late in Carter's term when 66 American hostages[20] were taken and held for more than a year in Iran. The incident left the public even more demoralized. When Reagan arrived on the scene, Americans readily turned to this man who was brimming with optimism about the future.

Reagan obtained early popularity, yet his first term was bumpy. He achieved some early successes, such as convincing Congress to reduce taxes by 25 percent across the board over the course of three years. This proposal, combined with the Tax Reform Act of 1986, would eventually reduce the top tax rate from 70 percent to 28 percent.[21] Reagan found another early victory in the area of defense spending. He obtained massive spending increases in this area, although he failed in his efforts to make parallel cuts in domestic spending.

A last early step taken by Reagan eventually tamed the nation's problem with escalating inflation rates, but not before many people incorrectly concluded that Reagan's policies had failed. Reagan supported efforts by Paul Volcker, then the Federal Reserve chairman, to raise interest rates soon after

Reagan entered office. The effort brought inflation down sharply, but it also triggered a short recession.[22]

The recession caused many to believe that Reagan's proposals should be abandoned, and his ideas were labeled "Reaganomics" by many critics. Reagan, however, refused to alter his course. He believed that his actions would alleviate the nation's financial difficulties, but he also knew that such a cure could not happen overnight. He steadfastly waited for recovery to come. In 1983, as Reagan's first round of tax cuts was finally phased in fully, the economy did begin to grow—and it grew rapidly. The economy grew for 15 straight years, creating 20 million new jobs between 1983 and 1989. The gross national product increased by one third during the rest of Reagan's presidency.[23] The so-called "misery index" (inflation plus rate of unemployment) dropped from 20.2 percent during October 1980 to 11.5 percent by 1984. Inflation, alone, decreased to less than five percent, although it had been more than 12 percent during Carter's tenure.[24] Reagan joked, "The best sign that our economic program is working is that they don't call it 'Reaganomics' anymore."[25]

By the time the 1984 election rolled around, Reagan was enormously popular with much of the public. (As with FDR, a smaller contingent of people hated him with an equal intensity.) For a country that had been dejected in the 1970s, Reagan was a refreshing change. He replaced pessimism with optimism. Americans believed in themselves and their country as they had not been able to do for years. In this sense, Reagan was similar to FDR. Each President restored confidence to the American people.

Reagan was inspired by his early hero, FDR, in other ways as well. He echoed FDR's fireside chats, often taking his case straight to the people through television addresses from the Oval Office or in his weekly radio broadcast. Reagan was hopeful about America's future, and his positive outlook spilled over onto voters. In many senses, Reagan campaigned on the idealism of "the future" as much as he campaigned on more tangible issues, such as the economy. His campaign slogan in 1984 was compatible with his sunny personality: "It's morning again in America!" Reagan biographer Lou Cannon has remarked on this Reagan trait: "When Reagan talked this way, in cadences that echoed the optimism of his old hero Franklin Roosevelt, he transcended partisan barriers."[26]

Walter Mondale, the Democratic nominee in 1984, probably never had a chance of defeating Reagan. Sixty percent of voters felt favorably toward Reagan in 1984. This number was higher than that for Mondale or either of the vice presidential candidates.[27] Not only was Reagan personally popular, but the economy was thriving for the first time in years. Most people believed that the economy had improved, and they credited Reagan with the improvement. Their approval of Reagan's economy management weighed more heavily even than their personal financial status when they went to the polls. Those who thought Reagan had helped the economy, even though their personal finances had not changed, voted nine to one for him.[28]

Mondale attempted to combat Reagan's strength in this area in several ways. First, he argued that the economy was not as good as it appeared—but voters didn't believe him.[29] Next, he argued that Reagan was merely rewarding the rich at the expense of the poor. While some voters believed Mondale, the argument did not seem to undermine Reagan's broad support base.[30] Last, Mondale attempted to pin the rising deficit on Reagan, but Americans instead blamed Congress. Approximately 50 percent of voters believed Democratic Congressmen were responsible for the deficit, compared to 30 percent who blamed Reagan.[31] Moreover, Mondale's solution to the deficit—spending cuts and a tax hike—also fell flat with voters, who preferred Reagan's arguments for reduced domestic spending. An ABC/*Washington Post* poll at the time of the election showed an overwhelming dislike for tax increases on the part of the electorate.[32] Mondale had hoped that his tax increase proposal would paint him as an honest man who was willing to be candid regarding the need to raise taxes. Instead, he alienated voters and gave Reagan grounds to compare him to the tax and spenders of the 1970s. Reagan, for his part, largely ignored the deficit during his campaign, instead focusing on the improved economy. His positive focus furthered the contrast between Reagan, the optimist, and Mondale, who increasingly began to look like just another pessimist.

Reagan had a further advantage over Mondale on foreign policy issues. When asked, voters sometimes evidenced disagreement with one or two elements of Reagan's policy, but overall, they liked the image of strength abroad that Reagan fostered. This perception crossed party lines. A plurality of Democrats, 42 percent, believed that a Republican administration would do more to keep the country strong.[33]

Although strong on both domestic and foreign issues, Reagan faced a bigger test with respect to a more personal issue: He would be almost 78-years old at the end of a second term in office, and some commentators argued that he was too old to run for President. Reagan, as always, was ever-ready with humor on the subject, which put people at ease. When accused of dozing during Cabinet meetings, he promptly responded to campaign workers: "'Some of you here were up all night . . . . And I can only tell you that, if I could manage it, I would schedule a Cabinet meeting so that we could all go over and take a nap together.'"[34] At a couple of points during the campaign, it seemed as if the age argument would make some headway. For instance, when Reagan did not perform well in the first presidential debate, the *Wall Street Journal* ran a headline that declared, "Is Oldest U.S. President Now Showing His Age?"[35] Reagan soon put the issue to rest with an improved second debate performance—and a joke. When asked about the age issue, he responded: "I want you to know that also I will not make age an issue of this campaign. I am not going to exploit for political purposes my opponent's youth and inexperience."[36] Even Mondale laughed at the line. Reagan's re-election was perhaps guaranteed in that moment.

"'Reagan is the most popular figure in the history of the United States,'" House Speaker Tip O'Neill observed after the election, "'No candidate we put up would have been able to beat Reagan this year.'"[37] His words accurately summarized the wide-ranging appeal that Reagan had successfully nourished. In 1984, Reagan was re-elected by an electoral vote of 525 to 13, and he secured 54,455,075 popular votes to Mondale's 37,577,185. His victory is notable for the diversity of people that it encompassed. Commentators often remark upon Reagan's ability to gain support from the so-called "Reagan Democrats." But his support crossed other lines as well. In 1984, Reagan won a majority of every region, every age group, and every occupation.[38] A majority of both men and women voted for Reagan.[39] Reagan made huge gains among Hispanics, although the Jewish and Black vote still went to Mondale. Reagan won a majority of the blue-collar vote; he was the first Republican to do so since Richard Nixon defeated George McGovern.[40]

George Shultz once stated, "Reagan trusted the American people, and because he did, the American people trusted him."[41] Reagan's concern for Americans was demonstrated in many small ways that added up over the years. For instance, he personally responded to thousands of letters that were written to him by his movie fans and constituents. In 1981, he wrote to a citizen, "You specified that you wanted to hear from me personally, so here I am."[42] This attitude marked his service to the country, and won him support at election time.

Vincent Rakowitz, a retired brewery worker in San Antonio, perhaps best summarized the appeal of Reagan to many voters in 1984: "'He really isn't like a Republican. He's more like an American, which is what we really need.'"[43]

◇

The elections of 1936 and 1984 stand as examples of Electoral College success. FDR and Reagan won by decisive electoral victories because they had successfully built inclusive national coalitions that appeared to embrace all Americans, as encouraged by the Electoral College system. Arguably, their success in coalition-building was due, at least in part, to the crises that gripped the nation in the 1930s and 1970s before their presidencies. Perhaps the people were more amenable to working together under one President during a time of disaster, as opposed to a time of prosperity. Yet each President also proved his talent for reaching across lines that normally divide the nation. Each demonstrated the success that can be obtained by any candidate who seeks to build upon the values that are shared by Americans, rather than the issues that divide them. Both FDR and Reagan personified the type of candidate that should win the presidency in a diverse, federalist republic. As a result, each was re-elected to the presidency with an electoral landslide.

CONCLUSION

T HE CONVENTIONAL WISDOM in 2004—supported by various polls—suggests that the nation remains "closely divided." A variety of issues sharply splits the nation. Should the Federal Marriage Amendment be passed? Is the failure to find Weapons of Mass Destruction an indictment on the Bush administration? Should Bush's tax cuts be made permanent? Is the economy improving or declining? As this book goes to press, most polls show President George W. Bush with a lead over Senator John Kerry in the national popular vote, although some polls show Kerry ahead in the electoral vote tally.

Regardless of which way the election comes out, voters can and should take comfort in the existence of the Electoral College. America's presidential election system is designed to identify the candidate best qualified to lead a nation composed of states, each with its own set of interests and its own set of subcultures. A winner will be chosen, even if individuals remain sharply divided on Election Day. The candidate obtaining a federal majority will be America's next President, just as the founding generation intended.

The Founders worked to create a government in which large and small sovereign states would be able to reside peacefully alongside each other. Their observations of history led them to conclude that pure democracies were inadequate to the task because they allow bare majorities to tyrannize over minority groups. Yet the Founders wanted to retain at least one important feature of these democracies: They wanted the people to have a voice in their government and, thus, in the selection of the nation's Chief Executive. How could this democratic principle be retained while minority groups were simultaneously protected?

The Founders' solution was to create a republican democracy, organized on federalist principles. Where possible, governance would be left close to home so the people could keep their representatives accountable to act wisely. Federal involvement would be relied upon only when necessary. Moreover, the federal Constitution, including its presidential election system, would contain a multitude of safeguards. The majority would retain enough power to rule, but the minority would be given many ways in which to make its voice heard. The freedom of all would thereby be protected.

The Electoral College operates in a different world than the one that existed in 1787. Modern Americans expect the federal government to involve itself in a wider range of activities. They likely possess a more populist mindset than their ancestors did, and they may not recognize the value of republican principles in government. Moreover, modern technological advancements have facilitated communication and commerce in ways that could not have been foreseen by those in the founding generation.

Contrary to the contentions of critics, these changes have not undermined the important benefits of America's unique presidential election system. In many ways, the advantages of the country's election process have instead strengthened over time as the two-party system has solidified and the winner-take-all rule has become the general procedure in presidential elections. The Electoral College, as it operates today, requires presidential candidates to build cross-regional coalitions before they can successfully win the White House. Moreover, the process reinforces the nation's two-party system, which promotes a spirit of moderation and compromise in politics. Last, the Electoral College promotes definitive election outcomes. Even when controversy or fraud becomes a factor, such disputes are isolated to one or a handful of states. The country is given as much stability and certainty as possible in a world full of ambitious politicians.

America conducts democratic presidential elections every four years. However, it conducts these democratic elections at the state level, rather than the national level, for an important reason: Conducting elections by states' votes, rather than individuals' votes, ensures that winning presidential candidates will be the best possible representatives for a nation composed of many diverse states. America's election system ensures that the country will be led by an American President, not a regional one.

The past pages have examined the valuable reasons for keeping the presidential election system instituted by the founding generation, and it has refuted the many criticisms that are often thrown at the Electoral College. This examination reveals that the Founders' faith in the Electoral College is still justified. The Founders would doubtless be proud to see their creation still successfully serving federalist, republican interests more than 200 years after it was first instituted.

The Electoral College has stood the test of time. It will serve the nation well long into the future, just as it has throughout American history.

APPENDIX A

Article II, Section 1.

CLAUSE 1: The executive Power shall be vested in a President of the United States of America. He shall hold his Office during the Term of four Years, and, together with the Vice President, chosen for the same Term, be elected, as follows:

CLAUSE 2: Each State shall appoint, in such Manner as the Legislature thereof may direct, a Number of Electors, equal to the whole Number of Senators and Representatives to which the State may be entitled in the Congress: but no Senator or Representative, or Person holding an Office of Trust or Profit under the United States, shall be appointed an Elector.

CLAUSE 3: The Electors shall meet in their respective States, and vote by Ballot for two Persons, of whom one at least shall not be an Inhabitant of the same State with themselves. And they shall make a List of all the Persons voted for, and of the Number of Votes for each; which List they shall sign and certify, and transmit sealed to the Seat of the Government of the United States, directed to the President of the Senate. The President of the Senate shall, in the Presence of the Senate and House of Representatives, open all the Certificates, and the Votes shall then be counted. The Person having the greatest Number of Votes shall be the President, if such Number be a Majority of the whole Number of Electors appointed; and if there be more than one who have such Majority, and have an equal Number of Votes, then the House of Representatives shall immediately chuse by Ballot one of them for President; and if no Person have a Majority, then from the five highest on the List the said House shall in like Manner chuse the President. But in chusing the President, the Votes shall be taken by States, the Representation from each State having one Vote; A quorum for this Purpose shall consist of a Member or Members from two thirds of the States, and a Majority of all the States shall be necessary to a Choice. In every Case, after the Choice of the President, the Person having the greatest Number of Votes of the Electors shall be the Vice President. But if there should remain two or more who have equal Votes, the Senate shall chuse from them by Ballot the Vice President.

CLAUSE 4: The Congress may determine the Time of chusing the Electors, and the Day on which they shall give their Votes; which Day shall be the same throughout the United States.

The 12th Amendment

The Electors shall meet in their respective states, and vote by ballot for President and Vice-President, one of whom, at least, shall not be an inhabitant of the same state with themselves; they shall name in their ballots the person voted for as President, and in distinct ballots the person voted for as Vice-President, and they shall make distinct lists of all persons voted for as President, and of all persons voted for as Vice-President, and of the number of votes for each, which lists they shall sign and certify, and transmit sealed to the seat of the government of the United States, directed to the President of the Senate;—The President of the Senate shall, in the presence of the Senate and House of Representatives, open all the certificates and the votes shall then be counted;—The person having the greatest number of votes for President, shall be the President, if such number be a majority of the whole number of Electors appointed; and if no person have such majority, then from the persons having the highest numbers not exceeding three on the list of those voted for as President, the House of Representatives shall choose immediately, by ballot, the President. But in choosing the President, the votes shall be taken by states, the representation from each state having one vote; a quorum for this purpose shall consist of a member or members from two-thirds of the states, and a majority of all the states shall be necessary to a choice. And if the House of Representatives shall not choose a President whenever the right of choice shall devolve upon them, before the fourth day of March next following, then the Vice-President shall act as President, as in the case of the death or other constitutional disability of the President. The person having the greatest number of votes as Vice-President, shall be the Vice-President, if such number be a majority of the whole number of Electors appointed, and if no person have a majority, then from the two highest numbers on the list, the Senate shall choose the Vice-President; a quorum for the purpose shall consist of two-thirds of the whole number of Senators, and a majority of the whole number shall be necessary to a choice. But no person constitutionally ineligible to the office of President shall be eligible to that of Vice-President of the United States.

APPENDIX B

Election Results: 1789-2000[1]

Candidate	Party	Electoral Votes		Popular Vote[2]	
		Actual[3]	Percent[4]	Actual	Percent
1789					
George Washington	F	69		.	
John Adams	F	34			
Others (10 candidates)	Misc.	35 (total)			
1792					
George Washington	F	132			
John Adams	F	77			
Others (3 candidates)	Misc.	55 (total)			
1796					
John Adams	F	71			
Thomas Jefferson	DR	68			
Others (11 candidates)	Misc.	137 (total)	.		
1800					
Thomas Jefferson	DR	73			
Aaron Burr	DR	73			
John Adams	F	65			
Others (2 candidates)	Misc.	65 (total)			
1804					
Thomas Jefferson	DR	162	92.0%		
Charles C. Pinckney	F	14	8.0%		

AI = American Independent	ID = Independent Democrat	R = Republican
AM = Anti-Mason	IDR = Ind. Dem.-Republican	SRD = States' Right Democrat
CU = Constitutional Union	L = Libertarian	SD = Southern Democrat
D = Democrat	NR = National-Republican	W = Whig
DR = Democratic-Republican	P = Progressive	WA = Whig-American
F = Federalist	PO = Populist	

ENLIGHTENED DEMOCRACY

| Candidate | Party | Electoral Votes | | Popular Vote[2] | |
		Actual[3]	Percent[4]	Actual	Percent
1808[5]					
James Madison	DR	122	69.3%		
Charles C. Pinckney	F	47	26.7%		
George Clinton	IDR	6	3.4%		
1812[6]					
James Madison	DR	128	58.7%		
De Witt Clinton	F / IDR	89	40.8%		
1816[7]					
James Monroe	DR	183	82.8%		
Rufus King	F	34	15.4%		
1820[8]					
James Monroe	DR	231	98.3%		
John Quincy Adams	IDR	1	0.4%		
1824[9]					
John Quincy Adams	DR	84	32.2%	113,122	30.9%
Andrew Jackson	DR	99	37.9%	151,271	41.3%
William H. Crawford	DR	41	15.7%	40,856	11.2%
Henry Clay	DR	37	14.2%	47,531	13.0%
1828					
Andrew Jackson	DR	178	68.2%	642,553	56.0%
John Quincy Adams	NR	83	31.8%	500,897	43.6%
1832[10]					
Andrew Jackson	D	219	76.0%	701,780	54.2%
Henry Clay	NR	49	17.0%	484,205	37.4%
John Floyd	ID	11	3.8%	—	—
William Wirt	AM	7	2.4%	100,715	7.8%
1836					
Martin Van Buren	D	170	57.8%	764,176	50.8%
William H. Harrison	W	73	24.8%	550,816	36.6%
Hugh L. White	W	26	8.8%	146,107	9.7%
Daniel Webster	W	14	4.8%	41,201	2.7%
William P. Mangum	ID	11	3.7%	—	—
1840					
William H. Harrison	W	234	79.6%	1,275,390	52.9%
Martin Van Buren	D	60	20.4%	1,128,854	46.8%
1844					
James K. Polk	D	170	61.8%	1,339,494	49.5%
Henry Clay	W	105	38.2%	1,300,004	48.1%
1848					
Zachary Taylor	W	163	56.2%	1,361,393	47.3%
Lewis Cass	D	127	43.8%	1,223,460	42.5%

Candidate	Party	Electoral Votes		Popular Vote[2]	
		Actual[3]	Percent[4]	Actual	Percent
1852					
Franklin Pierce	D	254	85.8%	1,607,510	50.8%
Winfield Scott	W	42	14.2%	1,386,942	43.9%
1856					
James Buchanan	D	174	58.8%	1,836,072	45.3%
John C. Fremont	R	114	38.5%	1,342,345	33.1%
Millard Fillmore	WA	8	2.7%	873,053	21.5%
1860					
Abraham Lincoln	R	180	59.4%	1,865,908	39.9%
John C. Breckinridge	SD	72	23.8%	848,019	18.1%
John Bell	CU	39	12.9%	590,901	12.6%
Stephen A. Douglas	D	12	4.0%	1,380,202	29.5%
1864[11]					
Abraham Lincoln	R	212	90.6%	2,218,388	55.0%
George B. McClellan	D	21	9.0%	1,812,807	45.0%
1868					
Ulysses S. Grant	R	214	72.8%	3,013,650	52.7%
Horatio Seymour	D	80	27.2%	2,708,744	47.3%
1872[12]					
Ulysses S. Grant	R	286	78.1%	3,598,235	55.6%
Thomas Hendricks	D	42	11.5%	—	—
B. Gratz Brown	D	18	4.9%	—	—
Charles J. Jenkins	D	2	0.5%	—	—
David Davis	D	1	0.3%	—	—
1876					
Rutherford B. Hayes	R	185	50.1%	4,034,311	48.0%
Samuel J. Tilden	D	184	49.9%	4,288,546	51.0%
1880					
James A. Garfield	R	214	58.0%	4,446,158	48.3%
Winfield S. Hancock	D	155	42.0%	4,444,260	48.3%
1884					
Grover Cleveland	D	219	54.6%	4,874,621	48.5%
James G. Blaine	R	182	45.4%	4,848,936	48.2%
1888					
Benjamin Harrison	R	233	58.1%	5,443,892	47.8%
Grover Cleveland	D	168	41.9%	5,534,488	48.6%
1892					
Grover Cleveland	D	277	62.4%	5,551,883	46.1%
Benjamin Harrison	R	145	32.7%	5,179,244	43.0%
James B. Weaver	PO	22	5.0%	1,024,280	8.5%
1896					
William McKinley	R	271	60.6%	7,108,480	51.0%
William J. Bryan	D / PO	176	39.4%	6,511,495	46.7%

Candidate	Party	Electoral Votes		Popular Vote[2]	
		Actual[3]	Percent[4]	Actual	Percent
1900					
William McKinley	R	292	65.3%	7,218,039	51.7%
William J. Bryan	D	155	34.7%	6,358,345	45.5%
1904					
Theodore Roosevelt	R	336	70.6%	7,626,593	56.4%
Alton B. Parker	D	140	29.4%	5,082,898	37.6%
1908					
William H. Taft	R	321	66.5%	7,676,258	51.6%
William J. Bryan	D	162	33.5%	6,406,801	43.0%
1912					
Woodrow Wilson	D	435	81.9%	6,293,152	41.8%
Theodore Roosevelt	P	88	16.6%	4,119,207	27.4%
William H. Taft	R	8	1.5%	3,486,333	23.2%
1916					
Woodrow Wilson	D	277	52.2%	9,126,300	49.2%
Charles E. Hughes	R	254	47.8%	8,546,789	46.1%
1920					
Warren G. Harding	R	404	76.1%	16,153,115	60.3
James M. Cox	D	127	23.9%	9,133,092	34.1
1924					
Calvin Coolidge	R	382	71.9%	15,719,921	54.0%
John W. Davis	D	136	25.6%	8,386,704	28.8%
Robert M. La Follette	P	13	2.4%	4,832,532	16.6%
1928					
Herbert C. Hoover	R	444	83.6%	21,437,277	58.2%
Alfred E. Smith	D	87	16.4%	15,007,698	40.8%
1932					
Franklin D. Roosevelt	D	472	88.9%	22,829,501	57.4%
Herbert C. Hoover	R	59	11.1%	15,760,684	39.6%
1936					
Franklin D. Roosevelt	D	523	98.5%	27,757,333	60.8%
Alfred M. Landon	R	8	1.5%	16,684,231	36.5%
1940					
Franklin D. Roosevelt	D	449	84.6%	27,313,041	54.7%
Wendell Willkie	R	82	15.4%	22,348,480	44.8%
1944					
Franklin D. Roosevelt	D	432	81.4%	25,612,610	53.4%
Thomas E. Dewey	R	99	18.6%	22,017,617	45.9%
1948					
Harry S. Truman	D	303	57.1%	24,179,345	49.6%
Thomas E. Dewey	R	189	35.6%	21,991,291	45.1%
J. Strom Thurmond	SRD	39	7.3%	1,176,125	2.4%

APPENDIX B

Candidate	Party	Electoral Votes		Popular Vote[2]	
		Actual[3]	Percent[4]	Actual	Percent
1952					
Dwight Eisenhower	R	442	83.2%	33,936,234	55.1%
Adlai Stevenson	D	89	16.8%	27,314,992	44.4%
1956					
Dwight Eisenhower	R	457	86.1%	35,590,472	57.4%
Adlai Stevenson	D	73	13.7%	26,022,752	42.0%
Walter B. Jones	D	1	0.2%	—	—
1960					
John F. Kennedy	D	303	56.4%	34,226,731	49.7%
Richard M. Nixon	R	219	40.8%	34,108,157	49.5%
Harry F. Byrd	D	15	2.8%	—	—
1964					
Lyndon B. Johnson	D	486	90.3%	43,129,566	61.1%
Barry M. Goldwater	R	52	9.7%	27,178,188	38.5%
1968					
Richard M. Nixon	R	301	55.9%	31,785,480	43.4%
Hubert H. Humphrey	D	191	35.5%	31,275,166	42.7%
George C. Wallace	AI	46	8.6%	9,906,473	13.5%
1972					
Richard M. Nixon	R	520	96.7%	47,169,911	60.7%
George S. McGovern	D	17	3.2%	29,170,383	37.5%
John Hospers	L	1	0.2%	3,673	<0.1%
1976					
Jimmy Carter	D	297	55.2%	40,830,763	50.1%
Gerald R. Ford	R	240	44.6%	39,147,793	48.0%
Ronald Reagan	R	1	0.2%	—	—
1980					
Ronald Reagan	R	489	90.9%	43,904,153	50.7%
Jimmy Carter	D	49	9.1%	35,483,883	41.0%
1984					
Ronald Reagan	R	525	97.6%	54,455,075	58.8%
Walter F. Mondale	D	13	2.4%	37,577,185	40.6%
1988					
George Bush	R	426	79.2%	48,886,097	53.4%
Michael S. Dukakis	D	111	20.6%	41,809,074	45.6%
Lloyd Bentsen	D	1	0.2%	—	—
1992					
Bill Clinton	D	370	68.8%	44,909,326	43.0%
George Bush	R	168	31.2%	39,103,882	37.4%
1996					
Bill Clinton	D	379	70.4%	47,402,357	49.2%
Bob Dole	R	159	29.6%	39,198,755	40.7%

Candidate	Party	Electoral Votes		Popular Vote[2]	
		Actual[3]	Percent[4]	Actual	Percent
2000[13]					
George W. Bush	R	271	50.4%	50,456,062	47.9%
Albert Gore, Jr	D	266	49.4%	50,996,582	48.4%

NOTES*

Introduction

1. THE FEDERALIST NO. 68, at 410 (Alexander Hamilton) (Clinton Rossiter ed., Signet Classic 2003) (1961). The "mode of appointment of the Chief Magistrate" refers to the election of the President.

2. The timeline for the networks' calls can be found in JEFFREY TOOBIN, TOO CLOSE TO CALL 17-25 (2001), among other sources.

3. *See, e.g.,* Matthew Cooper, *College Bound?*, TIME, Nov. 20, 2000, at 42, 42-43 (summarizing the election results as of November 11, 2000).

4. *See* Bush v. Gore, 531 U.S. 98 (2000) (per curiam); Bush v. Palm Beach County Canvassing Bd., 531 U.S. 70 (2000) (per curiam).

5. All election results cited in this book were obtained from Congressional Quarterly's *Presidential Elections* or the U.S. National Archives and Records Administration's website. *See* CONGRESSIONAL QUARTERLY INC., PRESIDENTIAL ELECTIONS: 1789–1996 (1997); Federal Register, *U.S. Electoral College*, U.S. Nat'l Archives & Records Admin., *at* http://www.archives.gov/federal_register/electoral_college (last visited Sept. 12, 2004).

6. A detailed discussion of the 1876 election can be found in WILLIAM H. REHNQUIST, CENTENNIAL CRISIS: THE DISPUTED ELECTION OF 1876 (2004); *see also* MICHAEL J. GLENNON, WHEN NO MAJORITY RULES: THE ELECTORAL COLLEGE AND PRESIDENTIAL SUCCESSION 16-17 (1992); ROBERT M. HARDAWAY, THE ELECTORAL COLLEGE AND THE CONSTITUTION: THE CASE FOR PRESERVING FEDERALISM 128-37 (1994); PAUL JOHNSON, A HISTORY OF THE AMERICAN PEOPLE 549 (1st U.S. ed., HarperCollins Publishers 1998) (1997).

The President of the Senate formally declared Hayes the new President when the electoral count was completed at about 4 a.m. on March 2, 1877—two days before Grant's term expired. Because March 4 fell on a Sunday that year, Hayes was sworn in privately at the White House. Formal inauguration ceremonies were held the following day. *See*

---

* This book is written by a lawyer, and thus uses legal citation forms. All endnotes follow the citation rules listed in *The Bluebook: A Uniform System of Citation*, published by the Harvard Law Review Association.

REHNQUIST, *supra*, at 178-79, 201.

7. The entire slates of electors in South Carolina, Florida, and Louisiana were disputed. One electoral vote was also undecided in Oregon due to a dispute regarding an elector who was deemed ineligible; however, the remainder of the state's vote was decided on Election Day. REHNQUIST, *supra* note 6, at 104-12.

8. *The Edge with Paula Zahn* (Fox television broadcast, Dec. 5, 2000). Gingrich's comments were made before California submitted amended vote totals on December 27, 2000. These amended totals increased Gore's margin over Bush in the popular vote totals, but only slightly. *See* Cooper, *supra* note 3, at 43 (showing Gore with a 1,199,404 lead over Bush in California at November 11, 2000); Federal Register, *2000 Presidential Election: Popular Vote Totals*, U.S. Nat'l Archives & Records Admin., *at* http://www.archives.gov/federal_register/electoral_college/2000/popular_vote.html (last visited Sept. 12, 2004) (showing Gore with a 1,293,774 lead over Bush in California, following submission of amended returns on December 27).

9. *See, e.g.*, ANN COULTER, SLANDER: LIBERAL LIES ABOUT THE AMERICAN RIGHT 81 (2002); BILL SAMMON, AT ANY COST : HOW AL GORE TRIED TO STEAL THE ELECTION 19 (2001). Other political scientists dismiss the idea that turnout was adversely affected.

10. One important difference between 1876 and 2000 is that Tilden voters were not primarily concerned about the difference between the electoral vote and the popular vote. Instead, they emphasized that they had, in fact, won the relevant states and had thus won the election.

11. Dick Polman, *Will This Become a War in Which All Sides Lose?*, PHILA. INQUIRER, Nov. 10, 2000, at A1 (emphasis added).

12. *Late Edition With Wolf Blitzer* (CNN television broadcast, Nov. 12, 2000).

13. The Gore team relied upon this "political imprimatur to keep the fight going" in talking points that it drafted the morning after the election. TOOBIN, *supra* note 2, at 30.

14. Susan Milligan, *The Electoral College: Move Is Afoot for Direct Vote*, B. GLOBE, Nov. 12, 2000, at A21.

15. 147 CONG. REC. S24 (daily ed. Jan. 4, 2001) (statement of Sen. Richard Durbin). Senator Durbin supported measures to abolish the Electoral College long before the election between Bush and Gore was held. *See, e.g.*, 146 CONG. REC. S11618-19 (daily ed. Dec. 6, 2000) (statement of Sen. Richard Durbin).

16. Carolina Gonzalez, *Electoral College's Time Is Past*, DAILY NEWS (New York), Nov. 13, 2000, at 22.

17. Ben Wildavsky, *School of Hard Knocks*, U.S. NEWS & WORLD REP., Nov. 20, 2000, at 52, 52.

18. J. M. Balkin, *The Constitution as a Box of Chocolates*, 12 CONST. COMMENT. 147, 148 (1995).

19. JAMES A. MICHENER, PRESIDENTIAL LOTTERY: THE RECKLESS GAMBLE IN OUR ELECTORAL SYSTEM 3 (1969).

20. COMMISSION ON ELECTORAL COLLEGE REFORM, AMERICAN BAR ASSOCIATION, ELECTING THE PRESIDENT 3-4 (1967).

21. SENATE COMM. ON THE JUDICIARY, 95TH CONG., DIRECT POPULAR ELECTION OF THE PRESIDENT AND VICE PRESIDENT OF THE UNITED STATES 8 (Comm. Print 1977).

NOTES

22. THE LEAGUE OF WOMEN VOTERS OF THE UNITED STATES, CHOOSING THE PRESIDENT 52 (1972).

23. Victor Williams & Alison M. MacDonald, *Rethinking Article II, Section 1 and Its Twelfth Amendment Restatement: Challenging Our Nation's Malapportioned, Undemocratic Presidential Election Systems*, 77 MARQ. L. REV. 201, 230 (1994) (citing The Civil Rights Cases, 109 U.S. 3 (1883)).

24. Abner J. Mikva, *Doubting Our Claims to Democracy*, 39 ARIZ. L. REV. 793, 799 (1997).

25. Bruce Bartlett, *How to Compound the Chaos*, WASH. TIMES, Nov. 20, 2000, at A18.

26. *Id.; see also* Byron York, *The Old College Try: How We Pick the Prez*, NAT'L REV., Dec. 4, 2000, at 24, 24.

27. *See* HARDAWAY, *supra* note 6, at 10.

28. A description of the 1968 election can be found at LAWRENCE D. LONGLEY & NEAL R. PEIRCE, THE ELECTORAL COLLEGE PRIMER 2000, at 59-69 (1999).

29. Frank Newport, *Americans Support Proposal to Eliminate Electoral College System*, Gallup Org., *at* http://www.gallup.com/content/login.aspx?ci=2140 (Jan. 5, 2001); *see also* Cragg Hines, *Let's Call It Our 'Be Kind to Pollsters' Quadrennium*, HOUS. CHRON., Jan. 28, 2001, at 3.

30. Time/*CNN Poll: America Shows Patience*, TIME, Nov. 20, 2000, at 41, 41.

31. THE FEDERALIST NO. 68, at 410 (Alexander Hamilton) (Clinton Rossiter ed., Signet Classic 2003) (1961).

32. Michael Kramer, *Bush Set to Fight an Electoral College Loss*, DAILY NEWS (New York), Nov. 1, 2000, at 6.

33. Mary Deibel, *Lawyers Loosed on Campaign Conumdrums*, SCRIPPS HOWARD NEWS SERVICE, Nov. 08, 2000; *see also* Jack Kemp, *Case of Civic Virtue vs. Civic Vice*, WASH. TIMES, Nov. 18, 2000, at A12 (discussing a "pre-election memo," prepared by former Solicitor General Walter Dellinger); Paul A. Gigot, *Two Countries, One System*, WALL ST. J., Nov. 9, 2000, at A26 (quoting Dellinger's statements in support of the Electoral College prior to the election).

34. This author attempted to contact former Solicitor General Walter Dellinger at his law firm, O'Melveny & Myers LLP, to confirm the existence of the memo that he allegedly prepared for Gore. Mr. Dellinger did not return emails seeking his comment; however, the author was able to contact one former Bush campaign official who confirmed that he had been told of the existence of the memo early in November 2000. This same former Bush official categorically denied that any plans to discredit the Electoral College were being prepared by the Bush campaign prior to the 2000 election. Karl Rove, chief strategist for the Bush campaign, also denied these rumors during a 2001 Philadelphia seminar analyzing the 2000 election results. *See* ELECTING THE PRESIDENT, 2000: THE INSIDERS' VIEW 217 (Kathleen Hall Jamieson & Paul Waldman eds., 2001) (quoting Karl Rove).

35. U.S. CONST. amend. IV.

36. *Cf.* Blakely v. Washington, 124 S. Ct. 2531, 2538-39 (2004) ("[The right of jury trial] is no mere procedural formality, but a fundamental reservation of power in our constitutional structure. Just as suffrage ensures the people's ultimate control in the

legislative and executive branches, jury trial is meant to ensure their control in the judiciary.").

37. THE FEDERALIST NO. 68, at 410 (Alexander Hamilton) (Clinton Rossiter ed., Signet Classic 2003) (1961).

Chapter One

1. U.S. CONST. amend. XII.

2. *Id.* art. II, § 1.

3. ROBERT M. HARDAWAY, THE ELECTORAL COLLEGE AND THE CONSTITUTION: THE CASE FOR PRESERVING FEDERALISM 91 (1994) (discussing the Federalist strategy in 1796); *see also* NEAL R. PEIRCE & LAWRENCE D. LONGLEY, THE PEOPLE'S PRESIDENT: THE ELECTORAL COLLEGE IN AMERICAN HISTORY AND THE DIRECT VOTE ALTERNATIVE 35 (rev. ed., Yale Univ. Press 1981) (1968) (same).

4. Descriptions of the election of 1800 can be found at: DAVID W. ABBOTT & JAMES P. LEVINE, WRONG WINNER: THE COMING DEBACLE IN THE ELECTORAL COLLEGE 13-14 (1991); DAVID P. CURRIE, THE CONSTITUTION IN CONGRESS: THE FEDERALIST PERIOD, 1789—1801, at 292-93 (1997); THOMAS FLEMING, DUEL: ALEXANDER HAMILTON, AARON BURR, AND THE FUTURE OF AMERICA 93-97, 101-02 (1999); HARDAWAY, *supra* note 3, at 91-92; PAUL JOHNSON, A HISTORY OF THE AMERICAN PEOPLE 241 (1st U.S. ed., HarperCollins Publishers 1998) (1997); 4 DUMAS MALONE, JEFFERSON AND HIS TIME: JEFFERSON THE PRESIDENT; FIRST TERM, 1801–1805, at 3-16 (1970); PEIRCE & LONGLEY, *supra* note 3, at 36-41.

5. Records of the voting can be found at: 10 ANNALS OF CONG. 1022-30 (1801). The voting ensued from February 11 to February 17, 1801. The House did not meet on February 15, which was Sunday. News reports discussing the voting on the floor are also included in a lengthy footnote in the Annals of Congress. *See id.* at 1028-33 (citing Feb 13, 16 and 18 reports of the *National Intelligencer*, including individual votes cast by representatives).

6. Letter from Thomas Jefferson to Dr. Benjamin Rush (Jan. 16, 1811), *in* THE LIFE AND SELECTED WRITINGS OF THOMAS JEFFERSON 607, 610 (Adrienne Koch & William Peden eds., 1944).

7. A description of these events can be found at MALONE, *supra* note 4, at app. I.

8. FLEMING, *supra* note 4, at 97 (citation omitted).

9. Donald Lutz et al., *The Electoral College in Historical and Philosophical Perspective, in* CHOOSING A PRESIDENT: THE ELECTORAL COLLEGE AND BEYOND 31, 37 (Paul D. Schumaker & Burdett A. Loomis eds., 2002) (discussing the negotiations over the 12th Amendment).

10. U.S. House of Representatives, *Amendments to the Constitution*, U.S. Cong., *at* http://www.house.gov/Constitution/Amend.html (last visited June 27, 2004).

11. U.S. CONST. amend. XII. Additional provisions, such as the timing for the Electoral College vote, can be found in Title 3 of the U.S. Code.

12. *See* U.S. CONST. art. II, § 1; *id.* amend. XII.

13. *See id.* art. II, § 1, cl. 2 & 4; *id.* amend. XII.

14. *Id.* art. II, § 1, cl. 2.

15. *See id.* art. I, § 2, cl. 3; *id.* art. I, § 3, cl. 1.

16. *Id.* amend XXIII, § 1.

17. Federal Register, *2004 List of States and Votes: Allocation of Electoral Votes Based on the 2000 Census,* U.S. Nat'l Archives & Records Admin., *at* http://www.archives.gov/federal_register/electoral_college/2004/allocation.html (last visited June 27, 2004).

18. U.S. CONST. art. II, § 1, cl. 2.

19. Bush v. Gore, 531 U.S. 98, 104 (2000) (per curiam).

20. *Id.; see also* McPherson v. Blacker, 146 U.S. 1, 34-35 (1892).

21. A discussion of the first several presidential elections can be found at *McPherson,* 146 U.S. at 29-32.

22. *See* L. PAIGE WHITAKER & THOMAS H. NEALE, CONGRESSIONAL RESEARCH SERV., THE ELECTORAL COLLEGE: AN OVERVIEW AND ANALYSIS OF REFORM PROPOSALS 2 (2001).

23. ME. REV. STAT. ANN. tit. 21-A, § 802 (West 1992); NEB. REV. STAT. § 32-1038 (1998).

24. Maine adopted its District Plan in 1969, putting it into effect for the first time during the 1972 presidential election. Nebraska adopted its plan in time for the 1992 presidential election. *See* LAWRENCE D. LONGLEY & NEAL R. PEIRCE, THE ELECTORAL COLLEGE PRIMER 2000, at 106-07 (1999) (discussing the circumstances under which Maine and Nebraska adopted procedures for awarding electoral votes by district).

25. *See, e.g.,* MICHAEL J. GLENNON, WHEN NO MAJORITY RULES: THE ELECTORAL COLLEGE AND PRESIDENTIAL SUCCESSION 35-44 (1992) (discussing the "constitutional minefield" that must be navigated when determining where the state's power to select electors ends and where congressional power to count electoral votes begins).

26. *See* WILLIAM H. REHNQUIST, CENTENNIAL CRISIS: THE DISPUTED ELECTION OF 1876, at 113-19 (2004).

27. Act of Feb. 3, 1887, ch. 90, 24 Stat. 373 (current version at 3 U.S.C. §§ 1-21 (2000)).

28. 3 U.S.C. § 1 (2000).

29. *See* AFTER THE PEOPLE VOTE: A GUIDE TO THE ELECTORAL COLLEGE app. C (John C. Fortier ed., 3d ed. 2004) (listing the states' procedures for including or excluding the names of electors on their presidential ballots).

30. 3 U.S.C. § 6.

31. For a listing of state laws on the subject, see Federal Register, *2000 Presidential Election: State Laws and Requirements,* U.S. Nat'l Archives & Records Admin., *at* http://www.archives.gov/federal_register/electoral_college/2000/laws.html (last visited June 27, 2004); *see also* AFTER THE PEOPLE VOTE, *supra* note 29, at app. C.

32. 3 U.S.C. § 7.

33. *Id.* §§ 9-11.

34. *See id.* §§ 12-13. This deadline falls on December 22 in 2004 and December 24 in 2008.

35. *See id.* § 15.

36. U.S. CONST. amend XII.

37. *See* Federal Register, *supra* note 17, at http://www.archives.gov/federal_register/electoral_college/2004/allocation.html.

38. U.S. CONST. amend XII.

39. *Id.*

40. These questions are discussed at length in HARDAWAY, *supra* note 3, at 55-61.

41. The 1825 House Rules are reprinted in PEIRCE & LONGLEY, *supra* note 3, at app. I (citation omitted).

42. *See, e.g.,* 10 ANNALS OF CONG. 1032-33 (1801) (quoting the *National Intelligencer*).

43. U.S. Const. amend. XX, § 1.

44. 3 U.S.C. § 15 (2000).

45. HARDAWAY, *supra* note 3, at 56 (discussing House deliberations in 1992).

46. MAX FARRAND, THE FRAMING OF THE CONSTITUTION OF THE UNITED STATES 175 (7th prtg. 1930).

Chapter Two

1. CLARENCE MANION, THE KEY TO PEACE 49 (1951).

2. This author performed a Lexis search in early 2004 and discovered two references to "democracy" in the states' constitutions. The Constitution of Puerto Rico also references "democracy." *See* CAL. CONST. art. IV, § 1.5; OR. CONST. art. XV, § 10; *see also* P.R. CONST. pmbl.; *id.* art. II, § 19.

3. Professor Judith Best also makes this point. *See* JUDITH A. BEST, THE CHOICE OF THE PEOPLE? DEBATING THE ELECTORAL COLLEGE 34-35 (1996). Actually, there were suggestions to give the colonies representation in the House of Commons. These proposals were initially championed by some colonists, including Benjamin Franklin. *See* GORDON S. WOOD, THE AMERICANIZATION OF BENJAMIN FRANKLIN 78, 115-16 (2004).

4. JAMES MADISON, NOTES OF DEBATES IN THE FEDERAL CONVENTION OF 1787, at 308 (Adrienne Koch ed., bicentennial ed., W.W. Norton & Co. 1987) (1966).

5. Denny Pilant, *No — The Electoral College Should Not Be Abolished, in* CONTROVERSIAL ISSUES IN PRESIDENTIAL SELECTION 216, 226 (Gary L. Rose ed., 1991).

6. Thomas Jefferson, Inauguration Address (Mar. 4, 1801), *in* THE LIFE AND SELECTED WRITINGS OF THOMAS JEFFERSON 321, 322 (Adrienne Koch & William Peden eds., 1944).

7. U.S. CONST. art. IV, § 4.

8. James A. Gardner, *Madison's Hope: Virtue, Self-Interest, and the Design of Electoral Systems*, 86 IOWA L. REV. 87, 126 (2000).

9. THE FEDERALIST NO. 10, at 76 (James Madison) (Clinton Rossiter ed., Signet Classic 2003) (1961).

10. MADISON, *supra* note 4, at 39.

11. *Id.* at 42.

12. *Id.* at 110.

13. *Id.* at 233.

14. Letter from James Madison to Thomas Jefferson (Oct. 17, 1788), *in* 11 THE PAPERS OF JAMES MADISON 295, 298 (Robert A. Rutland et al. eds., 1977).

15. 2 THE DEBATES IN THE SEVERAL STATE CONVENTIONS, ON THE ADOPTION OF THE FEDERAL CONSTITUTION, AS RECOMMENDED BY THE GENERAL CONVENTION AT PHILADELPHIA, IN 1787, at 253 (Jonathan Elliot ed., 2d ed. 1836) [hereinafter 2 ELLIOT'S

NOTES

DEBATES].

16. Letter from John Adams to John Taylor (Apr. 15, 1814), *in* 6 THE WORKS OF JOHN ADAMS, SECOND PRESIDENT OF THE UNITED STATES 447, 484 (Charles Francis Adams ed., 2d prtg. 1969).

17. Letter from Benjamin Rush to John Adams (July 21, 1789), *in* 1 LETTERS OF BENJAMIN RUSH 522, 523 (L. H. Butterfield ed., 1951).

18. JOHN WITHERSPOON, *Lecture XII of Civil Society, in* AN ANNOTATED EDITION OF LECTURES ON MORAL PHILOSOPHY 140, 144 (Jack Scott ed., 1982).

19. Fisher Ames, Speech in the Convention of Massachusetts, on Biennial Elections (Jan. 1788), *in* 2 WORKS OF FISHER AMES 3, 7 (Seth Ames ed., 1854).

20. PAUL JOHNSON, A HISTORY OF THE AMERICAN PEOPLE 179 (1st U.S. ed., HarperCollins Publishers 1998) (1997).

21. Patrick Henry, Speech before the Virginia Ratifying Convention (June 5, 1788), *in* THE ANTI-FEDERALIST PAPERS AND THE CONSTITUTIONAL CONVENTION DEBATES 199, 199 (Ralph Ketcham ed., Signet Classic 2003) (1986).

22. The Address and Reasons of Dissent of the Minority of the Convention of Pennsylvania to their Constituents (Dec. 18, 1787), *in* THE ANTI-FEDERALIST PAPERS AND THE CONSTITUTIONAL CONVENTION DEBATES, *supra* note 21, at 237, 242.

23. 3 THE DEBATES IN THE SEVERAL STATE CONVENTIONS, ON THE ADOPTION OF THE FEDERAL CONSTITUTION, AS RECOMMENDED BY THE GENERAL CONVENTION AT PHILADELPHIA, IN 1787, at 22 (Jonathan Elliot ed., 2d ed. 1836) (emphasis added).

24. *Id.*

25. "Brutus," *To the Citizens of the State of New York* (Oct 18, 1787), *reprinted in* THE ANTI-FEDERALIST PAPERS AND THE CONSTITUTIONAL CONVENTION DEBATES, *supra* note 21, at 270, 276.

26. *Id.* at 277.

27. Walter Berns, *Let's Hear It for the Electoral College, in* AFTER THE PEOPLE VOTE: A GUIDE TO THE ELECTORAL COLLEGE 51, 52-53 (John C. Fortier ed., 3d ed. 2004).

28. THE DECLARATION OF INDEPENDENCE para 2 (U.S. 1776).

29. MADISON, *supra* note 4, at 64.

30. *Id.* at 39.

31. *Id.*

32. *Id.*

33. *Id.*

34. *Id.* at 40.

35. *Id.*

36. THE FEDERALIST NO. 39, at 236 (James Madison) (Clinton Rossiter ed., Signet Classic 2003) (1961).

37. THE FEDERALIST NO. 49, at 314 (James Madison) (Clinton Rossiter ed., Signet Classic 2003) (1961).

38. 2 ELLIOT'S DEBATES, *supra* note 15, at 434.

39. *Id.*

40. *Id.*

41. WILLIAM G. CARR, THE OLDEST DELEGATE: FRANKLIN IN THE CONSTITUTIONAL CONVENTION 122 (1990) (citation omitted). Many Americans have misquoted this statement in recent years, instead stating that Benjamin Franklin responded: "A democracy, if you can keep it." The misquotes reflect many Americans' declining understanding of their heritage.

42. Indeed, the state legislatures elected each state's Senators until passage of the 17th Amendment provided for direct senatorial elections by the people of each state.

43. *But see* DAVID W. ABBOTT & JAMES P. LEVINE, WRONG WINNER: THE COMING DEBACLE IN THE ELECTORAL COLLEGE 91-93 (1991) (arguing that while Hispanics "have potentially great electoral leverage because of their geographical distribution," they are unable to take advantage of the benefit because of "political differentiations between [sic] Puerto Ricans, Cubans, and Mexican-Americans" and because many Hispanics are not citizens and, thus, cannot vote).

44. *See id.* at 86-87 (listing Jewish voters as an "advantaged group" under the Electoral College system).

45. CONGRESSIONAL QUARTERLY INC., PRESIDENTIAL ELECTIONS: 1789–1996, at 115 (1997).

46. Thurmond also received one vote from a fifth state. Preston Parks, a Truman elector in Tennessee, switched his vote to Thurmond. *See id.* at 15.

47. MADISON, *supra* note 4, at 308.

48. Gray v. Sanders, 372 U.S. 368, 376 n.8 (1963).

49. LUCIUS WILMERDING, JR., THE ELECTORAL COLLEGE 19 (1958).

50. THE FEDERALIST NO. 68, at 410 (Alexander Hamilton) (Clinton Rossiter ed., Signet Classic 2003) (1961).

51. 2 ELLIOT'S DEBATES, *supra* note 15, at 448.

52. SENATE COMM. ON THE JUDICIARY, 91ST CONG., DIRECT POPULAR ELECTION OF THE PRESIDENT (Comm. Print 1970) (Minority Views of Messrs. Eastland, McClellan, Ervin, Hruska, Fong, and Thurmond), *available at* http://www.claremont.org/writings/700814_minority.html.

Chapter Three

1. For information on the events that transpired before the Constitutional Convention commenced, see CATHERINE DRINKER BOWEN, MIRACLE AT PHILADELPHIA: THE STORY OF THE CONSTITUTIONAL CONVENTION MAY TO SEPTEMBER 1787 (2d prtg. 1986); CAROL BERKIN, A BRILLIANT SOLUTION: INVENTING THE AMERICAN CONSTITUTION (2003); ROBERT M. HARDAWAY, THE ELECTORAL COLLEGE AND THE CONSTITUTION: THE CASE FOR PRESERVING FEDERALISM 69-75 (1994); *see also* Roger A. Bruns, *A More Perfect Union: The Creation of the U.S. Constitution,* U.S. Nat'l Archives & Records Admin., *at* http://www.archives.gov/national_archives_experience/charters/constitution_history.html (last visited August 28, 2004).

2. THE FEDERALIST NO. 40, at 244 (James Madison) (Clinton Rossiter ed., Signet Classic 2003) (1961).

3. BOWEN, *supra* note 1, at 4.

4. JOSEPH J. ELLIS, FOUNDING BROTHERS: THE REVOLUTIONARY GENERATION 120 (15th prtg. 2001).

5. BOWEN, *supra* note 1, at 30.

6. Shlomo Slonim, *Designing the Electoral College, in* INVENTING THE AMERICAN PRESIDENCY 33, 33 (Thomas E. Cronin ed., 1989).

7. For detailed discussions of the Convention debates from a variety of viewpoints, see generally *id.* at 33-60; *see also* HARDAWAY, *supra* note 1, at 76-89; William Josephson & Beverly J. Ross, *Repairing the Electoral College*, 22 J. LEGIS. 145, 151-53 (1996); NEAL R. PEIRCE & LAWRENCE D. LONGLEY, THE PEOPLE'S PRESIDENT: THE ELECTORAL COLLEGE IN AMERICAN HISTORY AND THE DIRECT VOTE ALTERNATIVE 10-30 (rev. ed., Yale Univ. Press 1981) (1968).

8. Legislative selection, direct popular election, and the use of electors were the three primary modes of presidential election that were discussed by the Convention delegates. Although a variety of other proposals were made during the course of the Convention, most of these latter alternatives were rejected with little debate.

9. JAMES MADISON, NOTES OF DEBATES IN THE FEDERAL CONVENTION OF 1787, at 309 (Adrienne Koch ed., bicentennial ed., W.W. Norton & Co. 1987) (1966).

10. *Id.* at 306.

11. *Id.* at 307.

12. *Id.* at 306.

13. *Id.*

14. *Id.* at 326-27.

15. WILLIAM PETERS, A MORE PERFECT UNION 99 (1987).

16. *See* U.S. CONST. art I, § 2, cl.3; *id.* art. I, § 3, cl. 1; *id.* art II, § 1, cl. 2.

17. *See id.* art II, § 1, cl. 3 (amended 1804).

18. Letter from James Madison to Henry Lee (Jan. 14, 1825), *in* 9 THE WRITINGS OF JAMES MADISON 215, 217 (Gaillard Hunt ed., 1910).

19. LAWRENCE D. LONGLEY & NEAL R. PEIRCE, THE ELECTORAL COLLEGE PRIMER 2000, at 20 (1999).

20. PEIRCE & LONGLEY, *supra* note 7, at 30 (citation omitted).

21. *Id.*

22. MAX FARRAND, THE FRAMING OF THE CONSTITUTION OF THE UNITED STATES 164 (7th prtg. 1930).

23. U.S. CONST. art. II, § 1, cl. 3, (amended 1804).

24. SENATE COMM. ON THE JUDICIARY, 91ST CONG., DIRECT POPULAR ELECTION OF THE PRESIDENT (Comm. Print 1970) (Minority Views of Messrs. Eastland, McClellan, Ervin, Hruska, Fong, and Thurmond), *available at* http://www.claremont.org/writings/700814_minority.html (citation omitted).

25. McPherson v. Blacker, 146 U.S. 1, 27, 35 (1892).

26. There is, however, some evidence to suggest that the Court's enthusiasm for the Electoral College has become a bit diluted. Although the states' discretion is still the underlying foundation for presidential elections, some recent Court decisions reflect a dispute concerning the extent to which the Equal Protection Clause or the First

Amendment may or may not curb state discretion once a state legislature has chosen direct popular election as its method of appointing electors. A state legislature does not have to choose direct popular election; however, once it has done so, some federal constitutional rights may be held to attach. *See, e.g.,* Anderson v. Celebrezze, 460 U.S. 780, 794 n.18 (1983); Williams v. Rhodes, 393 U.S. 23, 29 (1968).

27. 531 U.S. 98, 104 (2000) (per curiam).

28. Hall v. Beals, 396 U.S. 45, 52 (1969) (Marshall, J., dissenting) (asserting that the case before the Court was not moot, as held by the majority).

29. BOWEN, *supra* note 1, at 33.

30. 4 THE DEBATES IN THE SEVERAL STATE CONVENTIONS, ON THE ADOPTION OF THE FEDERAL CONSTITUTION, AS RECOMMENDED BY THE GENERAL CONVENTION AT PHILADELPHIA, IN 1787, at 262 (Jonathan Elliot ed., 2d ed. 1836).

31. Texas Almanac: 2004-2005, *Facts, Profile & Rank,* Dallas Morning News, *at* http://www.texasalmanac.com/facts (last visited June 15, 2004).

32. *See* Federal Register, *2004 List of States and Votes: Allocation of Electoral Votes Based on the 2000 Census,* U.S. Nat'l Archives & Records Admin., *at* http://www.archives.gov/federal_register/electoral_college/2004/allocation.html (last visited June 27, 2004).

33. Texas Almanac: 2004-2005, *Elections,* Dallas Morning News, *at* http://www.texas almanac.com/politics/elections (last visited June 15, 2004).

34. One interesting twist on this principle could occur in New Hampshire. A group of libertarians is working to recruit 20,000 members to move to New Hampshire. Once there, these libertarians feel that the weight of their voices, together, will be enough to influence local elections, particularly since the population in that state is relatively small. From there, these libertarians hope to grow in influence until they have successfully reduced the size and scope of government, first in their cities and then in their newly adopted state. More information on this project is available at: http://www.free stateproject.org.

35. The Goldwater Institute reports that nearly 200,000 Californians moved to Arizona between 1995 and 2000, motivated at least in part by the lower taxes and pro-business environment. *See* Matthew Ladner, *Californians Drawn to Friendly Arizona—For Now,* Goldwater Inst. (May 27, 2004), *at* http://www.goldwaterinstitute.org/article.php/449.html. The report also compared the ten lowest-tax states with the ten highest-tax states and found that the low-tax states gained more than 1.3 million new residents, while the high-tax states lost more than 1.7 million. *See id.; see also* Matthew Ladner, *The Tax Man and the Moving Van: Fiscal Policy and State Population Shifts,* Goldwater Inst. (May 24, 2004), *at* http://www.goldwaterinstitute.org/article.php/444.html.

36. Arnold Schwarzenegger, *Arnold's Agenda to Bring California Back,* Join Arnold, *at* http://www.joinarnold.com/en/agenda (last visited July 1, 2004).

37. New State Ice Co. v. Liebmann, 285 U.S. 262, 311 (1932) (Brandeis, J., dissenting).

38. JUDITH A. BEST, THE CHOICE OF THE PEOPLE? DEBATING THE ELECTORAL COLLEGE 37-39 (1996).

39. Obviously, to the extent the judiciary arrogates to itself the power to legislate and oversee the other branches, the less force this argument will have. *See, e.g.,* Lawrence v. Texas, 539 U.S. 558 (2003); Roe v. Wade, 410 U.S. 113 (1973).

40. BEST, *supra* note 38, at 38.

41. HARDAWAY, *supra* note 1, at 77.

42. *Id.* at 76-77.

43. Following the 2000 election, several small states filed resolutions with the Congress in support of the Electoral College and the protections that it offers to small states. *See, e.g.,* 147 CONG. REC. S8,063 (daily ed. July 23, 2001); 147 CONG. REC. H2,148 (daily ed. May 14, 2001); 147 CONG. REC. S4,042 (daily ed. April 30, 2001).

Chapter Four

1. The phrase "one person, one vote" does not appear in the Constitution. It first appeared in a Supreme Court opinion in *Gray v. Sanders,* 372 U.S. 368, 381 (1963).

2. LAWRENCE D. LONGLEY & NEAL R. PEIRCE, THE ELECTORAL COLLEGE PRIMER 1-14 (1996).

3. *Proposals for Electoral College Reform: Hearings on H.J. Res. 28 and H.J. Res. 43 Before the Subcomm. on the Constitution of the House Comm. on the Judiciary,* 105th Cong. 48 (1997) (testimony of Professor Akhil Reed Amar, Yale University Law School), *available at* http://commdocs.house.gov/committees/judiciary/hju57219.000/hju57219_0f.htm.

4. U.S. CONST. amend. X.

5. *Id.* art I., § 8, cl. 3.

6. United States v. Lopez, 514 U.S. 549 (1995).

7. United States v. Morrison, 529 U.S. 598 (2000).

8. On the pretext of lightening the case load of older Justices, FDR proposed adding up to one additional Justice for every member of the Court who was seventy years of age or older. Up to six new Justices could have been appointed under the plan. *See* WILLIAM E. LEUCHTENBURG, FRANKLIN D. ROOSEVELT AND THE NEW DEAL: 1932-1940, at 231-38 (1963) (discussing FDR's battles with the Supreme Court); DIXON WECTER, THE AGE OF THE GREAT DEPRESSION: 1929-1941, at 104-06 (1948); John Wallace, *Stare Decisis and the Rehnquist Court: The Collision of Activism, Passivism and Politics in* Casey, 42 BUFFALO L. REV. 187, 223 (1994) (discussing the court packing plan).

9. 300 U.S. 379 (1937). Justice Roberts' opinion contradicted a stance that he had taken the year before in *Morehead v. New York,* 298 U.S. 587 (1936).

10. Some commentators include Chief Justice Hughes in the "switch in time that saved nine." Hughes did become a steadier ally of FDR's measures following the threatened court-packing plan, but his votes had sometimes fallen with the liberal Justices on other issues prior to FDR's proposal. Roberts, on the other hand, had been a firm ally of the conservative wing of the Court. Following *West Coast Hotel,* he instead became an ally of the liberal wing of the Court. *See* WECTER, *supra* note 8, at 106.

11. 301 U.S. 1 (1937).

12. *Id.* at 30.

13. *Id.*

14. Wickard v. Filburn, 317 U.S. 111 (1942).

15. Although recent instances of mob violence in various cities may suggest otherwise. *See, e.g., Schell Urges: Stay in Control,* SEATTLE TIMES, Dec. 2, 1999, at A1

(discussing the riots at World Trade Organization meetings in Seattle in 1999); *see also* Richard A. Serrano & Tracy Wilkinson, *All 4 in King Beating Acquitted: Violence Follows Verdicts: Guard Called Out*, L.A. TIMES, Apr. 30, 1992, at A1 (discussing the Los Angeles riots of 1992).

16. Ben Wildavsky, *School of Hard Knocks*, U.S. NEWS & WORLD REP., Nov. 20, 2000, at 52, 52.

17. *See* CONGRESSIONAL QUARTERLY INC., PRESIDENTIAL ELECTIONS: 1789–1996, at 87 (1997).

18. PAUL JOHNSON, A HISTORY OF THE AMERICAN PEOPLE 331 (1st U.S. ed., HarperCollins Publishers 1998) (1997) (citation omitted).

19. *Id.* at 332.

20. U.S. CONST. amend. XV.

21. *Id.* amend. XVII.

22. *Id.* amend. XIX.

23. Kevin Phillips, . . . *And Its Musty Old Quirks*, TIME, Nov. 20, 2000, at 67, 67.

Chapter Five

1. RONALD REAGAN, REAGAN, IN HIS OWN HAND 243 (Kiron K. Skinner et al. eds., 2001) (strikeouts in original eliminated and abbreviations expanded).

2. Jeff Greenfield, *The Hidden Beauty of the System*, TIME, Nov. 20, 2000, at 66, 66.

3. *See, e.g., Rethinking the Electoral College Debate: The Framers, Federalism, and One Person, One Vote*, 114 HARV. L. REV. 2526, 2532 & n.31 (2001).

4. LAWRENCE D. LONGLEY & NEAL R. PEIRCE, THE ELECTORAL COLLEGE PRIMER 2000, at 136 (1999).

5. Federal Register, *2000 Presidential Election: Popular Vote Totals*, U.S. Nat'l Archives & Records Admin., *at* http://www.archives.gov/federal_register/electoral_college/2000/popular_vote.html (last visited Aug. 28, 2004).

6. Federal Register, *Electoral Votes for President and Vice President: Election for the Fifty-Fourth Term, 2001-2005*, U.S. Nat'l Archives & Records Admin., *at* http://www.archives.gov/federal_register/electoral_college/votes/2000_2005.html#2000 (last visited Aug. 28, 2004).

7. *See* U.S. CONST. art. II, § 1, cl. 2.

8. *Id.*

9. Kathryn Jean Lopez, *Hillary Is Wrong: An Interview with Charles R. Kesler*, NAT'L REV. ONLINE (Nov. 13, 2000), *at* http://www.nationalreview.com/interrogatory/interrogatory111300.shtml.

10. JAMES MACGREGOR BURNS, THE DEADLOCK OF DEMOCRACY: FOUR-PARTY POLITICS IN AMERICA 251 (1963), *quoted in* JUDITH BEST, THE CASE AGAINST DIRECT ELECTION OF THE PRESIDENT: A DEFENSE OF THE ELECTORAL COLLEGE 66 (1975).

11. *Id.*

12. *Id.*

13. *See* Akhil Reed Amar, *Presidents Without Mandates (With Special Emphasis on*

Ohio), 67 U. CIN. L. REV. 375, 391 (1999) (asserting that the popular vote winner is usually the Electoral College winner, and, thus, it is hard to see why campaign strategies would change).

14. The World Series example is often used as an analogy for the Electoral College. One recent example can be found at: Michael Herz, *How the Electoral College Imitates the World Series*, 23 CARDOZO L. REV. 1191 (2002).

15. REAGAN, *supra* note 1, at 243 (strikeouts in original eliminated and abbreviations expanded).

16. As this book goes to press, President Bush has just completed a campaign stop in Poplar Bluff, Missouri (population 16,651, as of the 2000 Census), a city that just happens to be the hometown of this Author's family, on the paternal side. *See* U.S. Census Bureau, *Table DP-1. Profile of General Demographic Characteristics: 2000*, U.S. Dep't of Commerce, *at* http://censtats.census.gov/data/MO/1602959096.pdf (last visited Sept. 14, 2004) (listing population figures). Are we really to believe that presidential candidates would take the time to swing by such small cities for a visit if the country employed a direct popular vote system? Wouldn't candidates prefer to spend time in the City of New York (population 8,008,278), or Houston, Texas (population, 1,953,631)? *See* U.S. Census Bureau, *Population Change and Distribution: Census 2000 Brief*, U.S. Dep't of Commerce (Apr. 2001), *at* http://www.census.gov/prod/2001pubs/c2kbr01-2.pdf (reciting population figures).

17. *E.g.*, Patrice Hill, *W.Va. Miners Favor Bush Over Gore on Fossil Fuels*, WASH. TIMES, Oct. 11, 2000, at A12.

18. ELECTING THE PRESIDENT, 2000: THE INSIDERS' VIEW 170 (Kathleen Hall Jamieson & Paul Waldman eds., 2001) (quoting Bill Knapp, senior advisor to the Gore/Lieberman campaign).

19. *Id.* at 204 (quoting Karl Rove).

20. *See, e.g.*, Adam Nagourney, *Candidates Face Sprawling and Complex Electoral Map*, N.Y. TIMES, May 12, 2004, at A18 (listing West Virginia as a battleground state and noting that the Democratic Party is attempting to regain its support in the state).

21. BEST, *supra* note 10, at 139 (discussing Texas in the early part of the century as a "stalwartly Democratic state").

22. U.S. Census Bureau, *State and County QuickFacts: California*, U.S. Dep't of Commerce, *at* http://quickfacts.census.gov/qfd/states/06000.html (last visited Mar. 9, 2004).

23. *See* Federal Register, *2004 List of States and Votes: Allocation of Electoral Votes Based on the 2000 Census*, U.S. Nat'l Archives & Records Admin., *at* http://www.archives.gov/federal_register/electoral_college/2004/allocation.html (last visited June 27, 2004).

24. U.S. Census Bureau, *State and County QuickFacts: Wyoming*, U.S. Dep't of Commerce, *at* http://quickfacts.census.gov/qfd/states/56000.html (last visited Mar. 9, 2004).

25. Federal Register, *supra* note 23, at http://www.archives.gov/federal_register/electoral_college/2004/allocation.html.

26. *See* JUDITH A. BEST, THE CHOICE OF THE PEOPLE? DEBATING THE ELECTORAL COLLEGE 56-58 (1996).

27. *Id.* at 56.

28. Federal Register, *supra* note 23, at http://www.archives.gov/federal_register/ electoral_college/ 2004/allocation.html.

29. LONGLEY & PEIRCE, *supra* note 4, at 153-54.

Chapter Six

1. Arguably, neither Buchanan nor Nader was truly a "major" third-party candidate. Their runs for the presidency likely would have been inconsequential were it not for the close nature of the 2000 election.

2. Analysis after the election showed that, nationwide, Perot votes broke fairly equally between Clinton and Bush. However, the Center for Voting and Democracy reports that the Perot vote did not split equally in each state. To the contrary, Perot's candidacy seems to have worked to Bush's disadvantage in several states that Bush won in 1988 and might otherwise have been expected to win in 1992. *See Plurality Wins in the 1992 Presidential Race: Perot's Contribution to Clinton's Victory*, Ctr. for Voting & Democracy, *at* http://www.fairvote.org/plurality/perot.htm (last updated Apr. 2, 2004).

3. *Cf.* James Risen & Karen Tumulty, *Politicians Rally Around Plan to Balance Budget*, L.A. TIMES, May 17, 1992, at A1 (reporting on the then-building momentum for a balanced budget constitutional amendment, based at least in part on the pressure created as Ross Perot "hammer[s] away at the skyrocketing deficit as a metaphor for Washington's failure to deal with the nation's most serious economic problems" a message that has caused him to surge in the polls).

4. Omnibus Budget Reconciliation Act of 1993, Pub. L. No. 103-66, 107 Stat. 312.

5. U.S. House of Representatives, *Republican Contract with America*, U.S. Cong., *at* http://www.house.gov/house/Contract/CONTRACT.html (last visited June 17, 2004).

6. For more information on the 1912 election, see NATHAN MILLER, THEODORE ROOSEVELT: A LIFE 519-31 (1992).

7. For more information on the 1836 election, see MAJOR L. WILSON, THE PRESIDENCY OF MARTIN VAN BUREN 14-20 (1984); *see also* PAUL F. BOLLER, JR., PRESIDENTIAL CAMPAIGNS 60-64 (rev. ed. 1996)

8. For more information on the 1840 election, see BOLLER, *supra* note 7, at 65-77.

9. *See, e.g.,* ROBERT M. HARDAWAY, THE ELECTORAL COLLEGE AND THE CONSTITUTION: THE CASE FOR PRESERVING FEDERALISM 20 (1994) ("The Electoral College lesson has been clear throughout American history: accommodate, compromise, merge, persuade, build, and achieve a consensus.").

10. *See, e.g.,* NEAL R. PEIRCE & LAWRENCE D. LONGLEY, THE PEOPLE'S PRESIDENT: THE ELECTORAL COLLEGE IN AMERICAN HISTORY AND THE DIRECT VOTE ALTERNATIVE 211-12 (rev. ed., Yale Univ. Press 1981) (1968). Longley and Peirce instead contend that the two national parties are in decline due to the advances made in mass communication in recent years. *Id.*

11. *Id.* at 209.

12. *Id.* at 211.

13. *Id.* at 209.

14. For a discussion of this topic, see Tara L. Branum, *President or King? The Use and*

Abuse of Executive Orders in Modern-day America, 28 J. LEGIS. 1 (2002).

15. U.S. CONST. art. II, § 2, cl. 2.

16. *Id.* art. II, § 2, cl. 1; *see also id.* art. II, § 3.

17. *See, e.g.*, Branum, *supra* note 14, at 31 n.144 and accompanying text.

18. 102 CONG. REC. 5150 (Mar. 20, 1956) (statement of Senator John F. Kennedy).

19. PEIRCE & LONGLEY, *supra* note 10, at 220-22.

20. *Id.*

21. JUDITH A. BEST, THE CHOICE OF THE PEOPLE? DEBATING THE ELECTORAL COLLEGE 55 (1996); *see also* HARDAWAY, *supra* note 9, at 21 ("What the advocates of direct election fail to take into account, however, is that *these consistently large pluralities and majorities are the result of the very Electoral College system they are seeking to destroy.*").

22. Michael J. Glennon, *Nine Ways to Avoid a Train Wreck: How Title 3 Should Be Changed*, 23 CARDOZO L. REV. 1159, 1159 (2002).

23. One commentator rejected the contention that multiple candidacy runoffs will grow into a problem, asserting that a 40 percent requirement should do the trick. So lightly did he take the problem of multiple candidacies that he devoted only one small six-sentence paragraph in a 38-page law review article to consideration of the subject. *See* Ky Fullerton, *Bush, Gore, and the 2000 Presidential Election: Time for the Electoral College to Go?*, 80 OR. L. REV. 717, 744-45 (2001).

24. Fifty-six political parties exist, according to one weblogger, who lists them all on his website. *See* Ron Gunzburger, *Directory of U.S. Political Parties*, Ron Gunzburger's Politics1.com, *at* http://www.politics1.com/parties.htm (last visited July 5, 2004).

25. *See Official Web Site*, The American Nazi Party, *at* http://www.americannaziparty.com (last visited July 5, 2004).

26. *See Official Web Site*, The Prohibition Party, *at* http://www.prohibition.org (last visited July 5, 2004).

27. *See Official Web Site*, The Knights Party, *at* http://www.kkk.com (last visited July 5, 2004).

28. *See Official Web Site*, The Pansexual Peace Party, *at* http://members.tripod.com/Hail_Eris/eris/PPPP/homey.htm (last visited July 5, 2004).

29. BEST, *supra* note 21, at 57.

30. HARDAWAY, *supra* note 9, at 18-19. Professor Hardaway also argues that Hitler relied upon a similar system to establish a minority power base in Germany that eventually allowed him to rise to power. *Id.* at 18.

Chapter Seven

1. NEAL R. PEIRCE & LAWRENCE D. LONGLEY, THE PEOPLE'S PRESIDENT: THE ELECTORAL COLLEGE IN AMERICAN HISTORY AND THE DIRECT VOTE ALTERNATIVE 228 (rev. ed., Yale Univ. Press 1981) (1968).

2. For a discussion of the discrepancy that typically exists between popular vote totals and Electoral College vote totals, see JUDITH A. BEST, THE CHOICE OF THE PEOPLE? DEBATING THE ELECTORAL COLLEGE 9-15 (1996); ROBERT M. HARDAWAY, THE ELECTORAL COLLEGE AND THE CONSTITUTION: THE CASE FOR PRESERVING FEDERALISM 125-28 (1994).

3. As Nixon did in 1960. *See* discussion *infra* notes 9-10 and accompanying text.

4. *See, e.g.*, JUDITH BEST, THE CASE AGAINST DIRECT ELECTION OF THE PRESIDENT: A DEFENSE OF THE ELECTORAL COLLEGE 191-204 (1975) (noting the ability of the Electoral College to isolate incidents of fraud); *see also* HARDAWAY, *supra* note 2, at 25-28 (discussing the 1960 election and the uncertainty that could have resulted from the close count and the alleged fraud).

5. Federal Register, *2000 Presidential Election: Popular Vote Totals*, U.S. Nat'l Archives & Records Admin., *at* http://www.archives.gov/federal_register/electoral_college/2000/popular_vote.html (last visited Aug. 28, 2004).

6. Texas then had 24 electoral votes and Illinois had 27. Had those votes been cast for Nixon, rather than Kennedy, the final election tally would have been: Nixon, 270, and Kennedy, 252.

7. Nixon lost Texas by 46,257 votes and Illinois by 8,858 votes. *See* CONGRESSIONAL QUARTERLY INC., PRESIDENTIAL ELECTIONS: 1789–1996, at 118 (1997).

8. *See* discussion *supra* note 4 and accompanying text.

9. Richard Reeves, *There's Always the Option of Giving In*, N.Y. TIMES, Nov. 10, 2000, at A33.

10. RICHARD NIXON, THE MEMOIRS OF RICHARD NIXON 224 (1978).

11. *See* CONGRESSIONAL QUARTERLY INC., *supra* note 7, at 118.

12. Recounts in New Mexico were briefly discussed, but were not pursued. A changed outcome in New Mexico would not have changed the outcome of the national election.

Chapter Eight

1. *E.g.*, Bruce Bartlett, *Waffling Electors*, TOWNHALL.COM (Dec. 18, 2000), *at* http://www.townhall.com/columnists/brucebartlett/bb20001218.shtml; Diane Rado, *Electors Are Thrust Into Prominence*, ST. PETERSBURG TIMES (Florida), Dec. 18, 2000, at 1B.

2. U.S. CONST. art. II, § 1, cl.3.

3. *Id.* amend. XII.

4. LAWRENCE D. LONGLEY & NEAL R. PEIRCE, THE ELECTORAL COLLEGE PRIMER 2000, at 104 (1999); *see also* JUDITH A. BEST, THE CHOICE OF THE PEOPLE? DEBATING THE ELECTORAL COLLEGE 43-45 (1996).

5. *See, e.g.*, ROBERT M. HARDAWAY, THE ELECTORAL COLLEGE AND THE CONSTITUTION: THE CASE FOR PRESERVING FEDERALISM 85-87 (1994); *see also* Luis Fuentes-Rohwer & Guy-Uriel Charles, *The Electoral College, the Right to Vote, and Our Federalism: A Comment on a Lasting Institution*, 29 FLA. ST. U. L. REV. 879, 896 & n.102 (2001).

6. LONGLEY & PEIRCE, *supra* note 4, at 104.

7. *E.g.*, LONGLEY & PEIRCE, *supra* note 4, at 102; *see also* L. PAIGE WHITAKER & THOMAS H. NEALE, CONGRESSIONAL RESEARCH SERV., THE ELECTORAL COLLEGE: AN OVERVIEW AND ANALYSIS OF REFORM PROPOSALS 2 (2001); BEST, *supra* note 4, at 44.

8. LONGLEY & PEIRCE, *supra* note 4, at 102.

9. *See* AFTER THE PEOPLE VOTE: A GUIDE TO THE ELECTORAL COLLEGE app. C (John C. Fortier ed., 3d ed. 2004) (listing the method of nomination in each state).

10. *See id.* (delineating which electors are bound and how, by state).

11. Ray v. Blair, 343 U.S. 214 (1952).

12. *Id.* at 215.

13. *Id.*

14. *Id.* at 231.

15. For more information on the difficulties associated with forcing electors to abide by pledges, see HARDAWAY, *supra* note 5, at 50.

16. LONGLEY & PEIRCE, *supra* note 4, at 24, 113. According to Longley and Peirce, the count is as low as nine or as high as 17, depending on whether the disputed votes in 1824 are counted. *Id.*

17. *See* WHITAKER & NEALE, *supra* note 7, at 10; *see also* AFTER THE PEOPLE VOTE, *supra* note 9, at app. G (listing faithless electors); LONGLEY & PEIRCE, *supra* note 4, at 111-13 (same).

18. LONGLEY & PEIRCE, *supra* note 4, at 107.

19. *See* AFTER THE PEOPLE VOTE, *supra* note 9, at app. C; THOMAS H. NEALE, CONGRESSIONAL RESEARCH SERV., THE ELECTORAL COLLEGE: HOW IT WORKS IN CONTEMPORARY PRESIDENTIAL ELECTIONS 3 (2003).

20. *The NewsHour with Jim Lehrer* (PBS television broadcast, Nov. 7, 2000).

21. *See, e.g.,* NEAL R. PEIRCE & LAWRENCE D. LONGLEY, THE PEOPLE'S PRESIDENT: THE ELECTORAL COLLEGE IN AMERICAN HISTORY AND THE DIRECT VOTE ALTERNATIVE 160 (rev. ed., Yale Univ. Press 1981) (1968) (opposing the Automatic Plan and relating comments of other opponents).

22. For more information regarding the problems caused by the death of a candidate, see Akhil Reed Amar, *Presidents, Vice Presidents, and Death: Closing the Constitution's Succession Gap*, 48 ARK. L. REV. 215 (1995); BEST, *supra* note 4, at 46-49; John C. Fortier & Norman J. Ornstein, *If Terrorists Attacked Our Presidential Elections*, ELECTION L.J. (forthcoming fall 2004).

23. U.S CONST. amend. XX § 3. In the event that a Vice President-elect was inaugurated as President through operation of the 20th Amendment, the 25th Amendment would then allow him to designate a new Vice President following his inauguration. *See* U.S CONST. amend. XXV § 2.

24. *See, e.g.,* CONGRESSIONAL QUARTERLY INC., PRESIDENTIAL ELECTIONS: 1789–1996, at 11 (1997) (discussing the 1872 election); *see also* Amar, *supra* note 22, at 218-19 (discussing confusion among Greeley electors); Fortier & Ornstein, *supra* note 22 (same); Beverly J. Ross & William Josephson, *The Electoral College and the Popular Vote*, 12 J.L. & POL. 665, 706-07 (1996) (same); Stephen A. Siegel, *The Conscientious Congressman's Guide to the Electoral Count Act of 1887*, 56 FLA. L. REV. 541, 581-82 (2004) (noting 1872 election timeline).

25. *See* GLYNDON G. VAN DEUSEN, HORACE GREELEY, NINETEENTH-CENTURY CRUSADER 424 (1953) (relating the circumstances of Greeley's death).

26. Akhil Reed Amar, *This Is One Terrorist Threat We Can Thwart Now*, Yale Law Sch. (Nov. 11, 2001), *at* http://www.law.yale.edu/outside/html/Public_Affairs/134/yls_article.htm.

27. Professor Judith Best has made this suggestion as well. *See* BEST, *supra* note 4, at

48.

28. A separate constitutional provision applies when no candidate receives a majority of the electoral votes and one candidate dies before the contingent election is held. Congress may "by law provide for the case of the death" of such a candidate. U.S. CONST. XX § 4. For a discussion of automated secondary election procedures that could be designed to work hand in hand with the Automatic Plan, see Chapter Nine.

Chapter Nine

1. Richard C. Baker, *On Becoming President by One Vote*, 48 A.B.A. J. 455, 456 (1962).

2. MARTIN DIAMOND, AM. ENTER. INST., TESTIMONY IN SUPPORT OF THE ELECTORAL COLLEGE 7 (1977).

3. U.S. CONST. art. II, § 1, cl. 3.

4. *Id.* amend. XII; *see also* AFTER THE PEOPLE VOTE: A GUIDE TO THE ELECTORAL COLLEGE 17-19 (John C. Fortier ed., 3d ed. 2004) (describing the contingent election procedures).

5. U.S. CONST. amend. XX.

6. Pub. L. No., 80-199, 61 Stat. 380 (codified as amended at 3 U.S.C. § 19(a)(1) (2000)).

7. *See, e.g.,* JUDITH A. BEST, THE CHOICE OF THE PEOPLE? DEBATING THE ELECTORAL COLLEGE 13-15 (1996) (relating the primary complaints made about the contingent election procedure).

8. *See* discussion *supra* notes 18-19 (Ch. 4) and accompanying text.

9. *See, e.g.,* NEAL R. PEIRCE & LAWRENCE D. LONGLEY, THE PEOPLE'S PRESIDENT: THE ELECTORAL COLLEGE IN AMERICAN HISTORY AND THE DIRECT VOTE ALTERNATIVE 177-79 (rev. ed., Yale Univ. Press 1981) (1968) (discussing reforms that have been proposed to the contingent election procedure); *see also* JUDITH BEST, THE CASE AGAINST DIRECT ELECTION OF THE PRESIDENT: A DEFENSE OF THE ELECTORAL COLLEGE 83-123 (1975) (analyzing various reform proposals for the contingent election procedure); ROBERT M. HARDAWAY, THE ELECTORAL COLLEGE AND THE CONSTITUTION: THE CASE FOR PRESERVING FEDERALISM 153-55 (1994) (same).

10. *Cf.* BEST, *supra* note 9, at 104-05 (noting that run-offs "extend[ ] the electorate's uncertainty" and "would weaken or alter our two-party system"); *see also* HARDAWAY, *supra* note 9, at 154.

11. Professor Best refers to the "second-chance psychology" that can "infect both candidates and voters" when run-offs are introduced into the equation. BEST, *supra* note 9, at 117.

12. *See, e.g., id.* at 85.

13. *See id.* at 13-15 (arguing that the contingent election procedure is not usually needed and does not need to be changed).

14. *See* discussion *supra* notes 40-45 (Ch. 1) and accompanying text.

15. DAVID MCCULLOUGH, JOHN ADAMS 475 (2001). Although some might argue that no great harm comes from having Presidents and Vice Presidents of different parties. The President does not have to assign duties to Vice Presidents, although they sometimes do so. As a constitutional matter, the most important task of a Vice President is to be

available to serve as President in the event that a President passes away. Moreover, as a historical matter, many Vice Presidents have found themselves in the same situation as Jefferson, even when they were members of the same political party as the President. For instance, Theodore Roosevelt served briefly as Vice President prior to his presidency. He had few responsibilities as Vice President and was reportedly bored and frustrated with his role. *See* NATHAN MILLER, THEODORE ROOSEVELT: A LIFE 346 (1992) (describing Vice President Roosevelt as "[f]rustrated," "feeling unused," and looking for ways to fill his time).

16. *See, e.g.*, HARDAWAY, *supra* note 9, at 153-55, 166-68 (arguing that the contingent election procedure should not be changed).

Chapter Ten

1. Steven Thomma, *Possibility of a President Who Lost Popular Vote Triggers Crisis of Legitimacy*, KNIGHT RIDDER/TRIB. NEWS SERVICE, Nov. 9, 2000.

2. *Id.*

3. Michael Kramer, *Time to Ax Electoral College*, DAILY NEWS (New York), Nov. 9, 2000, at 10.

4. Arthur M. Schlesinger, Jr., *Not the People's Choice: How to Democratize American Democracy*, AM. PROSPECT, Mar. 25, 2002, at 23.

5. *See, e.g.*, Michael Herz, *How the Electoral College Imitates the World Series*, 23 CARDOZO L. REV. 1191 (2002).

6. Joy McAfee, *2001: Should the College Electors Finally Graduate?: The Electoral College: An American Compromise From Its Inception to Election 2000*, 32 CUMB. L. REV. 643, 661-62 (2001).

7. *Id.* at 662.

8. *See, e.g.*, JUDITH BEST, THE CASE AGAINST DIRECT ELECTION OF THE PRESIDENT: A DEFENSE OF THE ELECTORAL COLLEGE 46 (1975) ("[M]any critics seem to believe that the objection to a minority President need only be stated, not argued."); *see also* ROBERT M. HARDAWAY, THE ELECTORAL COLLEGE AND THE CONSTITUTION: THE CASE FOR PRESERVING FEDERALISM 13 (1994) ("[Such claims] raise the perfectly legitimate question of what is a 'majority.' More precisely, one may ask, a majority of what?").

9. NEAL R. PEIRCE & LAWRENCE D. LONGLEY, THE PEOPLE'S PRESIDENT: THE ELECTORAL COLLEGE IN AMERICAN HISTORY AND THE DIRECT VOTE ALTERNATIVE 236 (rev. ed., Yale Univ. Press 1981) (1968).

10. Paul Starr, *Mr. Bush Gets His Honeymoon*, AM. PROSPECT, Feb. 26, 2001, at 6 (internal citation omitted).

11. Alexander Keyssar, *The Majority's Rules*, L.A. TIMES, May 25, 2003, at R12.

12. Many Internet sites, for instance, still denounce the outcome of the 2000 election. These Internet sites include: http://www.geocities.com/countercoup, http://www.iknow whatyoudidlastelection.com, http://www.legitgov.org, and http://www.impeachbush.tv/el2000, among others.

13. *E.g.*, Richard L. Berke, *Bucking History, Tossup States Increase, Forcing Candidates to Rethink Strategies*, N.Y. TIMES, Oct. 27, 2000, at A27.

14. *See* discussion *supra* notes 32-34 (Introduction) and accompanying text.

15. BEST, *supra* note 8, at 47-48.

16. *Id.* at 48.

17. *Id.*

18. *See id.* at 48-49.

19. Herz, *supra* note 5, at 1196 (quoting Albert R. Hunt, *The Electoral College: Legitimate but Anachronistic*, WALL ST. J., Oct. 26, 2000, at A27).

Chapter Eleven

1. *See generally* WINNER TAKE ALL: REPORT OF THE TWENTIETH CENTURY FUND TASK FORCE ON REFORM OF THE PRESIDENTIAL ELECTION PROCESS (1978) (proposing the Bonus Plan); *see also* NEAL R. PEIRCE & LAWRENCE D. LONGLEY, THE PEOPLE'S PRESIDENT: THE ELECTORAL COLLEGE IN AMERICAN HISTORY AND THE DIRECT VOTE ALTERNATIVE 176 (rev. ed., Yale Univ. Press 1981) (1968) (describing the Bonus Plan and how it came to be proposed).

There is nothing intuitive about the number 102, although proponents argue that the two votes represent each state's two senators (plus two for the District of Columbia). Why not one extra vote per state and the District of Columbia, for an electoral bonus of 51? Or three votes (representing two Senators and one Congressman), for an electoral bonus of 153?

2. *See* JUDITH A. BEST, THE CHOICE OF THE PEOPLE? DEBATING THE ELECTORAL COLLEGE 62 (1996). Currently, 538 electoral votes are awarded, which means that 270 votes are needed to win. The Bonus Plan would bring the total number of votes to 640. A majority of 640 is 321, which means that 219 state electoral votes plus the 102 bonus votes would lead to victory. *Id.*

3. Paul Schumaker, *Not the People's Choice*, AM. PROSPECT, May 6, 2002, at 5.

4. *See* L. PAIGE WHITAKER & THOMAS H. NEALE, CONGRESSIONAL RESEARCH SERV., THE ELECTORAL COLLEGE: AN OVERVIEW AND ANALYSIS OF REFORM PROPOSALS 17-18 (2001) (reporting the arguments of District Plan proponents).

5. *See, e.g., id.; see also* DAVID W. ABBOTT & JAMES P. LEVINE, WRONG WINNER: THE COMING DEBACLE IN THE ELECTORAL COLLEGE 126 (1991) (discussing the "crucial shortcoming" of the District Plan: It "does nothing to correct the wrong-winner perversion"); PEIRCE & LONGLEY, *supra* note 1, at 142 (discussing the disparities that would still exist between the popular and electoral vote totals under a District Plan).

6. *See, e.g.,* Ky Fullerton, *Bush, Gore, and the 2000 Presidential Election: Time for the Electoral College to Go?*, 80 OR. L. REV. 717, 734 (2001) (citing Rhodes Cook, *This Just In: Nixon Beats Kennedy*, WASH. POST, Mar. 25, 2001, at B2). Bush would have won 288 to 250 in the electoral vote. Cook, *supra*, at B2.

7. Proponents sometimes argue that the District Plan would prevent campaigning from focusing on swing states. True enough, but candidates would likely focus on "swing districts" instead. *See* PEIRCE & LONGLEY, *supra* note 1, at 142.

8. *See* BEST, *supra* note 2, at 61-62 (discussing the increased incentives for gerrymandering).

9. Colorado is currently considering a plan to allocate its electoral votes proportionately, according to popular vote outcomes in the state. *See* discussion *infra* notes 15-19 and accompanying text. Colorado's proposal leaves electoral votes as whole numbers and does not consider awarding tenths or hundredths of an electoral vote. Electoral votes, after all, cannot be divided to hundredths or tenths unless the casting of electoral votes is first automated. A tenth or hundredth of an elector cannot attend a meeting of the Electoral College in December and cast his one tenth or one hundredth of an electoral vote. Only whole persons can attend the meetings of the Electoral College each presidential election year.

10. WHITAKER & NEALE, *supra* note 4, at 19-20 (relating the logistics proposed for a proportional division of electoral votes).

11. *Id.*

12. *E.g.*, ABBOTT & LEVINE, *supra* note 5, at 121-25.

13. *See* BEST, *supra* note 2, at 61-62.

14. *Id.* at 61.

15. Valerie Richardson, *Group Seeks to Split Colorado Electors*, WASHINGTONTIMES.COM (June 16, 2004), *at* http://www.washingtontimes.com/national/20040615-111043-1798r.htm.

16. *E.g.*, *Colorado to Vote on Reform of Winner-Take-All Approach to Electoral Votes*, ASSOCIATED PRESS, Aug. 17, 2004; John J. Sanko, *Voting Reform Reaches Ballot: If Plan Passes, Winner-Take-All System Would End*, ROCKY MOUNTAIN NEWS, Aug. 14, 2004, at 8A.

17. *See* U.S. CONST. art. II, § 1, cl.2 ("Each State shall appoint, *in such Manner as the Legislature thereof may direct*, a Number of Electors, equal to the whole Number of Senators and Representatives to which the State may be entitled in the Congress.") (emphasis added).

18. Hawke v. Smith, 253 U.S. 221, 226 (1920).

19. *Id.* at 227.

20. *See* Robert W. Bennett, *Popular Election of the President Without a Constitutional Amendment*, 4 GREEN BAG 2D 241 (2001) [hereinafter Bennett, *Popular Election*]; Robert W. Bennett, *State Coordination in Popular Election of the President Without a Constitutional Amendment*, 5 GREEN BAG 2D 141 (2002); *see also* Akhil Reed Amar & Vikram David Amar, *How to Achieve Direct National Election of the President Without Amending the Constitution: Part Three of a Three-Part Series on the 2000 Election and the Electoral College*, FINDLAW'S WRIT (Dec. 28, 2001), *at* http://writ.news.findlaw.com/amar/20011228.html; *Rethinking the Electoral College Debate: The Framers, Federalism, and One Person, One Vote*, 114 HARV. L. REV. 2526, 2549 n.112 (2001).

21. Bennett, *Popular Election*, *supra* note 20, at 241.

22. *See* U.S. CONST. art. V.

23. Bennett, *Popular Election*, *supra* note 20, at 241.

24. *See supra* note 20.

25. The 11 most populous states, following the 2000 Census, are: California (55 electoral votes), Texas (34), New York (31), Florida (27), Pennsylvania (21), Illinois (21), Ohio (20), Michigan (17), New Jersey (15), Georgia (15), and North Carolina (15).

26. The academics who propose this idea note that these 11 colluding states could

either award electors based upon the national popular vote, unconditionally, or they could enact statutes that would allow their votes to be awarded according to the popular vote only if a critical mass of other states chooses to do so as well.

Professors Akhil and Vikram Amar argue that such state statutes would not constitute an interstate compact requiring congressional approval under Article I, section 10 of the Constitution, since each state "would retain complete unilateral freedom to switch back to its older system for any future election, and the coordinated law creates no new interstate governmental apparatus." Amar & Amar, *supra* note 20, at http://writ.news.findlaw.com/amar/20011228.html.

27. *Id.*

Chapter Twelve

1. Following the 2000 Census, these states are: California (55 electoral votes), Texas (34), New York (31), Florida (27), Pennsylvania (21), Illinois (21), Ohio (20), Michigan (17), Georgia (15), North Carolina (15), and New Jersey (15). *See* Federal Register, *2004 List of States and Votes: Allocation of Electoral Votes Based on the 2000 Census*, U.S. Nat'l Archives & Records Admin., *at* http://www.archives.gov/federal_register/electoral_college/2004/allocation.html (last visited Sept. 12, 2004).

2. SENATE COMM. ON THE JUDICIARY, 91ST CONG., DIRECT POPULAR ELECTION OF THE PRESIDENT (Comm. Print 1970) (Minority Views of Messrs. Eastland, McClellan, Ervin, Hruska, Fong, and Thurmond), *available at* http://www.claremont.org/writings/700814_minority.html.

3. *See, e.g.*, DAVID W. ABBOTT & JAMES P. LEVINE, WRONG WINNER: THE COMING DEBACLE IN THE ELECTORAL COLLEGE 51-58 (1991) (discussing the elections of 1948, 1960, and 1968); NEAL R. PEIRCE & LAWRENCE D. LONGLEY, THE PEOPLE'S PRESIDENT: THE ELECTORAL COLLEGE IN AMERICAN HISTORY AND THE DIRECT VOTE ALTERNATIVE 58-84 (rev. ed., Yale Univ. Press 1981) (1968) (analyzing the elections of 1916, 1948, 1960, 1968 and 1976); *see also Proposals for Electoral College Reform: Hearings on H.J. Res. 28 and H.J. Res. 43 Before the Subcomm. on the Constitution of the House Comm. on the Judiciary*, 105th Cong. 26 (1997) (statement of Becky Cain, President, League of Women Voters), *available at* http://commdocs.house.gov/committees/judiciary/hju57219.000/hju57219_0f.htm [hereinafter Statement of Becky Cain].

4. PEIRCE & LONGLEY, *supra* note 3, at 59; *see also* Statement of Becky Cain, *supra* note 3, at 26.

5. PEIRCE & LONGLEY, *supra* note 3, at 62; *see also* Statement of Becky Cain, *supra* note 3, at 26; ABBOTT & LEVINE, *supra* note 3, at 52-53 (stating that shifts in California and Ohio would have prevented either Truman or Dewey from gaining an electoral majority, thus throwing the election into the House contingent election).

6. PEIRCE & LONGLEY, *supra* note 3, at 84; *see also* Statement of Becky Cain, *supra* note 3, at 26.

7. *See* JUDITH BEST, THE CASE AGAINST DIRECT ELECTION OF THE PRESIDENT: A DEFENSE OF THE ELECTORAL COLLEGE 72-80 (1975).

8. *Id.* at 79.

9. *Id.* at 72-74.

10. Or perhaps he had good ideas that would have served the country well, but he communicated them in a way that failed to gain the trust of voters in many parts of the country.

11. Others have reached the conclusion that the Electoral College cannot properly be blamed if, in fact, popular vote winners did not win the presidency in 1824 and 1876. *E.g., id.* at 24-25, 52-54; *see also* ROBERT M. HARDAWAY, THE ELECTORAL COLLEGE AND THE CONSTITUTION: THE CASE FOR PRESERVING FEDERALISM 4 (1994); Denny Pilant, *Should the Electoral College Be Abolished? —No, in* CONTROVERSIAL ISSUES IN PRESIDENTIAL SELECTION 216, 219-20 (Gary L. Rose ed., 1991); Grant M. Dixton, *Book Review: The Electoral College Primer*, 34 HARV. J. ON LEGIS. 293, 298 (1997); Arthur Schlesinger, Jr., *It's a Mess, But We've Been Through It Before*, TIME, Nov. 20, 2000, at 64, 65. Others include these elections as ones in which the will of the people was "frustrated." *E.g.*, PEIRCE & LONGLEY, *supra* note 3, at 5; *see also* Akhil Reed Amar, *Presidents Without Mandates (With Special Emphasis on Ohio)*, 67 U. CIN. L. REV. 375, 391 (1999) (referring to Hayes, along with Harrison, as a "clear popular loser"); Abner J. Mikva, *Doubting Our Claims to Democracy*, 39 ARIZ. L. REV. 793, 799 (1997) (discussing the 1876 election).

12. A discussion of the 1824 election can be found at PAUL F. BOLLER, JR., PRESIDENTIAL CAMPAIGNS 33-41 (rev. ed. 1996); MICHAEL J. GLENNON, WHEN NO MAJORITY RULES: THE ELECTORAL COLLEGE AND PRESIDENTIAL SUCCESSION 15-16 (1992); HARDAWAY, *supra* note 11, at 123-25.

13. A discussion of the 1876 election can be found at WILLIAM H. REHNQUIST, CENTENNIAL CRISIS: THE DISPUTED ELECTION OF 1876 (2004); *see also* BOLLER, *supra* note 12, at 133-41; GLENNON, *supra* note 12, at 16-17; HARDAWAY, *supra* note 11, at 128-37.

14. *See* REHNQUIST, *supra* note 13, at 176-79 (discussing the filibusters); *see also* HARDAWAY, *supra* note 11, at 134-35 (same).

15. PAUL LELAND HAWORTH, THE HAYES-TILDEN DISPUTED PRESIDENTIAL ELECTION OF 1876, at 340-41 (1906), *cited by* BEST, *supra* note 7, at 53.

16. Nixon lost Massachusetts and the District of Columbia. He also lost one electoral vote when a faithless elector in Virginia cast a vote for Libertarian candidate John Hospers. Nixon's popular vote total was also a landslide: 47,169,911 to 29,170,383. *See* CONGRESSIONAL QUARTERLY INC., PRESIDENTIAL ELECTIONS: 1789–1996, at 69, 121 (1997).

17. *Editorial: Ronald Reagan, 1911-2004*, LAS VEGAS REV.-J., June 7, 2004, at 6B.

18. *Id.*

19. *The NewsHour with Jim Lehrer* (PBS television broadcast, June 7, 2004).

20. Peggy Noonan, *The Ben Elliott Story: What I Saw at the Funeral*, OPINIONJOURNAL.COM (June 14, 2004), http://www.opinionjournal.com/columnists/pnoonan/?id=110005212.

Chapter Thirteen

1. JUDITH BEST, THE CASE AGAINST DIRECT ELECTION OF THE PRESIDENT: A DEFENSE OF THE ELECTORAL COLLEGE 67 (1975).

2. *See* CONGRESSIONAL QUARTERLY INC., PRESIDENTIAL ELECTIONS: 1789–1996, at 48,

100 (1997) (reporting 1888 election totals).

3. *See id.* at 100.

4. *See id.*

5. For more information on Cleveland's first term and the 1888 election, see DOROTHY BURNE GOEBEL & JULIUS GOEBEL, JR., GENERALS IN THE WHITE HOUSE 250-54 (1945); HORACE SAMUEL MERRILL, BOURBON LEADER: GROVER CLEVELAND AND THE DEMOCRATIC PARTY 102-34 (1957); RICHARD E. WELCH, JR., THE PRESIDENCIES OF GROVER CLEVELAND 93-99 (1988); *see also* HARRY J. SIEVERS, S.J., BENJAMIN HARRISON: HOOSIER STATESMAN 357-427 (1959); HOMER E. SOCOLOFSKY & ALLAN B. SPETTER, THE PRESIDENCY OF BENJAMIN HARRISON 1-18 (1987).

6. MERRILL, *supra* note 5, at 116.

7. Franklin Delano Roosevelt issued more total vetoes, but they were issued over the course of his more than three terms in office. A list of presidential vetoes can be found at Office of the Clerk, *Presidential Vetoes*, U.S. House of Representatives, *at* http://clerk.house.gov/histHigh/Congressional_History/vetoes.html (last modified Nov. 7, 2003).

8. MERRILL, *supra* note 5, at 107.

9. *Id.* at 108.

10. GOEBEL & GOEBEL, *supra* note 5, at 250.

11. MERRILL, *supra* note 5, at 128.

12. *Id.*

13. SOCOLOFSKY & SPETTER, *supra* note 5, at 12 (citation omitted).

14. R. HAL WILLIAMS, YEARS OF DECISION: AMERICAN POLITICS IN THE 1890'S, at 3 (1978); *see also* SIEVERS, *supra* note 5, at 371. Harrison did not travel to give his speeches. Voters traveled to see him in Indianapolis, and he gave speeches (often tailored to his audience) from his doorstep.

15. SIEVERS, *supra* note 5, at 369.

16. *Id.* at 357.

17. *The Early Show* (CBS television broadcast, Dec. 14, 2000).

18. *Talk of the Nation* (NPR radio broadcast, Dec. 12, 2000).

19. Jack Mabley, *U.S. May Be Divided, But It's Not Unhealthy*, CHI. DAILY HERALD, Dec. 13, 2000, at 16.

20. *E.g.*, JAMES W. CEASER & ANDREW E. BUSCH, THE PERFECT TIE: THE TRUE STORY OF THE 2000 PRESIDENTIAL ELECTION (2001) [hereinafter PERFECT TIE].

21. Stephen Goode, *For the People: Interesting Numbers in* Bush v. Gore, INSIGHT ON THE NEWS (Jan. 15, 2001), *at* http://www.insightmag.com/news/2001/01/15/ForThePeople/For-The.People-210830.shtml.

22. *Id.*

23. *Id.*

24. State vote totals for both the Bush and Gore charts are obtained from the U.S. National Archives and Records Administration website. *See* Federal Register, *2000 Presidential Election: Popular Vote Totals*, U.S. Nat'l Archives & Records Admin., *at* http://www.archives.gov/federal_register/electoral_college/2000/popular_vote.html (last

visited July 23, 2004). For each candidate, the percent of votes won also takes into account those votes cast for third-party candidates, although the popular vote tallies of these latter candidates are not listed in the charts.

25. *Breaking Down the Electorate*, TIME, Nov. 20, 2000, at 74, 74 (reporting Voter News Service exit polls). Only 26% of the same population voted for Bush. *Id.*

26. *Id.*

27. Henry C. Kenski et al., *Explaining the Vote in a Divided Country: The Presidential Election of 2000, in* THE 2000 PRESIDENTIAL CAMPAIGN: A COMMUNICATION PERSPECTIVE 225, 232-37 (Robert E. Denton, Jr. ed., 2002) [hereinafter 2000 PRESIDENTIAL CAMPAIGN].

28. PERFECT TIE, *supra* note 20, at 28 tbl. 1.2.

29. *See* ELECTING THE PRESIDENT, 2000: THE INSIDERS' VIEW 212 (Kathleen Hall Jamieson & Paul Waldman eds., 2001) (quoting Karl Rove) [hereinafter ELECTING THE PRESIDENT].

30. PERFECT TIE, *supra* note 20, at 28-29 (discussing Bush' strategy for competing with Gore on economic issues).

31. *Id.* at 29-31 (discussing the importance of values during the campaign); *see also* DAVID FRUM, THE RIGHT MAN: THE SURPRISE PRESIDENCY OF GEORGE W. BUSH 7-9 (2003) (same).

32. *See* 2000 PRESIDENTIAL CAMPAIGN, *supra* note 27, at 229-30.

33. George W. Bush, Nomination Acceptance Speech at the Republican National Convention in Philadelphia, Pennsylvania (Aug. 3, 2000) (transcript available at http://www.pbs. org/newshour/election2000/gopconvention/george_w_bush.html).

34. PERFECT TIE, *supra* note 20, at 30 (quoting Richard Cheney).

35. John F. Harris, *Scrambling on "Friendly" Turf: In Full Roar, Gore Tries To Rally Tennessee Again*, WASH. POST, Oct. 26, 2000, at A1, *quoted in* 2000 PRESIDENTIAL CAMPAIGN, *supra* note 27, at 260.

36. PERFECT TIE, *supra* note 20, at 28 tbl. 1.2.

37. *Exit Polls: Results*, CNN.COM, *at* http://www.cnn.com/ELECTION/2000/results/index.epolls.html (last visited Sept. 10, 2004).

38. *Id.*

39. *Id.* Twenty-four percent deemed the scandals "very important," while 20 percent rated the scandals "important." *Id.*

40. George W. Bush, The First Gore-Bush Presidential Debate in Boston, Massachusetts (Oct. 3, 2000) (transcript available at http://www.debates.org/pages/trans2000a.html).

41. Albert Gore, The First Gore-Bush Presidential Debate in Boston, Massachusetts (Oct. 3, 2000) (transcript available at http://www.debates.org/pages/trans2000a.html).

42. ELECTING THE PRESIDENT, *supra* note 29, at 206 (quoting Karl Rove); *see also* 2000 PRESIDENTIAL CAMPAIGN, *supra* note 27, at 227-28.

43. *See* PERFECT TIE, *supra* note 20, at 35-36.

44. ELECTING THE PRESIDENT, *supra* note 29, at 203-04 (quoting Karl Rove).

45. *See* 2000 PRESIDENTIAL CAMPAIGN, *supra* note 27, at 229.

Chapter Fourteen

1. More information on FDR's presidency and the 1936 election can be found at: CONRAD BLACK, FRANKLIN DELANO ROOSEVELT: CHAMPION OF FREEDOM 388-92 (2003); PAUL F. BOLLER, JR., PRESIDENTIAL CAMPAIGNS 240-49 (rev. ed. 1996); KENNETH S. DAVIS, FDR, THE NEW DEAL YEARS, 1933-1937: A HISTORY 603-648 (1986); WILLIAM E. LEUCHTENBURG, FRANKLIN D. ROOSEVELT AND THE NEW DEAL: 1932-1940, at 175-96 (1963); DIXON WECTER, THE AGE OF THE GREAT DEPRESSION: 1929-1941, at 101-04 (1948).

2. *See, e.g., Great Depression*, BRITANNICA CONCISE ENCYCLOPEDIA, *at* http://www.britannica.com/ebc/print?eu=391338 (last visited July 20, 2004).

3. *Past Presidents: Franklin D. Roosevelt*, The White House, *at* http://www.whitehouse.gov/history/presidents/fr32.html (last visited July 20, 2004).

4. BOLLER, *supra* note 1, at 240.

5. Some have disputed this number, including welfare recipients among those who were "productively employed" during the 1930s. Jim Powell, *Tough Questions for Defenders of the New Deal*, WALL ST. J., Nov. 6, 2003, at A15; *see also* JIM POWELL, FDR'S FOLLY: HOW ROOSEVELT AND HIS NEW DEAL PROLONGED THE GREAT DEPRESSION (2003); GENE SMILEY, RETHINKING THE GREAT DEPRESSION (2002); Bruce Bartlett, *Understanding the Great Depression and New Deal*, TOWNHALL.COM (Nov. 8, 2003), *at* http://www.townhall.com/columnists/brucebartlett/bb20031108.shtml.

6. LEUCHTENBURG, *supra* note 1, at 194; Miller Center of Public Affairs, *Franklin Delano Roosevelt (1933-1945)*, Univ. of Va., *at* http://www.americanpresident.org/history/franklindelanoroosevelt/biography/CampaignsElections.common.shtml (last visited July 23, 2004)

7. Some Republicans hoped that challenges from dissident elements within the Democratic Party would undermine FDR's candidacy and allow a Republican challenger to squeak through to victory. LEUCHTENBURG, *supra* note 1, at 179. Democratic Senator Huey Long, for instance, had offered an alternative solution to the economic problems gripping the country, and his "Share the Wealth" program had many supporters across the country. Unfortunately for those who did not approve of the New Deal, Long's presidential aspirations were abruptly cut short when he was assassinated in September 1935. *Id.* at 179-80.

8. BOLLER, *supra* note 1, at 242.

9. LEUCHTENBURG, *supra* note 1, at 175 (citations omitted).

10. Eleanor Roosevelt National Historic Site, *Alfred M. Landon (1887-1987)*, Nat'l Park Serv., *at* http://www.nps.gov/elro/glossary/landon-alfred.htm (last visited July 23, 2004).

11. WECTER, *supra* note 1, at 102.

12. *Id.* at 103; *see also* BLACK, *supra* note 1, at 389; LEUCHTENBURG, *supra* note 1, at 184.

13. WECTER, *supra* note 1, at 103. Although it should be noted that Roosevelt nevertheless won a surprising number of voters from prosperous Americans. For instance, Boston merchant Edward Filene stated, "Why shouldn't the American people take half my money from me? I took all of it from them." LEUCHTENBURG, *supra* note 1, at 190.

14. LEUCHTENBURG, *supra* note 1, at 193.

15. *Id.*

16. BOLLER, *supra* note 1, at 247 (citation omitted).

17. Miller Center of Public Affairs, *supra* note 6, at http://www.americanpresident. org/history/franklindelanoroosevelt/biography/CampaignsElections.common.shtml; *see also* BLACK, *supra* note 1,at 391 (reporting post-election poll results, which indicated that Roosevelt gained more support among Catholics, Jews, blacks, and southern whites).

18. LEUCHTENBURG, *supra* note 1, at 184; *see also* BLACK, *supra* note 1, at 391.

19. BOLLER, *supra* note 1, at 355 (citation omitted).

20. Sixty-six hostages were originally seized. Fourteen were released during 1979 and 1980, but the remaining 52 hostages remained in captivity until January 20, 1981. *Iran Hostage Crisis*, BRITANNICA CONCISE ENCYCLOPEDIA, *at* http://www.britannica.com/ebc/ article?eu=393470 (last visited Sept. 11, 2004).

21. Dinesh D'Souza, *How Reagan Reelected Clinton*, dinesh-dsouza.com (Nov. 3, 1997), *at* http://www.dinesh-dsouza.com/articles/reaganreelected.html.

22. *See, e.g.*, James K. Glassman, *Reagan Whipped Inflation*, NAT'L REV. ONLINE (June 16, 2004), *at* http://www.nationalreview.com/nrof_glassman/glassman200406160818.asp (discussing actions that brought inflation under control during the 1980s).

23. D'Souza, *supra* note 21, at http://www.dinesh-dsouza.com/articles/reagan reelected.html.

24. Scott Keeter, *Public Opinion in 1984, in* THE ELECTION OF 1984, at 91, 93 (Marlene Michels Pomper ed., 1985).

25. D'Souza, *supra* note 21, at http://www.dinesh-dsouza.com/articles/reagan reelected.html.

26. LOU CANNON, PRESIDENT REAGAN: THE ROLE OF A LIFETIME 435 (2d ed., PublicAffairs 2000) (1991).

27. Keeter, *supra* note 24, at 93.

28. *Id.* at 99.

29. *See id.* at 95.

30. *See id.* at 97.

31. *Id.* at 95.

32. *Id.* at 96. tbl.4.1.

33. *Id.* at 100.

34. BOLLER, *supra* note 1, at 370 (citation omitted).

35. *Id.* at 371.

36. Ronald Reagan, Second Presidential Debate in Kansas City, Missouri (Oct. 28, 1984) (transcript available at http://www.pbs.org/newshour/debatingourdestiny/84 debates/2prez1.html).

37. BOLLER, *supra* note 1, at 373 (citation omitted).

38. CANNON, *supra* note 26, at 434. Reagan did not win a majority of votes among the unemployed. *Id.*

39. Keeter, *supra* note 24, at 101. An ABC/*Washington Post* poll showed that 54 percent of women supported Reagan, compared to 62 percent of men. By contrast,

Mondale received support from 46 percent of women and 38 percent of men. *Id.* at 102 tbl. 4.3.

40. CANNON, *supra* note 26, at 434.

41. Peter Roff, *UPI's White House Watch*, WASHINGTONTIMES.COM (June 14, 2004), *at* http://washingtontimes.com/upi-breaking/20040611-064937-2389r.htm.

42. RONALD REAGAN, A LIFE IN LETTERS xiii (Kiron K. Skinner et al. eds., 2003).

43. CANNON, *supra* note 26, at 435.

Appendices

1. For election results, see CONGRESSIONAL QUARTERLY INC., PRESIDENTIAL ELECTIONS: 1789–1996, at 115 (1997) (reporting electoral and popular vote totals).

2. No record of the popular vote was kept until 1824.

3. A list of faithless electors can be found in Chapter Eight.

4. Due to the combined voting procedure for President and Vice-President, this figure is not useful until after adoption of the Twelfth Amendment in 1804.

5. The total number of available elector votes was 176; however, only 175 votes were cast because one Kentucky elector did not vote.

6. The total number of available elector votes was 218; however, only 217 votes were cast because one Ohio elector did not vote.

7. The total number of available elector votes was 221; however, only 217 votes were cast because one Delaware elector and three Maryland electors did not vote.

8. The total number of available elector votes was 235; however, only 232 votes were cast because three electors—from Mississippi, Pennsylvania, and Tennessee—did not vote.

9. The election of 1824 was decided in the House contingent election, since no presidential candidate received a majority of electoral votes. John Q. Adams received the votes of 13 state delegations; Jackson, 7; and Crawford, 3.

10. The total number of available elector votes was 288; however, only 286 votes were cast because two Maryland electors did not vote.

11. The total number of available elector votes was 234; however, only 233 votes were cast because one Nevada elector did not vote.

12. The total number of available elector votes was 366; however, only 349 votes were cast and counted. The Democratic candidate, Horace Greeley, died between the time of the popular vote and the meeting of the presidential electors. Sixty-three of his electors voted for alternative candidates, but three electors determined to cast their votes for Greeley despite his death. Congress refused to count these last three votes, since they had been cast for a deceased candidate. In addition, Congress refused to accept votes from Arkansas and Louisiana due to disruptive conditions resulting from Reconstruction.

13. Results for the 2000 election were obtained from the U.S. National Archives and Records Administration website. *See* Federal Register, *2000 Presidential Election: Popular Vote Totals*, U.S. Nat'l Archives & Records Admin., at http://www.archives. gov/federal_register/electoral_college/2000/popular_vote.html (last visited Sept. 7, 2004).

INDEX

INDEX

249